African-American Pioneers in Anthropology

African-American Pioneers in Anthropology

Edited by

Ira E. Harrison and

Faye V. Harrison

University of Illinois Press • Urbana and Chicago

Manufactured in the United States of America

1 2 3 4 5 C P 5 4 3 2 1

This book is printed on acid-free paper.

Library of Congress Cataloging-in-Publication Data
African-American pioneers in anthropology / edited by
Ira E. Harrison and Faye V. Harrison.
p. cm.
Includes bibliographical references.
ISBN 0-252-02430-3 (cloth : acid-free paper)
ISBN 0-252-06736-3 (pbk. : acid-free paper)
1. Afro-American anthropologists.
2. Anthropology—United States—History.
3. Ethnology—United States—History.
I. Harrison, Ira E.
II. Harrison, Faye V.
GN17.3.U6 A37 1999
301'.089'96073—ddc21
98-19724
CIP

Contents

Acknowledgments

We wish to acknowledge the sustained support we received from both the Department of Anthropology at the University of Tennessee at Knoxville and the University of Illinois Press toward completion of this work. Also the many valuable contributions that Glenn Jordan made in the early phases of organizing this book are deeply appreciated. Finally, our special thanks go to Elizabeth Dulany for midwifing the project through a labor much more lengthy than we care to admit. Thanks Liz!

Introduction

Anthropology, African Americans, and the Emancipation of a Subjugated Knowledge

Faye V. Harrison and Ira E. Harrison

African Americans, and subordinate-group analysts generally, have historically occupied a largely peripheral and, using W. E. B. Du Bois's insightful metaphor, *veiled* or hidden position within the hierarchical order of knowledge that anthropology represents. As a consequence, much of the scholarship they have produced has been rendered largely invisible in the texts and discourses that define anthropology as the authoritative—yet overwhelmingly Eurocentric and masculinist—study of humankind. The marginal positioning of African-American as well as other subordinated knowledges has begun receiving some needed attention (e.g., Adams 1987; Drake 1980; F. Harrison 1988; Jones [1970] 1988; Jordan 1982). Various critical anthropological projects—feminist, Marxist, post-Marxist, postmodernist, and indigenous—are problematizing the boundaries and parameters that have historically demarcated and hierarchized anthropological inquiry and investigation.[1] As Renato Rosaldo (1993:xviii) points out, the current trend of blurring ethnography's boundaries has created space for historically subordinated, or *subaltern,* scholarship. Subaltern viewpoints warrant valorization because they can enrich—as well as complicate—anthropological analysis. Rosaldo underscores this value: "[anthropology] only stands to lose by ignoring how the oppressed analyze their own situation. Indeed, the dominated usually understand the dominant better than the reverse. In coping with their daily lives, they simply must" (189).

Accordingly, the recapturing of subjugated knowledges should be an integral component of any genuinely critical project designed to reinvent, decolonize, and transform anthropology (Hymes 1972; Fox 1991; F. Harrison 1991b). The intellectual biographies compiled in this volume repossess and reposition the African-American intellectual lineage within the history of anthropology. These biographies conjure long-forgotten skeletons out of their hiding places in "the anthropological closet" (cf. Willis 1974).[2] These life stories, career paths, and intellectual agendas from the black experience in American anthropology provide an invaluable view of the discipline's history from below. This book represents a collaborative effort to trace and document intellectual history by following Laura Nader's important directive of "studying up" (1972) from a "frog's perspective," as William S. Willis Jr. (1972:121) allegorically phrased it (see also Sanday's chapter).

One of anthropology's most respected historiographers, George Stocking Jr., describes his agenda as writing the history of "major figures in the succession of dominant paradigmatic viewpoints in hegemonic anthropological traditions" (1992:8). In the course of situating and defending his commitment to the mainstream while still part of an intellectual milieu in which decentering and diversifying authority and voice have a growing appeal, he concedes that "[his work] has not sought to rescue neglected precursors of paradigmatic alternatives once lost and now to be regained . . . nor to examine anthropology historically from the perspective of those who have been its subject 'others.' . . . *[However,] these, and other alternative histories, can be fruitful and indeed necessary historiographical or critical enterprises*" (8; emphasis ours). Toward this end, *African-American Pioneers in Anthropology* represents one of many responses to the expanded space and critical possibilities created by the disruptions and transfigurations the discipline has experienced since the 1960s.

Late-Twentieth-Century Climate and Challenge

Like all other disciplines, anthropology has always been situated in wider fields of discourse and power (Trouillot 1991). Indeed, power assumes multiple forms, ranging from discursive varieties to those that Wolf (1990) characterizes as organizational and structural. These varying modes of ideological, cultural, and politico-economic power, which are inextricable, are implicated in the socially constructed disparities of race as well as gender and class, among other dimensions of hierarchical differentiation. Since the 1960s, anthropologists have intensely debated the epistemological, political, and moral bases of the truth and knowledge claims made by the discipline that developed as "the handmaiden of colonialism." Whether an agent for or against an imperialist agenda, anthropology has been at once destabilized and enriched by its embeddedness in "the real world." At this juncture in world history, the real world is shaped by continuing struggles for decolonization and rights of citizenship and human integrity, by the dilemmas and constraints of postcolonial sovereignty and development, and by the destabilizing effects of, on the one hand, ethno-nationalist resurgence and, on the other, transnationalism and globalization. In light of this climate, the discipline's credibility and authority have been seriously contested from both within and without. Indeed, in this current postcolonial, postmodern, post–cold war era, confidence in the coherence and efficacy of all "master narratives" and what Foucault (1980:80) called "global, totalitarian theories" (e.g., psychoanalysis, Marxism, neoclassical development discourse) has greatly subsided. The interrogation and displacement of established intellectual conventions, including anthropology's dominant conventions, have contributed to an extreme state of skepticism that informs much of the construction and deconstruction of knowledge today. Assumptions concerning what constitutes knowledge and what can be known, which are basic questions of epistemology, are fervently debated across polarized lines.

In light of the pronounced vulnerability to criticism and political impotence so characteristic of this era (Foucault 1980:80; West 1991), some social analysts recognize the need for restoring confidence in the production of explanatory accounts of both local and global sociocultural terrains. As West has argued, there is a need for "social theory wedded in a nuanced manner to concrete historical analyses"—rather than for universalizing and totalizing paradigms offering transcendent explanations for all phenomena (1991:xxii). How else can the sociocultural terrain and "ethnoscape" (Appadurai 1991) of the end of the twentieth century and the beginning of the next be illuminated and, through more effective struggle, reconfigured?

The critical theory for which Cornel West and other analysts call is not to be undergirded by positivist assumptions that objectivity lies outside the realm of values and politics and that the observer must be "disconnected from the social processes that condition the observed object of study" (F. Harrison 1993:405; see also Giddens 1976, 1977, 1979).

To the contrary, critical theorists recognize that knowledge production and sociopolitical engagement (in one form or another) are dialectically interrelated and mutually reinforcing (Leacock 1987). Following the reasoning of the feminist historian of science Donna Haraway (1991), one should also understand that "objective" knowledge is always partial, positioned in some specific social location, and engaged in "webs of connections" and "shared conversations" with other differentially "situated knowledges" (see also Wilson 1988).

Epistemological instability notwithstanding, anthropology is strategically situated at a potentially reconstructive "crossroads of knowledge production" (di Leonardo 1991:1; F. Harrison 1993:401). Grounded in intersecting subdisciplinary paths, anthropology's "paradigmatic reintegration" (Stocking 1992:370) might well be achieved through the synthesis and reconciliation of divergent, yet potentially complementary, modes of analysis and theorizing. As an example, Robert Ulin (1991) argues in favor of bridging the current gap between political economy and postmodernism. Faye V. Harrison (1991a, 1993) has already proposed that projects committed to decolonizing and democratizing anthropology produce syntheses incorporating elements from political economy, reflexive and interpretive ethnography, a race- and class-conscious feminism, and radical traditions of scholarship by blacks and other peoples of color both inside and outside the West. In other words, we should go beyond Ulin's and many other radical anthropologists' largely Eurocentric and masculinist vision of critical anthropology by acknowledging and coming to terms with anthropology's gender and racial politics. Because of these politics, much of the work that women and peoples of color have produced has been virtually erased from anthropology's canon (Behar 1993; Behar and Gordon 1995; F. Harrison 1988, 1991a, 1993; Lutz 1990).

Anthropology, like all other disciplines, is produced and reproduced in a wider order of power that hierarchically positions multiple knowledges by valorizing some and subjugating others (Foucault 1980:82–85). This process appropriates, disguises, and buries certain knowledges within the body of systematizing theory. It also disqualifies and relegates other knowledges to marginal ranks. It has the power to canonize as well as to make invisible. For anthropology to be successfully reinvented, recaptured, and decolonized, it must come to terms with its hierarchy-producing discourses and practices and emancipate its subjugated knowledges and "the historical memories of struggles and hostile encounters" that they embody (Foucault 1980:83, 85).

Organizing a Black Presence in a Rehistoricized Anthropology

Anthropology's critical reconstruction and decolonization necessitate that it become more "attuned to the politics of its history" (Vincent 1991:45). This can be achieved only through a rethought historicism, a rehistoricization that repossesses both exposed and hidden dimensions of the past. According to Joan Vincent (1991:46–49) (who draws on the thinking of Levinson 1989), the key components of this process of rehistoricization are skepticism, contextualism, processualism, criticism, and engagement. Critical historians of anthropology must question the autonomy of ethnographic texts and individual authors. They must understand that ethnography is a socially constructed historical phenomenon grounded in the material circumstances of both the profession and the wider world. They must consider that once ethnographies are written, the prejudices and judgments of readers determine their reception. Reader-text interaction, or reception, governs whether texts are incorporated into the canon, whose disciplinary significance is reproduced over time.

In light of the politics of reception, rehistoricists must critically reposition the significance of the "classics." They must also, however, recognize the importance of recapturing works deemed "less significant" by historically specific canonical criteria. Finally, critical historicists must "feed upon [partisan] engagement, . . . address the politics around the writing of the text, the politics of reading the text, and the politics of its reproduction" (Vincent 1991:49). Moreover, critical rehistoricization projects must be grounded in "constant and sustained engagement with ethnographic subjects and . . . observations, inferences, and interpretations [embedded] within that engagement" (Roseberry 1989:x–xi qtd. in Vincent 1991:49).

African-American Pioneers in Anthropology was conceived and implemented with the clear intent of rehistoricizing the "racial economy" of anthropological science (Harding 1993) as well as the strategies and tactics blacks have employed to resist and subvert it. This rehistoricization effort is more than the sum of its individual biographies. It has been a concerted effort subsumed within the politicized development of the Association of Black Anthropologists (ABA), a national organization dedicated to advancing the status of blacks in the profession. Initially emerging from the Minority Caucus at the 1968 American Anthropological Association (AAA) meeting in Seattle, Washington, the ABA was officially founded in 1973 to provide much needed moral support to the few blacks in the field as well as to encourage a more critical and decolonized anthropology of Blacks worldwide and of other racially subjugated peoples subjected to oppression" (I. Harrison 1987).

In the 1980s, the ABA organized sessions on black anthropologists' "ancestors and elders" at annual meetings of the AAA. As Ira E. Harrison's (1987) instructive historical sketch of the ABA indicates, study of the history of blacks in anthropology emerged early as a dominant and continuous theme. Sheila Walker, who was involved in the early development of the ABA, explains:

> When we formed this organization . . . we talked about the need to create a forum for communication among members of the Black Anthropological Community and of the need to work together to make anthropology relevant to Black people. Most of us obviously thought that the latter was possible. . . . We each also thought that we were absolutely unique and original in having such a thought in the late sixties since few, if any, of us were aware that there already existed a whole tradition of Afro-American anthropology. St. Clair Drake, in his "Reflections on Anthropology and the Black Experience," however, made it quite clear that we were not the least bit original. In discussing the history of Blacks in anthropology he said, "A few of us chose careers in anthropology forty to forty-five years ago because we believed the discipline had relevance for the liberation of Black people from the devastating consequences of white racism" (Drake 1978:86).
>
> So, we weren't the first Black anthropologists to think our thoughts, but we were the first group fortunate enough to constitute a critical mass large enough to organize themselves for the purpose of trying to make Anthropology positively meaningful to Black people. One first step . . . was to discover the intellectual heritage already created for us by our elders such as St. Clair Drake, W. Montague Cobb, Irene Diggs, and our other forefathers and foremothers in the U.S. and beyond. (1982:1–2)

African-American Pioneers in Anthropology aims to make more visible, to situate, and to consolidate the considerable interest in anthropology's black "ancestors and elders" that has already yielded a number of important publications.[3] While this volume focuses primarily on African Americans, a more comprehensive history would include extensive discussion of the ethnological traditions that developed in the Caribbean, especially in Haiti (see Drake 1980, 1990b; Carnegie 1992; Sanjek 1993). The delineation of the "triangular trade" in the various knowledges of the black or pan-African world is clearly a worthy project, especially in light of anthropologists' growing interests in diasporas and transnational social fields and identities (Drake 1975, 1982; F. Harrison 1988; Basch, Schiller, and Blanc 1994; Sutton 1987; Khan 1994).

The biographies in this collection raise and attempt to answer several questions: Who were the black American pioneers attracted to anthropology from the 1920s to the early 1950s? What were their objectives, both intellectual and activist? Why and how did they decide to become anthropologists, when most of their black peers inclined toward social analysis chose sociology, history, or literature? How did their lives and work reflect the institutional structure of professional anthropology at that time? What were their lived experiences in professional anthropology? How did they cope with, resist, or contest anthropology's ideological and institutional racism and, in the case of the few women, anthropology's racially specific sexism? How did they resist victimization and express proactive agency? What contributions to knowledge have the pioneers made to anthropological science and the fellowship of anthropologists? How can their legacy serve as a basis for future scholarship?

Framework for Repossessing Black Pioneers

When writing or rewriting intellectual history, the analyst must locate the ideas and the producers and consumers of those ideas in a chronology of analytically relevant time. The historical analyst must also position researchers and their research objectives in genealogically significant disciplinary territory, multidisciplinary crossroads, and interdisciplinary borderlands.

In repossessing the historical agency of African-American anthropologists, several analytical distinctions can be made. First, there are three relevant categories of intellectuals who can be positioned in the broadest possible genealogy:

1. formally trained anthropologists, including those with graduate training who worked as anthropologists in such roles as university professors, researchers, and consultants and those who received graduate training but were not employed as anthropologists;
2. academic scholars in cognate fields (e.g., history, linguistics, sociology, and medicine) who made considerable use of anthropology in their scholarship and, in some instances, have contributed anthropologically relevant knowledge; and

3. intellectuals and "para-intellectuals" outside academia who were active consumers of anthropological knowledge and have used that knowledge for scholarly or activist purposes.

This collection of biographies is concerned primarily with the first category of individuals, who are the black classmates and counterparts of some of American anthropology's most recognized and esteemed (white) anthropologists. Unfortunately, relatively equal educational opportunities did not result in an equality of career outcomes.

The second set of important analytical distinctions that can be made concerns periodization. The period in which training and employment are obtained conditions the production and reproduction of careers as well as knowledge in historically specific ways. Four major time periods are discernible:

1. the mid-1800s through the end of World War I;
2. the post–World War I period up to 1955;
3. 1956–68; and
4. 1968 to the present.[4]

The anthropologists on which this book focuses were trained during the period after World War I, when blacks began earning Ph.D.'s in the field. The persons identified as members of this historic cohort are

1. Caroline Bond Day (1920s–1930s); Harvard University (physical anthropology with Earnest Hooton)
2. Mark Hanna Watkins (1920s–1933); University of Chicago (anthropological linguistics with Edward Sapir)
3. Zora Neale Hurston (1920s); Columbia University (folklore with Franz Boas)
4. Louis Eugene King (1920s–1930s); Columbia University (Afro-American community study with Franz Boas and Melville Herskovits)
5. Laurence Foster (1920s–1930s); University of Pennsylvania (folklore, Afro-American–Indian relations with A. Irving Hallowell)
6. W. Montague Cobb (1930–32); Case Western Reserve University (physical anthropology, gross anatomy with T. Wingate Todd)
7. Katherine Dunham (1930s–1940s); University of Chicago (ethnology with Robert Redfield)

8. Ellen Irene Diggs (1930s–1940s); University of Havana (ethnology with Fernando Ortiz)
9. Allison Davis (1930s–early 1940s); London School of Economics, Harvard University, and University of Chicago (social anthropology with W. Lloyd Warner)
10. Arthur Huff Fauset (1930s–1940s); University of Pennsylvania (ethnology, folklore with Frank G. Speck)
11. Manet Fowler (1937–52); Columbia University and Cornell University (cultural and applied anthropology, race relations, and industrial relations with E. Adamson Hoebel, Ralph Linton, Alexander Leighton, and William Foote Whyte)
12. St. Clair Drake (1937–54); University of Chicago (social anthropology with W. Lloyd Warner, Robert Redfield)
13. Hugh Smythe (1940s); Northwestern University (cultural anthropology, African ethnology with Melville Herskovits)
14. William S. Willis Jr. (1945–55); Columbia University (ethnohistory, history of anthropology, New World Indians, New World Negroes with Morton Fried)
15. Hubert B. Ross (1948–54); Columbia University (cultural anthropology, New World Negro with Charles Wagley, Gene Weltfish, and Joseph Greenberg)
16. Elliot Skinner (1950s–1955); Columbia University (Caribbean and African ethnology, political organization with Charles Wagley, Julian Steward, and Joseph Greenberg)
17. Council Taylor (1950s–1955); Yale University (Caribbean ethnology, with Sidney Mintz)

Of the above individuals, only Day, Hurston, and Dunham did not earn doctorates.[5] Because a few blacks may have "passed" as white[6] or remain unaccounted for this list may be incomplete, but it most likely contains the majority of blacks who became anthropologists during the pioneering period.[7] Unfortunately, due to the unevenness of the historiographical record, biographies of Mark Hanna Watkins (who, for many years, taught at Howard University), Hugh Smythe (who taught at Brooklyn College and served as an ambassador to Syria, 1965–67, and to Malta, 1967–69), Manet Fowler (who worked mainly outside academia as a practicing anthropologist), and Council Taylor (who taught at the University of California at Los Angeles and the State University of New York at Old Westbury) are not included here. Provided additional data are eventually uncovered, ongoing biographical projects on Watkins and Fowler will be completed (Wright n.d.; F. Harrison n.d.).[8]

The conditions for a second generation of professional anthropologists were set in 1953 when the Ford Foundation, responding to the forces of decolonization and the resultant shifts in international affairs, established a fellowship fund to increase the number of Africanists across a number of disciplines. This led to the emergence of a group of well-trained black experts on Africa, at least a dozen of whom were anthropologists (e.g., Niara Sudarkasa [Gloria Marshall], Johnnetta Cole, James Gibbs, and William Shack).[9] This second generation was trained between the mid-1950s and 1968.

In 1968, which in many respects was a watershed year, historically white universities began accepting black students in record numbers. This development, and the subsequent institutionalization of black studies programs throughout the United States, had major implications for the subsequent training and career options of African-American anthropologists. Since 1968 a much more sizable—and more diverse in terms of research expertise—third generation of black anthropologists has emerged. Over the course of the century, the number of black anthropologists has grown from the seventeen or so pioneers to well over one hundred and moving toward two hundred strong.

Repossessing Anthropology's Interfaces and Borderlands

St. Clair Drake's seminal historiography of anthropology's relationship with black intellectuals illuminates the remarkable breadth of the discourse that has informed the contents and contours of African Americans' anthropological scholarship (1974, 1978, 1980, 1984, 1987, 1990b). In his view, this field of knowledge transcends conventional disciplinary and professional boundaries. Historically, the discursive domain of African-American anthropology has accommodated the participation of the formally trained as well as the self-educated. It has encompassed the activist scholarship of academicians with doctorates as well as lay analysts, some with degrees in cognate disciplines.

This concern with the wider intellectual and political environment within which black anthropologists have lived and worked is premised on the recognition that anthropology is not autonomous but is produced and reproduced—or buried, erased, or negated—in a mutifaceted structure of intellectual production that organizes relations among diverse forms of knowledges—the "qualified," "disqualified," and "unqualified," from "normal" (Kuhn 1962) science's privileged point of view. Drake's analysis is especially important because it contests the academic hierarchy negating the theoretical merit and historical significance of ideas produced outside anthropology's restricted professional settings (e.g., university departments, museums, and government bureaus). After all, several African-American pioneers were unable to work (e.g., Day and King) or, perhaps in a few cases, *chose* not to work (e.g., Fauset, Fowler, Dunham, and Hurston) as anthropologists. Most who managed to obtain academic positions found themselves placed in sociology departments (Diggs, Drake, Foster, Watkins, and Ross) or in even more interdisciplinary settings such as schools of education (Davis), where they applied their anthropological perspectives and methods to and fused them into cognate disciplines. Hence, some of these pioneering anthropologists gained reputations primarily as sociologists (e.g., Diggs, Drake, and Smythe) or psychologists (e.g., Davis).[10] And, of course, Hurston and Dunham have long been better known for fiction and dance than for anthropology.

Other important figures also played central roles in configuring the interface between broader black intellectual concerns—anchored in antiracist struggle—and anthropology. This category predominated before the pioneering generation emerged in the aftermath of World War I. Although without formal credentials in anthropology, some of those oppositional analysts devoted to vindicating their race (e.g., Frederick Douglass, Martin Delaney, and W. E. B. Du Bois) articulated, and in some cases theorized, anthropologically relevant concerns that could be considered *ethnography* today. Why should such individuals be denied recognition within anthropology when the acknowledged forerunners (e.g., Durkheim and Morgan) and even some of the founders (e.g., Boas) of the discipline were not trained in anthropology? In Drake's history of African-American anthropological ideas there is clearly a visible place for black scholars (Drake 1980, 1987, 1990b), who, unlike their Euro-American counterparts, lacked the institutionalized recognition, support, and power for producing and reproducing their work as "anthropology." They were denied entrance into the fraternity of anthropologists because of the constraints of a racially segmented intellectual labor market. Another barrier to the formal anthropological pipeline was the ideologically constructed assumption concerning the necessary distinction and distance between the "purity" of science and the "pollution" of the partisan advocacy often embodied in subjugated knowledges. This dichotomy was further underpinned with racist and masculinist presuppositions concerning white males' inherent rationalism (and authority to universalize objective truths from their partial points of view) and blacks' and women's natural emotionalism (cf. Trinh 1989). This separation of powers is also reflected in later periods when "natives" were recruited to serve as fieldwork assistants and as Ph.D credentialed "key informants" expected to provide data for white anthropologists to interpret and explain (see F. Harrison 1991a, 1993; Jones [1970] 1988; Obbo 1990; Sanjek 1993).[11] This pattern of appropriation and exploitation is clearly revealed, for example, in Caroline Bond Day's relationship with Earnest Hooton, who regularly appropriated Radcliffe students' work (see Ross, Adams, and Williams's chapter). Boas's students similarly relied widely on "insiders" or "natives" in their field research. Boas himself depended upon the expertise and ethnographic labor of Native American field assistants, such as Ella Deloria (Finn 1993; Sanjek 1993). As students, both Louis King and Zora Neale Hurston assisted the "father of Afro-American anthropology," Melville Herskovits, by collecting the physical measurements and genealogical evidence for his first book about African Americans, *The American Negro: A Study in Racial Crossing* ([1928] 1964).

Continuities and Legacies

Perhaps the clearest continuity in African-American intellectual history over the past few centuries is a tradition of racial vindication (Drake 1971, 1980, 1984; Skinner 1983). Vindicationism emerged in reaction to racist assertions that Africans are degraded savages, that Africans and African Americans have no culture, that blacks are inherently inferior, and that miscegenation is degenerative to whites and white culture. African Americans have developed a deeply rooted humanistic tradition that directly opposes such ideas. St. Clair Drake (1987) has explicitly situated his work in this tradition, and Faye V. Harrison (1992) has argued that a number of pioneers (especially Day, Diggs, Davis, and Drake) were either directly or indirectly influenced by the specific vindicationist scholarship and political journalism of W. E. B. Du Bois, whose prodigious intellectual production ranged extensively, encompassing fiction, ethnography, physical anthropology, historiography, political criticism, sociology, and philosophy.

In the late nineteenth century and well into the twentieth, the most articulate and prominent "defender of the race" was, of course, Du Bois (see, e.g., 1899, [1903] 1961, [1939] 1970), who, Council Taylor (1971) and Faye V. Harrison (1992) have argued, should be positioned in the black anthropological lineage as well as in anthropology's wider genealogy as an ancestor—or at least an interlocutor. Drake (1980, 1987), Allison Davis (1983), and George Bond (1988) categorize Du Bois as a sociologist and historian who *consumed* anthropology in his vindicationist praxis. The argument that Du Bois should be considered an anthropologist points to several substantive and methodological aspects of his work. He accepted the principle of psychic unity. He was critical of speculative thinking and armchair theorizing. He embraced an inductive methodology that entailed prolonged direct observation and social description and explanation grounded in historical depth. His *Philadelphia Negro* (1899) was just as much ethnography as empirical sociology, and his research-driven critiques of scientific and popular racism paralleled and indeed intersected with Boasianism (Muller 1992; Baker 1994a, 1994c, 1998). His legacy within African-American anthropology is reflected in a number of features in the scholarship of several pioneers:

1. research is conceived and conducted as a form of activism;
2. historical and comparative methods are emphasized;
3. racism is seen as a central problem in the contemporary world;
4. race's intersection with class on both national and international levels is stressed; and
5. divergent theoretical strategies are synthesized or reconciled.

In at least implicit respects, a Du Boisian legacy is inscribed in the texts that many African-American anthropologists and other social analysts have written and continue to write (F. Harrison and Nonini 1992).

The tradition of racial vindication, however, preceded Du Bois by many years. With origins in the eighteenth century among free persons and preachers, it became increasingly visible during the nineteenth century as part of the reaction to the virulent racist ideology that reached its zenith during that period. According to Drake:

> A trend was set in the 1840s among Afro-American intellectuals—a very large proportion of whom were preachers—of using both Biblical and "scientific" data in a type of writing that I have called "vindicationist," i.e., a rebuttal of the criticism, slurs, ridicule and racist derogation that was hurled upon black people as the contest between abolitionists and defenders of slavery sharpened. "Vindicationists" were concerned with sins of omission, too, e.g., the failure to recognized the contributions black people had made in the Nile Valley civilizations. (1984:11)

Prominent nineteenth-century activist-intellectuals in the vindicationist tradition include Martin Delany, Frederick Douglass, and Edward Wilmot Blyden. Nineteenth-century adherents utilized biblical and classical Greek and Roman evidence (Drake 1971) as well as contemporary eyewitness accounts of how Africans lived (e.g., Delaney and Campbell [1860] 1971). Drake (1990b) points out that some of these accounts were quite rich in ethnographic description and analytical insights. Despite the religious and cultural biases, they were probably less distorted and more sympathetic than the standard racist colonial travelogues and missionary reports that came to inform the speculative theorizing of armchair ethnologists. Indeed, African-American missionaries working in colonial Africa during the late nineteenth century and in the early twentieth had a record of antiracist and anticolonial subversion that prompted colonial governments to try to bar them from African missions. As Drake (1990b) emphasizes, this early ethnographic record embedded in black missionary reports and diaries remains to be rescued from the black mainline churches' national archives.

It is important to note that, especially between 1850 and the early 1900s, the history of African-American vindicationism was significantly interwoven with the history of mainstream anthropology. One task of nineteenth-century African-American intellectuals was to counter the racist claims of Josiah Nott, Samuel Morton, George Gliddon, and the American ethnological school (Drake 1980, 1984, 1990b; Frederickson 1971). A most compelling example of this antiracist impetus is Douglass's eloquent 1854 (1950) critique of ethnology. Based on a sophisticated synthesis of sociocultural analysis and political economy, that address may have initiated the nature-nurture debate in U.S. public culture (personal communication with Michael Blakey, Nov. 23, 1994). A more positive and cooperative interaction between the vindicationist tradition and institutionalized anthropology developed in the early twentieth century between Du Bois and Boas (Baker 1998; Drake 1980; Muller 1992).[12]

Other prominent African-American activist-intellectuals who appropriated anthropological knowledge for their purposes include the self-trained historian Joel A. Rogers and the Puerto Rican–born bibliophile Arturo Schomberg, after whom the New York City Public Library's Schomberg Center for Research in Black Culture is named. Another key member of this group was Carter G. Woodson, the Harvard-trained historian who founded the Association for the Study of Negro Life and History along with the *Journal of Negro History* and Associated Publishers.

There is also a well-established African-American tradition of university-based scholars in the humanities, medicine, and the biological sciences who have been both active consumers and shapers of anthropological knowledge. Prime examples include Julian Herman Lewis (a physician), W. Montague Cobb (a physical anthropologist who was also a physician), Lorenzo Turner (a linguist), Frank Snowden (a classicist), and William Leo Hansberry (a historian).[13] Within professional anthropology, the best known of these individuals is Cobb. A philosopher-scientist-activist, Cobb was esteemed as a distinguished scholar for several decades. He was elected vice president of the American Association of Physical Anthropologists in 1948 and president of that organization in 1957. Until Yolanda T. Moses became the American Anthropological Association's president in 1995, Cobb had been the only black ever elected to the highest office of a major anthropological association in the United States.

The humanistic tradition of racial vindication continues today as the raison d'être for black studies programs, and, as suggested above, aspects of this tradition are also found in the work of most African-American scholars and activist-intellectuals who give their attention to the black experience. The critical rehistoricization that *Pioneers* represents is rooted ultimately in the vindicationist terrain sowed by, among others, Delaney, Douglass, and Du Bois.

Biographical Windows on the Black Experience in Anthropology

"Stamp of Approval," a front-page article in the *Anthropology Newsletter*, announces:

> Allison Davis, *one of the most influential anthropologists and educators of his day*, is the first anthropologist to be featured on a US commemorative stamp. Davis took his place on February 1 as the 17th and most recent honoree of the US Postal Service's annual Black Heritage stamp series. He was chosen as a stamp subject for his *pioneering work* in education and the social sciences. . . . *His work helped to* [*abolish legal*] *racial segregation* and contributed to contemporary thought on valuing the capabilities of youth from diverse background. (1, 6; emphasis ours)

An article published around the same time in the *Journal of Blacks in Higher Education* highlights Davis's achievements in these terms: "Davis was one of the first critics of cultural biases in intelligence tests. . . . *His thesis* that social class, rather than race [as a so-called biological phenomenon], was the determining factor in black educational inequality *formed the basis for the federal antipoverty programs' Operation Head Start*, a major and durable achievement that seeks to get disadvantaged children started off on the right educational foot" ("Black Heritage Award":23; emphasis ours).[14] Despite his accomplishments, Davis had more impact on educational research and public policy than on mainstream anthropology. For the most part, his ethnographically rich analysis of the political economy and social structure of racial caste and class in the Deep South (Davis, Gardner, and Gardner 1941) as well as his cross-race and cross-class scholarship in personality development and childhood socialization have not been integrated into graduate curricula or mainstream discourse and citations (see Browne's chapter). The *Anthropology Newsletter* article probably introduced most of the publication's readers to Davis. Although the *Anthropology Newsletter* and the AAA may have been opportunistically jumping on the bandwagon driven by the federal government and black lobbyists, these few words of recognition and approval were certainly better late than never. The brief article underscores the need to fill in the race-coded gaps in anthropology's history and demonstrate the wide range of influence from the many neglected pioneers.

Indeed, as Lee Baker's (1994b) archival research indicates, Louis King, another anthropologist who has remained unknown, contributed to the success of the historic 1954 *Brown* case. As Ira E. Harrison highlights in his chapter, King's West Virginia ethnography helped corroborate Otto Klineberg's research in *Negro Intelligence and Selective Migration* (1935). Baker demonstrates that Klineberg's study was used by the National Association for the Advancement of Colored People Legal Defense Fund's lawyers in their argument that environmental factors rather than race conditioned differences in whites' and blacks' IQ scores and academic performances. Harrison's biography indicates that Klineberg had corroborated his thesis that selective migration did not account for the higher scores of black migrants in the North by citing King's dissertation, which demonstrated no marked differences between those who migrated and those who remained.

According to the biographies compiled here, several other pioneers were involved in activism, advocacy, and public service. For instance, both Yolanda T. Moses and Carole H. Carpenter underscore the importance of political engagement in their chapters. Laurence Foster combined an academic career with community activism, and Arthur Huff Fauset's self-identification was not as an anthropologist but as a "campaigner for social justice." Lesley M. Rankin-Hill and Michael L. Blakey portray W. Montague Cobb as a public intellectual active in both professional and civil rights organizations. His leadership in implementing seven Imhotep National Conferences "to compile and disseminate otherwise scant information on African-American health" contributed to the passage of the 1964 Civil Rights Act and the 1965 Medicare Bill. Determined to get the word out, Cobb regularly published information on health and race in black journals and popular magazines. As Gwendolyn Mikell's and Joyce Aschenbrenner's biographies illuminate, other popular vehicles that raised the public's social and cultural consciousness were Zora Neale Hurston's fiction and Katherine Dunham's dance theater. Hugh Smythe and Elliot Skinner both exhibited their commitment to improving world affairs and to promoting a black presence in U.S. foreign policy by serving as ambassadors (Drake 1980:24; Mwaria's chapter).

Willie L. Baber points out that while St. Clair Drake was being initiated into anthropological fieldwork in Mississippi by his mentor, Allison Davis, he committed time to organizing sharecroppers. During his Africa phase, he conducted policy-related applied research in Ghana while working with pan-Africanists Kwame Nkrumah and George Padmore. Later, when living in Chicago, Drake organized unemployed workers and joined with several civil rights organizations. A few months before his death in 1990, the Society for Applied Anthropology commended Drake's activist-driven scholarship by conferring on him the Bronislaw Malinowski Award (also see F. Harrison 1990b).

Katherine Dunham's activism was most recently exhibited in the early 1990s during a life-threatening hunger strike in which she expressed her outrage against the U.S. government's policy on Haitian refugees and Haitian political repression. Throughout her career, she served as an advocate for the Haitian people and protested against the segregation of dance companies and their audiences. She also brought her sociopolitical sensibilities to her cultural work with youth gangs in East St. Louis (see Aschenbrenner's chapter).

The pioneers' shared commitment to fighting racism and instigating meaningful social change is also reflected in the contents of their scholarship. Davis's interrogation of racial caste and its relationship with social class in a southern town embedded in a regional plantation system stemmed from his motivation to understand and expose the injustices of racial inequality for the purpose of undermining it. Davis's analysis of the political and economic underpinnings of southern racism and its terror was unparalleled in the literature of that time; yet, *Deep South* never received the attention that Hortense Powdermaker's (1939) and John Dollard's (1937) work did (Drake 1974). In his approach to caste, Davis attempted to bring some of the concerns of radical, even Marxist, social analysis to the then dominant social structuralist paradigm. The resulting analytical tensions were not unlike those found in several pioneers' work, as they disrupted the coherence of conventional theory with their attempts to bring new issues to research and explain the forces of racist oppression, colonial expansion, biological variation, and cultural resistance from more critical, nondeterministic perspectives.

Accordingly, analysts such as Laurence Foster and William S. Willis Jr. pushed against the limits of established frameworks. They applied questions concerning racial oppression and Anglo-American colonial expansion to their respective studies of Native Americans and the relations between Native Americans and African Americans. Unlike many, if not most, of their white contemporaries, they related issues of Native American cultural and social change to race and power. According to Willis (1969, 1975), despite its antiracist underpinnings, Boasian ethnology and folklore fell short of adequately dealing with the impact racism and antiracism had on sociocultural change. For instance, the sociocultural context of black folklore was not conceived widely enough to include white supremacy and segregation; consequently, mainstream interpretations of the black folk tradition "distorted important dimensions" and "severely restricted . . . insights into the black experience [and struggle for survival and freedom under] slavery and . . . Jim Crow" (1975:326–27). While Boasian antiracism attracted Davis, Drake, and perhaps other pioneers into anthropology, its liberalist limitations spurred them to address white racism in less uncertain and less compromised terms.

Carolyn Bond Day and W. Montague Cobb stretched physical anthropology's limits by critically interrogating the racial determinism so widespread in mainstream studies of human biological variation. Day's critique, however, was only implicitly embedded in her book but quite forthright in the NAACP's magazine, *Crisis* (see Ross, Adams, and Williams's chapter). This suggests the importance of examining both academic and popular writings when discerning the conceptual and political underpinnings of this vindicationist literature.

Irene Diggs's Latin American research was driven, in part, by a Du Boisian agenda for understanding the variation in the sociohistorical construction of race and blackness internationally (see Bolles's chapter; Bolles 1989; F. Harrison 1992). This comparative approach to blacks in the Western Hemisphere is also at least implicitly characteristic of Hurston's and Dunham's research in folklore, religion, and dance. However, it appears much more explicitly in Drake's work. Drawing upon his rich research experiences in the United States, Great Britain, and Africa, he devoted several years to an extensive historicized investigation of Africa and the black diaspora, resulting in two encyclopedic tomes, one of which he was unable to complete before his death. As Jordan (1982, 1983, 1990) and Baber's biography elucidate, in this impressive manuscript Drake explored the comparative dynamics of racial domination and the diverse forms of accommodation and resistance they engendered across time and space.

It is noteworthy that many of the features of anthropology's recent "postmodernist turn" and "experimental moment" (e.g., ethnography viewed as literary text, social analysis informed or framed by reflexivity, and texts written in multiple voices and in dialogic context) were foreshadowed in Zora Neale Hurston's work, which dramatically blurred the boundaries between social science and art, folklore and fiction, ethnography and autobiography, and social analysis and journalism. Such genre blurring was also characteristic of Manet Fowler's holographic writing (F. Harrison n.d.) and Katherine Dunham's choreography and narrative ethnography. Hurston, Fowler, and Dunham belong to a "women's tradition" in ethnographic writing, which has addressed both academic and popular audiences and has been much "more open about [issues of] positionality [and] less assertive [about] scientific authority" (Abu-Lughod 1991:152). At the time they were developing their careers, this creative intellectual expressiveness was not considered a desirable credential for gaining entry into the established academic fraternity of anthropologists. Moreover, in Hurston's case, her work also departed from established conventions due to its concern with questions of gender, as Mikell argues in her chapter. Hurston's sensitive depiction of women and her concern with male-female relations represented an important precursor of more recent contributions that black women and, more generally, women of color have made. These contributions have prompted feminist analysts to confront the ways in which race intersects gender and differentially shapes women's (and men's) lives.

Anthropology's racial division of labor has historically assigned most analysts of color to the study of their own or similar cultures, while whites have been expected to cross racial lines to study dominated peoples, who for the most part are peoples of color.[15] Not surprisingly, then, most of the pioneers specialized in the study of blacks[16] and, hence, produced situated knowledge informed by their sociopolitical positions as men and women of African descent[17]—as racial others and outsiders in Eurocentrically constructed anthropological discourse. Foster and Willis, however, were trained as Native Americanists (perhaps in the tradition of "buffalo soldiers"), and Smythe, although trained as an Africanist, conducted research in Japan as well as Africa. Perhaps more than any other pioneer, Davis went against the grain of research convention. By working with a biracial research team of two married couples, he, as the senior researcher (another anomaly), analyzed and theorized the interacting structures of racial caste and social class in the experience of *both blacks and whites* in "Old City," Mississippi. In his later investigations, he continued studying multiple dimensions of race, class, and even gender (F. Harrison 1992:250). Despite his work, his alternative approach to research conceptualization and design has not been well received or reproduced (cf. Vincent 1991:47–48) as an integral and, indeed, central part of mainstream anthropology's development.

Early African-American interest in sub-Sahara Africa also led to new directions in social analysis. Cheryl B. Mwaria's portrayal of Elliot Skinner's distinguished career demonstrates how in his political ethnography of the Mossi he was able to transcend many of the limits of conventional Africanist anthropology, which—especially among British-trained and influenced anthropologists—was largely grounded in an ahistoric and equilibrium model of society. Departing from the discourse that eroticized primitive and tribal others, Skinner studied the continuities and discontinuities within an African kingdom that had endured in spite of the disintegrative forces engendering the decline of the historic empires of Mali and Songhai. In later work, he embedded his ethnography of local everyday life in a macrostructural treatment of a postcolonial city and nation-state, producing an exemplary mode of analysis that refashioned anthropological holism.

St. Clair Drake's work also helped to take African studies in important new directions. His deconstruction of the myth concerning the so-called Hamitic origins of African civilizations cleared the conceptual ground for thinking more critically and productively about questions of agency and the ability of ordinary African peoples to generate social action and change. In his work on the political transition of early postcolonial states he analyzed the power struggles between the new elites and traditional authorities (e.g., chieftaincies) and elucidated how traditional structures of power were accommodated and, in the most successful instances, mobilized in planned social and economic development (Drake 1960).

While African-American anthropologists have been largely marginal to anthropology's central discourses, this relative position has not precluded specific cases of academic success in anthropology. For instance, Skinner, Drake, and Cobb achieved considerable esteem within prestigious institutions or professional organizations and Hurston has received heightened interest (Dorst 1987; Gordon 1990; Hernández 1993; Mikell 1982, 1983). These instances do not, however, negate the ambivalent relationship, at best, that black subaltern analysis has with mainstream anthropology, whose "racial economy of science" (Harding 1993) needs to be confronted and dismantled.

No Longer "People without History"

African-American Pioneers in Anthropology—like its feminist counterparts (Golde 1970; Gacs et al. 1989; F. Harrison and Nonini 1992; Behar and Gordon 1995)—questions anthropology's conventional wisdom and its taken-for-granted knowledge of its past. Moreover, it recovers some of the excluded voices of anthropologists whose scholarship has been "hidden in the closet." This project, which privileges the situated experiences and partial perspectives of "frogs" (who see the world around them from below), has substantiated *the fact* that contemporary as well as past black anthropologists are not (drawing on Wolf's [1982] book title) "people without history."

In the spirit of this neglected history, Johnnetta Cole accepted the AAA's 1993 Distinguished Service Award with the powerful declaration that she is the product of a dual legacy: "As I receive this award, I am standing on the institution and work of men who taught me the stuff of anthropology: George Eaton Simpson, Melville Herskovits, Paul Bohannan. But when you see me you must also see mighty women, women whom I never met in a classroom, but whose work and whose lives convinced me that I too could become an anthropologist. Let me call the names of two of those she-roes of mine: Zora Neale Hurston and Vera Green" ("Until Difference":3).[18]

On the same evening that the AAA conferred its highest honors on Cole and Claude Lévi-Strauss, Yolanda T. Moses, an African-American woman of similar intellectual genealogy, was inducted as the association's next president. Undeniably, anthropology has multiple lineages.[19] It cannot adequately come to terms with the multidimensionality and the politics of its past, present, and future unless it acknowledges and embraces this diversity—both its enriching breadth and its troubling complications.

Notes

This essay has undergone several stages of writing and rewriting. We owe a debt of gratitude to Glenn Jordan for the invaluable input he provided during the earliest phases of this book's development cycle. The book has its origins in two AAA sessions in 1981 and 1983 that Ira Harrison conceived and organized under the aegis of the ABA. Three biographies (I. Harrison 1983; Mikell 1983; Moses 1983) from these sessions were published in the *Western Journal of Black Studies.* The idea of a book came out of Ira Harrison's discussions with Jordan, whose writings (1982, 1983) on the sociology of anthropological knowledge built on the approach of his mentor, St. Clair Drake. The original pioneers project spawned a number of subsequent sessions and publications. In 1985 Ira Harrison organized a AAA session on Howard University's contributions to anthropology, and Glenn Jordan and Faye Harrison (both of whom had studied under Drake at Stanford University) co-organized a session on Drake's distinguished body of work. For that same AAA meeting, Faye Harrison and Dallas Browne co-organized an urban-focused session in honor of the fortieth anniversary of *Black Metropolis* (1945), the classic that Drake had co-authored with the sociologist Horace Cayton. This session resulted in a special issue of *Urban Anthropology: Studies in Cultural Systems and World Economic Development* that Faye Harrison edited. In the introduction to that volume (F. Harrison 1988), she elaborated a diaspora perspective informed by Drake's pan-Africanist approach, and she presented a conceptual framework for analyzing the relations between anthropology's core and peripheral discourses. While exposing the discipline's hierarchy-producing and racializing practices, she conceptualized the periphery as a significant locus of innovative and activist scholarship. In 1990 Faye Harrison joined her colleague Ira Harrison as co-editor of this book, replacing Jordan, who had settled in Wales.

This introduction is the product of the collaborative efforts outlined above, but Faye Harrison assumed final responsibility for framing and fleshing out the essay, which situates *Pioneers* vis-à-vis recent trends in critically reconstructing anthropology.

1. See di Leonardo (1991) and Moore (1988) for overviews of feminist anthropology's development and current trends. See Fahim (1982), Fahim and Helmer (1980), Jones [1970] (1988), D. Lewis (1973), Limón (1991), Rosaldo (1993), Ohnuki-Tierney (1984), Owusu (1978, 1979), and Walker (1982) for treatments of "native" or indigenous anthropologies. See Hakken and Lessinger (1987), Leacock (1982), O'Laughlin (1975), Ulin (1991), and Wolf (1982) for Marxist and post-Marxist analyses. See Clifford and Marcus (1986) and Marcus and Fischer (1986) for insights into the ethnography-as-text movement.

2. The omission or erasure of black (e.g., African, African-American, and Caribbean) anthropologists is characteristic of the literature in the history of anthropology (see Lowie 1932; Harris 1968; Kaplan and Manners 1972; Hatch 1973; Voget 1975; Honigman 1976; Kuper 1983; Helm 1985; Stocking 1968, 1987, 1992). Barrett (1984) also omits black anthropologists' contributions although he does underscore anthropology's responsibility to research and theorize such neglected subjects as racism and inequality.

3. For intellectual biographies and biographically grounded essays see Baber (1990), Bolles (1986, 1989), Bolles and Moses (1989), I. Harrison (1983), Jordan (1982, 1983, 1990), Mikell (1982, 1983, 1989), Moses (1983), and Rankin-Hill and Blakey (1994). For an interview with Drake on his career, see Bond (1988). For extremely informative essays on the black experience in anthropology, see Drake (1974, 1978, 1980, 1984, 1990b). Willis (1972, 1975) also contributed essays on anthropology's history from the vantage point of "skeletons in the closet" and "frogs." For perspectives on black contributions to the history of urban anthropology, Du Bois's influence on several black pioneers, and the racial and gendered politics of writing ethnography and theorizing culture, see F. Harrison (1988, 1992, 1993). For obituaries on Mark Hanna Watkins, Vera Green, and St. Clair Drake see Wright (1976), Cole (1982), and F. Harrison (1990a, 1990c). Also see "Until Difference" (1994), Dorst (1987), Gordon (1990), and Sanjek (1993) for treatments of Allison Davis, Zora Neale Hurston, and African and African-American ethnographers neglected in the record. Also see Baker (1994a, 1998) for an insightful social history of anthropology's constructions of race and for a critical assessment of Boas's relationship to African Americans' struggle against racism. Hsu's view (1973) on prejudice's effects on American anthropology is also of relevance.

4. This chronology differs somewhat from that which Drake (1990b) proposes. In his view the pioneering period fell between the two world wars.

5. It is reputed that although Day wrote a dissertation, she never received her doctorate (personal communication with Michael Blakey, Nov. 23, 1994).

6. Although the issue of passing does not appear to be of major concern, it is relevant. At a commemorative event in honor of Council Taylor's seventy-fifth birthday, he revealed that in his youth and young adulthood, he, with his family's support, passed for white to maximize his educational and occupational opportunities. His public racial persona became more consistent with his private identity during the 1960s when, in the context of the civil rights and Black Pride and Black Power movements, blackness underwent radical redefinition and reevaluation, and opportunities for black social mobility expanded. Taylor was among the black intellectuals who founded the Institute of the Black World, which engaged in activist research.

7. Most of the pioneers were trained in the major anthropology programs in the country. More than half of them studied at Columbia and Chicago alone; consequently, these schools were key pipelines into, and gatekeepers of, African-American anthropology. However, before graduate school many pioneers had

been inspired—without benefit of formal anthropology curricula—to document black culture by their prior education in historic black institutions: Day, Diggs, and Smythe at Atlanta University (now Clark-Atlanta University); Hurston, King, and Willis at Howard University; Foster at Lincoln University; Watkins at Prairie View State College (now Prairie View University); and Drake at Hampton Institute (now Hampton University).

Beyond the setting of top-ranking universities, anthropology was also taught in seminaries preparing missionaries for work overseas. According to Duberman's (1989) biography of Paul Robeson and entries in Hine's (1993) and Smith's (1993) encyclopedias on African-American women in the United States, during the 1930s and 1940s Eslanda Goode Robeson, Paul Robeson's wife, pursued doctoral studies in anthropology at London University, the London School of Economics, and finally at the interdenominational Hartford Seminary Foundation in Connecticut. There she took classes on Africa, India, and China and drafted a doctoral dissertation (Duberman 1989:292), which seminary records indicate that she never completed (personal communication with Karen B. Rollins, registrar, Hartford Seminary, Oct. 21, 1997). Although none of the above sources indicates anything about the focus of her dissertation, it seems likely that it concerned some aspect of African ethnology. In 1936 she visited Africa, where her experiences strengthened her commitment to pan-Africanism and internationalism. Nine years later, she published *African Journey* (1945), which chronicled her travels on the continent and the development of her thinking on African affairs.

Robeson's decision to attend the seminary rather than an established Ph.D. program at a major university may perhaps be attributed, in part, to her belief that before World War II "the only people who were even vaguely aware of Africans as human beings were missionaries. Tourists, businessmen, government officials, and politicians . . . considered the Africans . . . savages, labor fodder and pawns" (qtd. in Smith 1993:444). Also Duberman suggests that the Hartford Seminary Foundation may have been appealing because its dean, Malcolm S. Pitt, had been Paul Robeson's classmate at Rutgers. Further, in *African Journey* Eslanda Robeson expressed her dissatisfaction with the training she received while in London. She found her professors' and classmates' interpretations of Africa to be ideological apologia for a racist colonial world order. As a consequence of that experience, among others, her evaluation of established anthropology departments, whether in Europe or the United States, was decidedly critical. It appears that she wanted the freedom to pursue her interests in a supportive and flexible environment. Not surprisingly, Robeson's academic interests were solidly grounded in her political activism. In 1941 she collaborated with her husband to found the Council on African Affairs, an organization that promoted decolonization. For her, a doctorate in anthropology was not a means to a university appointment. Instead, it represented an opportunity to strengthen her political role in the international arena. This activist orientation was exhibited during the early postwar period, when she traveled throughout central Africa to collect data that she later used "to argue and discuss the problems of the region before the United Nations Trusteeship Council" (Smith 1993:445).

8. In a AAA meeting paper Muhammad (1985) points out that Watkins (1903–76) did his thesis and dissertation (1933) research on Chechewa Bantu grammar. This research culminated in *A Grammar of Chechewa* (1937a). In later years he furthered his research interests in African languages (Watkins 1962) and the languages of the Americas by conducting field studies in South Africa, Haiti, Mexico, Guatemala, and Costa Rica. Over the years, Watkins taught sociology at Municipal College in Louisville, Kentucky; sociology and anthropology at Fisk University in Nashville, Tennessee; for short periods at Georgetown and the University of Chicago; and from 1947 to 1973 at Howard University, where he developed the anthropology curriculum, one of only two programs (until 1978 when Fisk included one) offered at historically black colleges during Watkins's tenure as a college professor (see Watkins 1937b). See Wright (1976) for an obituary written from the vantage point of a junior colleague—the black anthropologist who replaced Watkins at Howard. Wright points out that Watkins, who "was a splendid teacher," was "not a prolific writer" (1976:889). To a considerable extent, the constraints of working in a historically black university, where teaching was emphasized and the infrastructure for research underdeveloped, accounts for this (also see I. Harrison's chapter on Ross).

Manet Fowler (1916–) was probably the first black woman to receive a Ph.D. in anthropology from a U.S. university. She wrote prizewinning short stories (Fowler 1938a, 1938b) and worked in journalism and public relations before becoming an anthropologist. She conducted her dissertation research on a "human relations situation" grounded in labor, racial, and interpersonal conflicts. As an applied researcher, her objective was to offer insights for more effective labor management policy. In her holographically written dissertation (Fowler 1952), she provided remarkably thick description of a 1950 labor relations conflict between service workers and their employer, a major university. She treated the university as "big business," an industrial organization marked by increasingly centralized and depersonalized control and hierarchical relations between managers and subordinate employees. Her window on the strike was the life story of "Chef A," a middle-aged black kitchen worker who joined the union just a month before the strike and became one of its leaders. Besides providing ethnographic details on the psychological and social dynamics of the conflict, Fowler explained the multiple causes and consequences of the strike by synthesizing her professors' theoretical frameworks: anthropologist-psychiatrist Alexander Leighton's personality/life history analysis and sociologist-ethnographer William Foote Whyte's social interaction/social situation framework. Her analysis demonstrated the inadequacy of an economistic approach in theorizing and resolving industrial conflict. She also demonstrated the usefulness of the very life history techniques applied to Chef A for illuminating the partial, situated theoretical perspectives of Leighton and Whyte. Although Fowler taught anthropology and

African-American studies at a number of colleges and universities for short periods, she devoted most of her career to applied work. For example, in the early 1950s she worked on a Tuskegee Institute rural health project on black sharecroppers and tenant farmers; in the late 1950s and early 1960s she worked with the New York State Department of Health's Office of Professional Training and its Public Health Research, Program Development, and Evaluation Group; and in the late 1960s and early 1970s she worked on a project on racial and gender aspects of aging at Syracuse University's Family Service Center (F. Harrison n.d.).

9. Shack began his graduate training at Northwestern but, upon advice from Drake and others, completed it at the University of London in 1961. Other black Americans who were trained in social anthropology and African studies in England were Audrey Smedley, who in the late 1950s studied with Max Gluckman at Manchester, and George Bond, who took his degree in 1968 from the University of London.

10. St. Clair Drake's reputation as a sociologist is reflected in his receipt of the American Sociological Association's prestigious Du Bois–Johnson–Frazier Award in 1973. Drake (1980:24) points out that Hugh Smythe, who did research in Africa and Japan, is listed in *Who's Who in America* as a sociologist. Allison Davis has been described in print as a psychologist. An article in the *Journal of Blacks in Higher Education* (1994) on the black heritage stamp honoring Davis characterizes him as a "distinguished anthropologist, social psychologist, and early advocate of the need to eliminate cultural bias in intelligence testing" ("Black Heritage Award":23).

11. St. Clair Drake often related his observations on anthropology's politics to his students. He once stated that he was recognized as an "area man," one who had collected ethnographic data on a specific culture area (in his case Africa and the African diaspora) and contributed to a specific area study, such as African studies. He claimed that area scholars are differentiated from anthropology's "theory men," whose work is received as theoretically significant. For the most part black anthropologists are positioned as area researchers often able to collect data that may be unavailable to whites. Very little black scholarship is received as a source of useful theory construction, regardless of the actual substance and theoretical underpinnings of that scholarship. Joan Vincent (1991:47) points out that ethnography is the medium through which most sociocultural anthropologists describe cultural processes as well as theorize. If this is generally the case, then we should expect the ethnography that blacks produce to embody theory reflective of blacks' locations and experiences in both "the field" (of primary data collection) and the wider world of structured inequality. This theory needs to be excavated by an "archaeology" of subjugated knowledges.

12. The relationship between Du Bois and Boas needs further examination. Muller (1992) points to archival material that suggests that Du Bois may have influenced Boas's views on race and culture though Boas never acknowledged this influence in citations. Baker (1994a, 1998) provides a textured picture of Boas's re-

lationship with the African-American struggle against racism. He points to Monteiro (1990:22) and Baltzell (1967:xxvi) for claims "that Boas's chapter in *The Mind of Primitive Man* entitled 'The Race Problem in Modern Society' was influenced by Du Bois' *Philadelphia Negro* and the Atlanta Studies" (214). That substantial intellectual cross-fertilization took place across the color line is evident in Herskovits's case. Jackson (1986) has documented the protracted dialogue Herskovits had with African-American scholars (e.g., "New Negro" movement philosopher and architect Alain Locke), who challenged him to move beyond the assimilationism informing and limiting his early research (see F. Harrison 1992:256n1).

13. Julian Lewis was an associate professor at a white institution (a rare achievement at that time) who, in 1942, published *The Biology of the Negro.* Drake points out that Lewis's book merited inclusion in any bibliography of the field—"not because of any empirical contributions he had made, but because the work did precisely what he said he was trying to do: . . . [assemble observations] and reported facts . . . [on] the biology, including the pathology, of the Negro" (1990b:2). Lorenzo Dow Turner's work is much better known among anthropologists and African-Americanists than Lewis's. Drawing on his vast knowledge of the languages of west and central Africa, Turner produced the classic *Africanisms in the Gullah Dialect* (1949). Howard-based Frank Snowden is perhaps the leading authority on the "black" presence in ancient Greek and Roman societies. His book *Blacks in Antiquity: Ethiopians in the Greco-Roman Experience* (1970) was immediately recognized as a definitive contribution. William Leo Hansberry, through his years of work at Howard University, forged an intellectual tradition in the field of history. Hansberry devoted most of his scholarly career to the interrelationships between ancient Ethiopia (i.e., Nubia or Kush) and the surrounding areas in Africa as well as with the classical world. He pioneered during a period when scant recognition was given to the peoples and cultures of that area as compared with the intensive concentration on Egyptology. See Drake (1987, 1990a) for an insightful analysis of African-American classicists and Egyptologists.

14. Kluger (1976) points out that Allison Davis was among thirty-five or so social scientists who filed an amicus brief included as an appendix with the *Brown* case material. Also, in the early 1950s Thurgood Marshall hired the political scientist John A. Davis—Allison Davis's brother—to head a research task force to substantiate the NAACP's Legal Defense Fund's case with social science research. Of course, John Davis was informed by his brother's research on the socialization of "children of bondage" (e.g., Davis and Dollard 1940).

15. See Obbo (1990) for a poignant discussion of white anthropologists' attitudes toward African ethnographers. She also discusses her white American colleagues' negative reactions to her research on middle-class whites.

16. St. Clair Drake was unable to conduct his doctoral research in Africa because Melville Herskovits, one of the most prominent gatekeepers for Africanist anthropology, believed that black Americans could not be "objective" in the study of African societies. Perhaps in his view black Americans' nationalist proclivi-

ties or their tendency toward emotionalism precluded their objectivity. One of Herskovits's early black students, Hugh Smythe, was permitted to pursue a dissertation on Yoruba kinship, but through library research only. By the 1960s Herskovits's attitude had clearly changed. Johnnetta Cole was able to conduct her dissertation research in Liberia. At this later juncture, the Ford Foundation helped provide institutionalized incentives and support for a black American presence among Africanists.

17. See Whitehead and Conaway's volume (1986) on the impact of the gendered self on fieldwork as a reflexive and socially negotiated process. Some of the contributors also examine the racialized dimensions of selfhood.

18. Vera Mae Green was the first president of the Association of Black Anthropologists and a Caribbean and Latin America specialist. When an undergraduate at Roosevelt University in Chicago, she studied under St. Clair Drake, who inspired her to pursue further studies in anthropology. See Cole (1982) and I. Harrison (1982).

19. Sanjek (1996) rehistoricizes urban anthropology in terms of its multiple lineages, which encompass the contributions of Du Bois, Warner, Davis, and Drake.

References Cited

Abu-Lughod, Lila. 1991. "Writing against Culture." In *Recapturing Anthropology: Working in the Present.* Ed. Richard G. Fox. Santa Fe: School of American Research Press. 137–62.

Adams, Amelia M. 1987. "Blacks in Anthropology: Natives in Search of a Definition." Undergraduate thesis, Smith College.

Appadurai, Arjun. 1991. "Global Ethnoscapes: Notes and Queries for a Transnational Anthropology." In *Recapturing Anthropology: Working in the Present.* Ed. Richard G. Fox. Santa Fe: School of American Research Press. 191–210.

Baber, Willie L. 1990. "A Tribute to St. Clair Drake, Activist and Scholar." *Transforming Anthropology* 1 (2): 18–24.

Baker, Lee D. 1994a. "The Location of Franz Boas within the African-American Struggle." *Critique of Anthropology* 14 (2): 199–217.

———. 1994b. "Moving the History of Anthropology from the Memorial to the Contextual: The Case of Louis E. King." Paper presented at the annual meeting of the American Ethnological Society. Santa Monica, Calif. Apr. 14–16.

———. 1994c. "The Role of Anthropology in the Social Construction of Race, 1896–1954." Ph.D. diss., Temple University.

———. 1998. *From Savage to Negro: Anthropology and the Construction of Race, 1896–1954.* Berkeley:University of California Press.

Baltzell, E. Digby. 1967. Introduction to *The Philadelphia Negro* by W. E. B. Du Bois. New York: Schocken Books. ix–xliv.

———. 1998. *From Savage to Negro: Anthropology and the Construction of Race, 1896–1954*. Berkeley: University of California Press, 1998.

Barrett, Stanley. 1984. *The Rebirth of Anthropological Theory*. Toronto: University of Toronto Press.

Basch, Linda, Nina Glick Schiller, and Cristina Szanton Blanc. 1994. *Nations Unbound: Transnational Projects, Postcolonial Predicaments, and Deterritorialized Nation-States*. Basel, Switzerland: Gordon and Breach.

Behar, Ruth. 1993. "Introduction: Women Writing Culture: Another Telling of the Story of American Anthropology." *Critique of Anthropology* 13 (4): 307–25.

Behar, Ruth, and Deborah Gordon, eds. 1995. *Women Writing Culture: A Reader in Feminist Ethnography*. Berkeley: University of California Press.

"Black Heritage Award for an African-American Educator." 1994. *Journal of Blacks in Higher Education* 3 (Spring): 23.

Bolles, A. Lynn. 1986. "African-American Soul Force: Dance, Music, and Vera Mae Green." *Sage* 3 (2): 32–34.

———. 1989. "Ellen Irene Diggs." In *Women Anthropologists: Selected Biographies*. Ed. Ute Gacs, Aisha Khan, Jerrie McIntyre, and Ruth Weinberg. Urbana: University of Illinois Press. 59–64.

Bolles, A. Lynn, and Yolanda T. Moses. 1989. In "Vera Mae Green." *Women Anthropologists: Selected Biographies*. Ed. Ute Gacs, Aisha Khan, Jerrie McIntyre, and Ruth Weinberg. Urbana: University of Illinois Press. 127–32.

Bond, George C. 1988. "A Social Portrait of John Gibbs St. Clair Drake: An American Anthropologist." *American Ethnologist* 15 (4): 762–81.

Carnegie, Charles V. 1992. "The Fate of Ethnography: Native Social Science in the English-Speaking Caribbean." *New West Indian Guide* 66 (1–2): 5–25.

Clifford, James, and George E. Marcus, eds. 1986. *Writing Culture: The Poetics and Politics of Ethnography*. Berkeley: University of California Press.

Cole, Johnnetta B. 1982. "Obituary: Vera May Green." *American Anthropologist* 84 (3): 633–35.

Davis, Allison. 1983. *Leadership, Love, and Aggression*. New York: Harcourt, Brace, Jovanovich.

Davis, Allison, and John Dollard. 1940. *Children of Bondage: The Personality Development of Negro Youth in the Urban South*. Washington, D.C.: American Council on Education.

Davis, Allison, Burleigh B. Gardner, and Mary R. Gardner. 1941. *Deep South: A Social Anthropological Study of Caste and Class*. Chicago: University of Chicago Press.

Delaney, Martin, and Robert Campbell. [1860] 1971. *Search for a Place: Black Separatism*. Ann Arbor: University of Michigan Press.

di Leonardo, Micaela, ed. 1991. *Gender at the Crossroads of Knowledge: Feminist Anthropology in the Postmodern Era*. Berkeley: University of California Press.

Dollard, John. 1937. *Caste and Class in a Southern Town*. New Haven: Yale University Press.

Dorst, John. 1987. "Rereading *Mules and Men:* Toward the Death of the Ethnographer." *Cultural Anthropology* 2 (3): 305–18.

Douglass, Frederick. [1854] 1950. "The Claims of the Negro Ethnologically Considered." In *The Life and Writings of Frederick Douglass.* Ed. Philip S. Foner. New York: International Publishers. 289–309.

Drake, St. Clair. 1960. "Traditional Authority and Social Action in Former British West Africa." *Human Organization* 19 (3): 150–58.

———. 1971. *The Redemption of Africa and Black Religion.* Chicago: Third World Press.

———. 1974. "In the Mirror of Black Scholarship: W. Allison Davis and *Deep South.*" In *Education and Black Struggle: Notes from the Colonized World.* Ed. Institute of the Black World. Harvard Educational Review Monograph no. 2. Cambridge, Mass.: Harvard Educational Review. 42–54.

———. 1975. "The Black Diaspora in Pan-African Perspective." *Black Scholar* 7 (1): 2–13.

———. 1978. "Reflections on Anthropology and the Black Experience." *Anthropology and Educational Quarterly* 9 (2): 85–109.

———. 1980. "Anthropology and the Black Experience." *Black Scholar* 11 (7): 2–31.

———. 1982. "Diaspora Studies and Pan-Africanism." In *Global Dimensions of the African Diaspora.* Ed. Joseph E. Harris. Washington, D.C.: Howard University Press. 341–402.

———. 1984. "Further Reflections on Anthropology and the Black Experience." *ABA Occasional Papers* no. 3.

———. 1987. *Black Folk Here and There: An Essay in History and Anthropology.* Vol. 1. Los Angeles: Center for Afro-American Studies, University of California at Los Angeles.

———. 1990a. *Black Folk Here and There: An Essay in History and Anthropology.* Vol. 2. Los Angeles: Center for Afro-American Studies, University of California at Los Angeles.

———. 1990b. "Further Reflections on Anthropology and the Black Experience." Ed. Willie Baber. *Transforming Anthropology* 1 (2): 1–14.

Drake, St. Clair, and Horace Cayton. 1945. *Black Metropolis: A Study of Negro Life in a Northern City.* New York: Harcourt, Brace.

Duberman, Martin B. 1989. *Paul Robeson: A Biography.* New York: Ballentine Books.

Du Bois, W. E. B. 1899. *The Philadelphia Negro.* Philadelphia: University of Pennsylvania Press.

———. [1903] 1961. *The Souls of Black Folk: Essays and Sketches.* New York: Fawcett.

———. [1939] 1970. *Black Folk Then and Now: An Essay in the History of Sociology of the Negro Race.* New York: Octagon.

Fahim, Hussein, ed. 1982. *Indigenous Anthropology in Non-Western Countries.* Durham: Carolina Academic Press.

Fahim, Hussein, and Katherine Helmer. 1980. "Indigenous Anthropology in Non-Western Countries: A Further Elaboration." *Current Anthropology* 21 (5): 644–63.

Finn, Janet L. 1993. "Ella Cara Deloria and Mourning Dove." *Critique of Anthropology* 13 (4): 335–49.

Foucault, Michel. 1980. *Power/Knowledge: Selected Interviews and Other Writings, 1972–1977.* New York: Pantheon Books.

Fowler, Manet. 1938a. "Hall of Liberty." *Opportunity Journal of Negro Life* 16 (4): 112–15, 121.

———. 1938b. "Southern Circumstance." *Opportunity Journal of Negro Life* 16 (10): 310–11.

———. 1952. "The Case of Chef A: An Inquiry into and Analysis of Human Relations Situation." 2 vols. Ph.D. diss., Cornell University.

Fox, Richard G., ed. 1991. *Recapturing Anthropology: Working in the Present.* Santa Fe: School of American Research Press.

Frederickson, George. 1971. *The Black Image in the White Mind: The Debate on Afro-American Character and Destiny, 1817–1914.* New York: Harper Torchbooks.

Gacs, Ute, Aisha Khan, Jerrie McIntyre, and Ruth Weinberg, eds. 1989. *Women Anthropologists: Selected Biographies.* Urbana: University of Illinois Press.

Giddens, Anthony. 1976. *New Rules of Sociology Method: A Positive Critique of Interpretive Sociologies.* London: Hutchinson.

———. 1977. *Studies in Social and Political Theory.* London: Hutchinson.

———. 1979. *Central Problems in Social Theory: Action, Structure, and Contradiction in Social Analysis.* Berkeley: University of California Press.

Golde, Peggy, ed. 1970. *Women in the Field: Anthropological Experiences.* Chicago: Aldine.

Gordon, Deborah. 1990. "The Politics of Ethnographic Authority: Race and Writing in the Ethnography of Margaret Mead and Zora Neale Hurston." In *Modernist Anthropology: From Fieldwork to Text.* Ed. Marc Manganaro. Princeton: Princeton University Press. 146–62.

Hakken, David, and Hanna Lessinger, eds. 1987. *Marxist Perspectives in U.S. Anthropology.* Boulder: Westview Press.

Haraway, Donna. 1991. "Situated Knowledges: The Science Question in Feminism and the Privilege of Partial Perspective." *Simians, Cyborgs, and Women: The Reinvention of Nature.* New York: Routledge. 183–201.

Harding, Sandra, ed. 1993. *The "Racial" Economy of Science: Toward a Democratic Future.* Bloomington: Indiana University Press.

Harris, Marvin. 1968. *The Rise of Anthropological Theory: A History of Theories of Culture.* New York: Thomas Y. Crowell.

Harrison, Faye V. 1988. "Introduction: An African Diaspora Perspective for Urban Anthropology." *Urban Anthropology and Studies of Cultural Systems and World Economic Development* 17 (2–3): 111–41.

———. 1990a. "Death Notice: John Gibbs St. Clair Drake, Jr." *Anthropology Newsletter* 31 (9): 4.

———. 1990b. "From the President: In Memory of St. Clair Drake." *Transforming Anthropology* 1 (2): 28–29.

———. 1990c. "Obituary: John Gibbs St. Clair Drake, Jr." *Transforming Anthropology* 1 (2): 33–34.

———. 1991a. "Anthropology as an Agent of Transformation: Introductory Comments and Queries." In *Decolonizing Anthropology: Moving Further toward an Anthropology for Liberation.* Ed. Faye V. Harrison. Washington, D.C.: American Anthropological Association. 1–14.

———, ed. 1991b. *Decolonizing Anthropology: Moving Further toward an Anthropology for Liberation.* Washington, D.C.: American Anthropological Association.

———. 1992. "The Du Boisian Legacy in Anthropology." *Critique of Anthropology* 12 (3): 239–60.

———. 1993. "Writing against the Grain: Cultural Politics of Difference in the Work of Alice Walker." *Critique of Anthropology* 13 (4): 401–27.

———. n.d. "Manet Fowler: Living, Surviving, and Celebrating Professional Commitment to Anthropological Practice." Ms.

Harrison, Faye V., and Donald Nonini, eds. 1992. Special Issue on W. E. B. Du Bois and Anthropology. *Critique of Anthropology* 12 (3): 227–364.

Harrison, Ira E. 1982. "I Remember Vera." *Notes from the ABA* 8 (2): 4.

———. 1983. "Louis Eugene King, the Anthropologist Who Never Was." *Western Journal of Black Studies* 7 (1): 21–26.

———. 1987. "The Association of Black Anthropologists." *Anthropology Today* 3 (1): 17–21.

Hatch, Elvin. 1973. *Theories of Man and Culture.* New York: Columbia University Press.

Helm, June, ed. 1985. *Social Context of American Ethnology, 1840–1984.* Washington, D.C.: American Ethnological Society.

Hernández, Graciela. 1993. "Multiple Mediations in Zora Neale Hurston's *Mules and Men.*" *Critique of Anthropology* 13 (4): 351–62.

Herskovits, Melville J. [1928] 1964. *The American Negro: A Study in Racial Crossing.* Bloomington: Indiana University Press.

Hine, Darlene Clark, ed. 1993. *Black Women in America: An Historical Encyclopedia.* 2 vols. Brooklyn, N.Y.: Carlson.

Honigman, John. 1976. *The Development of Anthropological Ideas.* Homewood, Ill.: Dorsey Press.

Hsu, Francis. 1973. "Prejudice and Its Intellectual Effect in American Anthropology: An Ethnographic Report." *American Anthropologist* 75 (1): 1–19.

Hymes, Dell, ed. 1972. *Reinventing Anthropology.* New York: Pantheon Books.

Jackson, Walter. 1986. "Melville Herskovits and the Search for Afro-American Culture." In *Malinowski, Rivers, Benedict, and Others.* Ed. George W. Stocking Jr. Madison: University of Wisconsin Press. 95–126.

Jones, Delmos. [1970] 1988. "Towards a Native Anthropology." In *Anthropology for the Nineties: Introductory Readings.* Ed. Johnnetta B. Cole. New York: Free Press. 30–41.

Jordon, Glenn H. 1982. "Reading St. Clair Drake: A Methodological Essay with a Focus on *Black Metropolis.*" Urbana: Afro Scholar Working Papers, Afro-American Studies and Research Program, University of Illinois.

———. 1983. "Time, Space, and Basic Research Questions in the Writings of St. Clair Drake." *Notes from the ABA* 9 (1–2): 13–27.

———. 1990. "On Being a Committed Intellectual: St. Clair Drake and the Politics of Anthropology." *Transforming Anthropology* 1 (2): 15–18.

Kaplan, David, and Robert A. Manners. 1972. *Culture Theory.* Englewood Cliffs, N.J.: Prentice-Hall.

Khan, Aisha. 1994. "*Juthaa* in Trinidad: Food, Pollution, and Hierarchy in a Caribbean Diaspora Community." *American Ethnologist* 21 (2): 245–69.

Klineberg, Otto. 1935. *Negro Intelligence and Selective Migration.* New York: Columbia University Press.

Kluger, Richard. 1976. *Simple Justice.* New York: Alfred A. Knopf.

Kuhn, Thomas S. 1962. *The Structure of Scientific Revolutions.* Chicago: University of Chicago Press.

Kuper, Adam. 1983. *Anthropology and Anthropologists: The Modern British School.* London: Routledge and Kegan Paul.

Leacock, Eleanor. 1982. "Marxism and Anthropology." In *The Left Academy.* Ed. Bertell Ollman and Edward Vernoff. New York: McGraw Hill. 242–76.

———. 1987. "Theory and Ethics in Applied Urban Anthropology." In *Cities of the United States.* Ed. Leith Mullings. New York: Columbia University Press. 317–36.

Levinson, Marjorie. 1989. Introduction to *Rethinking Historicism: Critical Readings in Romantic History* by Marjorie Levinson, Marilyn Butler, Jerome McGann, and Paul Hamilton. Oxford: Basil Blackwell. 1–17.

Lewis, Diane. 1973. "Anthropology and Colonialism." *Current Anthropology* 14 (5): 581–91.

Lewis, Julian H. 1942. *The Biology of the Negro.* Chicago: University of Chicago Press.

Limón, Jose. 1991. "Representation, Ethnicity, and Precursory Ethnography: Notes of a Native Anthropologist." In *Recapturing Anthropology: Working in the Present.* Ed. Richard G. Fox. Santa Fe: School of American Research Press. 115–35.

Lowie, Robert. 1932. *History of Ethnological Theory.* New York: Farrar and Rinehart.

Lutz, Catherine. 1990. "The Erasure of Women's Writing in Sociocultural Anthropology." *American Ethnologist* 17 (4): 611–27.

Marcus, George, and Michael Fischer. 1986. *Anthropology as Cultural Critique.* Chicago: University of Chicago Press.

Mikell, Gwendolyn. 1982. "When Horses Talk: Reflections on Zora Neale Hurston's Haitian Anthropology." *Phylon* 43 (3): 218–30.

———. 1983. "The Anthropological Imagination of Zora Neale Hurston." *Western Journal of Black Studies* 7 (1): 27–35.

———. 1989. "Zora Neale Hurston." In *Women Anthropologists: Selected Biographies.* Ed. Ute Gacs, Aisha Khan, Jerrie McIntyre, and Ruth Weinberg. Urbana: University of Illinois Press. 160–66.

Monteiro, Tony. 1990. "Harvesting the Literary Legacy of W. E. B. Du Bois." *Political Affairs* 69 (2): 22–27.

Moore, Henrietta. 1988. *Feminism and Anthropology.* Minneapolis: University of Minnesota Press.

Moses, Yolanda T. 1983. "Laurence Foster, a Black Anthropologist: His Life and Work." *Western Journal of Black Studies* 7 (1): 36–42.

Muhammad, Khadijah Ansari [Louise M. Skinner]. 1985. "Mark Hanna Watkins, Anthropologist, Academician, Advocate." Paper presented at the annual meeting of the American Anthropological Association. Washington, D.C. Dec. 6.

Muller, Nancy Ladd. 1992. "Du Boisian Pragmatism and 'The Problem of the Twentieth Century.'" *Critique of Anthropology* 12 (3): 319–37.

Nader, Laura. 1972. "Up the Anthropologist—Perspectives Gained from Studying Up." In *Reinventing Anthropology.* Ed. Dell Hymes. New York: Pantheon Books. 284–311.

Obbo, Christine. 1990. "Adventures with Fieldnotes." In *Fieldnotes: The Makings of Anthropology.* Ed. Roger Sanjek. Ithaca: Cornell University Press. 290–302.

Ohnuki-Tierney, Emiko. 1984. "'Native' Anthropologists." *American Ethnologist* 11 (3): 584–86.

O'Laughlin, Bridget. 1975. "Marxist Approaches in Anthropology." *Annual Review of Anthropology* 4:341–70.

Owusu, Maxwell. 1978. "The Ethnography of Africa: The Usefulness of the Useless." *American Anthropologist* 80 (2): 310–34.

———. 1979. "Colonial and Postcolonial Anthropology in Africa: Scholarship or Sentiment." In *The Politics of Anthropology: From Colonialism and Sexism toward a View from Below.* Ed. Gerrit Huizer and Bruce Mannheim. The Hague: Mouton. 145–60.

Powdermaker, Hortense. 1939. *After Freedom: A Cultural Study in the Deep South.* New York: Viking Press.

Rankin-Hill, Lesley, and Michael Blakey. 1994. "W. Montague Cobb (1904–1990): Physical Anthropologist, Anatomist, and Activist." *American Anthropologist* 96 (1): 74–96.

Robeson, Eslanda Goode. 1945. *African Journey.* New York: John Day.

Rosaldo, Renato. 1993. *Culture and Truth: The Remaking of Social Analysis.* Boston: Beacon Press.

Roseberry, William. 1989. *Anthropologies and Histories: Essays in Culture, History, and Political Economy.* New Brunswick, N.J.: Rutgers University Press.

Sanjek, Roger. 1993. "Anthropology's Hidden Colonialism: Assistants and Their Ethnographers." *Anthropology Today* 9 (2): 13–18.

———. 1996. "Urban Anthropology." In *Encyclopedia of Social and Cultural Anthropology.* Ed. Alan Barnard and Jonathan Spencer. London: Routledge. 555–58.

Skinner, Elliot P. 1983. "Afro-Americans in Search of Africa: The Scholars' Dilemma." In *Transformation and Resiliency in Africa.* Ed. Pearl T. Robinson and Elliot P. Skinner. Washington, D.C.: Howard University Press. 3–26.

Smith, Jessie Carney, ed. 1993. *Epic Lives: One Hundred Black Women Who Made a Difference.* Detroit: Visible Ink Press.

Snowden, Frank. 1970. *Blacks in Antiquity: Ethiopians in the Greco-Roman Experience.* Cambridge, Mass.: Belknap Press of Harvard University Press.

"Stamp of Approval." 1994. *Anthropology Newsletter* 35 (4): 1, 6.

Stocking, George W., Jr. 1968. *Race, Culture, and Evolution: Essays in the History of Anthropology.* New York: Free Press.

———. 1987. *Victorian Anthropology.* New York: Free Press.

———. 1992. *The Ethnographer's Magic and Other Essays in the History of Anthropology.* Madison: University of Wisconsin Press.

Sutton, Constance. 1987. "The Caribbeanization of New York City and the Emergence of a Transnational Socio-cultural System." In *Caribbean Life in New York: Sociocultural Dimensions.* Ed. Constance Sutton and Elsa M. Chaney. New York: Center for Migration Studies of New York. 15–30.

Taylor, Council. 1971. "Clues for the Future: Black Urban Anthropology Reconsidered." In *Race, Change, and Urban Society.* Ed. Peter Orleans and William R. Ellis. Beverly Hills: Sage. 219–27.

Trinh T. Minh-ha. 1989. *Woman, Native, Other.* Bloomington: Indiana University Press.

Trouillot, Michel-Rolphe. 1991. "Anthropology and the Savage Slot: The Poetics and Politics of Otherness." In *Recapturing Anthropology: Working in the Present.* Ed. Richard Fox. Santa Fe: School of American Research Press. 17–44.

Turner, Lorenzo Dow. 1949. *Africanisms in the Gullah Dialect.* Chicago: University of Chicago Press.

Ulin, Robert. 1991. "Critical Anthropology Twenty Years Later: Modernism and Postmodernism in Anthropology." *Critique of Anthropology* 11 (1): 63–89.

"Until Difference Doesn't Make Any More Difference." 1994. *Anthropology Newsletter* 35 (1): 3.

Vincent, Joan. 1991. "Engaging Historicism." In *Recapturing Anthropology: Working in the Present.* Ed. Richard G. Fox. Santa Fe: School of American Research Press. 44–58.

Voget, Fred W. 1975. *A History of Ethnology.* New York: Holt, Rinehart, and Winston.

Walker, Sheila. 1982. "Reflections on Becoming an Afro-American Anthropologist." *ABA Occasional Papers* no. 1.

Watkins, Mark Hanna. 1937a. *A Grammar of Chechewa: A Bantu Language of British Central Africa.* Philadelphia: Linguistic Society of America.

———. 1937b. "A Place for Anthropology in the Negro College." *Quarterly Review of Higher Education among Negroes* 5 (2): 60–64.

———. 1962. "Bantu Languages." *Encyclopedia Britannica,* 14th ed.

West, Cornel. 1991. *Ethical Dimensions of Marxist Thought.* New York: Monthly Review Press.

Whitehead, Tony Larry, and Mary Ellen Conaway, eds. 1986. *Self, Sex, and Gender in Cross-Cultural Fieldwork.* Urbana: University of Illinois Press.

Willis, William, Jr. 1972. "Skeletons in the Anthropological Closet." In *Reinventing Anthropology.* Ed. Dell Hymes. New York: Pantheon Books. 121–52.

———. 1975. "Franz Boas and the Study of Black Folklore." In *The New Ethnicity: Perspectives from Ethnology.* Ed. John W. Bennett. St. Paul: West Publishers. 307–34.

Wilson, Lynn. 1988. "Epistemology and Power: Rethinking Ethnography at Greenham." In *Anthropology for the Nineties: Introductory Readings.* Ed. Johnnetta B. Cole. New York: Free Press. 42–58.

Wolf, Eric. 1982. *Europe and the People without History.* Berkeley: University of California Press.

———. 1990. "Distinguished Lecture: Facing Power—Old Insights, New Questions." *American Anthropologist* 92 (3): 586–96.

Wright, Jerome. 1976. "Obituary: Mark Hanna Watkins." *American Anthropologist* 78 (4): 889–90.

———. n.d. "Mark Hanna Watkins." Ms. Author's possession.

1

Caroline Bond Day: Pioneer Black Physical Anthropologist

Hubert B. Ross, Amelia Marie Adams, and Lynne Mallory Williams

Science is filled with research lines that eventually died out. Those who follow such trends tend to become lost and forgotten between the dusty pages of old journals as new and better theories develop. Such was the case with Caroline Bond Day, who received her master's degree in 1932, making her one of the first African Americans to receive a graduate degree in anthropology (Drake 1979). Her research on race crossing was published in 1932, was titled *A Study of Some Negro-White Families in the United States,* and included a foreword and notes on the anthropometric data by Earnest A. Hooton. Within this study, Day examined the morphological and sociological results of black and white race crossing. Her reason for conducting this study is evident from the opening statement:

> The people studied in this group are not, for the most part, the type with which the public is familiar individually, nor are they those used as literary material by the novelists and playwrights of today. Many of these families, especially those in the South, live in worlds of their own, tucked away here and there on some quiet street, or in little peaceful neighborhoods, frequently unknown and unobserved by those about them. The average tourist in the South never suspects their existence. If he is shown Negro life at all, he is usually conducted through a slum district, the squa-

Caroline Bond Day. (Courtesy of Radcliffe College Archives)

> lor of which probably seems heightened to him by the fact of physical differences. If he were to see this group, in which physical differences are less striking, he would probably be impressed with similarities to any other middle class group of American people, rather than differences. (1932:3)

For Day, the concepts of race and class were intertwined. The biological hybrids that she proposed to study were equivalent to a social middle class, and Day hoped to reveal the existence of a black middle class in the urban centers of America. This blurred division between biological and sociological constructs was characteristic of early scientific studies. Biologically oriented studies that used genealogical information, as Day had done, were hindered further by an erroneous understanding of the inheritance process. At the time of Day's research, most scientists believed that biological traits were inherited through the blood. For these reasons, among others, Caroline Bond Day has been all but forgotten to anthropologists of today.

Birth and Early Development

Caroline Bond Day was born Caroline Fagan Stewart to Georgia and Moses Stewart on November 18, 1889. By her own calculations Day was an approximate mulatto, having $\frac{7}{16}$ white blood, $\frac{1}{16}$ Indian blood, and $\frac{8}{16}$ Negro blood (1932:plate 34). After her father's death, her mother married John Bond, and Caroline changed her name to Caroline Stewart Bond (1932:plate 35). According to the genealogical plates included in her only book-length study, Caroline had two half-siblings through her mother's second marriage.

As a child Caroline attended Tuskegee elementary school, where her mother was a teacher. In 1905 she entered the first class of Atlanta University High School and she graduated in 1908. She then attended Atlanta University, receiving a bachelor's degree in 1912. At Atlanta University she took courses in drama and appeared in several productions of Shakespeare's plays. Although her major and courses are unknown, it is possible that she was influenced in her graduate school and career choices by W. E. B. Du Bois (Drake 1979).

Du Bois was a professor of economics and history at Atlanta University from 1896 to 1910, when he became editor of *Crisis.* Imbued with the scientific spirit of the period, Du Bois created a sociological laboratory to study firsthand the problems of the "American Negro." He hoped to generate enough information to refute racist scientific theories (Stephan and Gilman 1991). Du Bois "delineated four approaches to the study of the Negro as a social group: 1) historical study, 2) statistical investigation, 3) anthropological measurement, and 4) sociological interpretation" (Lange 1983:143). In an address to the American Academy of Political and Social Sciences, Du Bois maintained that although differences between the races surely existed, no one had scientifically shown what they were (Du Bois 1898).

Du Bois's study *The Health and Physique of the Negro American* ([1906] 1968) is an excellent example of his attempt to discredit the claims being made under the guise of science. Whether Du Bois's research was known to Day we do not know. She may have been exposed to these ideas in the classroom, however, because her study of mulatto families was similar to a section of Du Bois's study. Like Du Bois's, Day's methods and expectations also went far beyond the confines of both anthropometry and anthropology in exploring the issues of miscegenation and amalgamation. Hooton commented on Day's interest in sociological facts both in her study and in an article he wrote bringing attention to her work (Day 1932; Hooton 1930). While a direct connection is hard to establish, there is no doubt Day was at least indirectly influenced by Du Bois's call to scientifically study African Americans.

Hooton's and Day's Perspectives on Race

After graduating from Atlanta University in 1912, Day started making plans to attend Radcliffe College. She had hoped to obtain a graduate degree but ended up taking additional undergraduate courses because Radcliffe refused to give her credit for all her course work from Atlanta University (Alexander 1993). While at Radcliffe she took anthropology courses with Hooton, the physical anthropologist from Harvard who would later direct her research project. At that time Hooton was the only physical anthropologist employed by an academic department. As such, he trained all students interested in obtaining degrees in physical anthropology (Spencer 1981, 1982). It was during this period that Day began collecting data for her study on race crossing. This was no doubt the result of her association with Hooton, whose own work revealed a belief in physical inheritance as an explanation of mental and cultural difference between the races (Hooton 1930; Day 1932; Gossett 1963).

After she received her bachelor's degree from Radcliffe in 1919 Day's studies were temporarily suspended (Alexander 1993). Day held a variety of jobs over the next few years: at a World War I relief center for black soldiers, as a YWCA secretary, as the dean of women at Paul Quinn College in Waco, Texas, and as head of the English department at Prairie View College, also in Texas. On March 1, 1920, she married Aaron Day, an instructor at the college. Sometime during the mid-1920s Day returned to Atlanta University, where she served as both director of dramatics and an instructor of English.

The years from 1919 to 1932 were spent alternating between teaching positions at various institutions and graduate study in Hooton's lab. Day must have continued to collect anthropometric and genealogical data during this period since several of the families included in her research project were from Texas and her husband's genealogy also appears in the publication (Day 1932:plate 53). Hooton lobbied vigorously on Day's behalf and as a result she was able to receive funding twice to continue her graduate work (Hooton 1930; Roses and Randolph 1940; Alexander 1993). Day spent these years organizing the genealogical materials, calculating each person's ethnicity, and analyzing the sociological data she had collected.

During this period Day's interest in drama and literature, cultivated during her years at Atlanta University, continued, as did her concerns about being racially mixed in a race-conscious society. She published several articles on these topics as well as "A Fairy Story," a short fiction piece for children, and "What Shall We Play," a discussion of possible theater productions for African-American youth. "Educational Fruit," a description of a theater production by black youth in Washington, D.C., appeared in *Opportunity* in 1933.

In 1926 she won third place in the *Opportunity* fiction contest with her story "The Pink Hat." This story is, perhaps, her best creative work, and in some respects the most revealing of her worldview. From Day's perspective, white culture provided the role model to which blacks should aspire (Roses and Randolph 1993). "The Pink Hat" incorporates Day's scientific interest in hybridization with her understanding of current social attitudes toward people of mixed ancestry. It portrays her feelings about being a mulatto and the injustices of society she faced.

In 1930 Day published a short article in *Crisis* called "Race-Crossings in the United States." In it Day set the stage in the black community for her later study by reviewing previous ones. Anxious to have Day's study completed, and probably concerned about the length and sporadic nature of her progress, Hooton completed the statistical and anthropometric analysis with the aid of his other graduate students. The complete study was published in 1932 as part of the Harvard African Studies series, of which Hooton was the editor. Upon its publication, Day received her master's degree (Alexander 1993).

Day continued to teach English and drama at Atlanta University, and she also taught one course in anthropology. However, at the end of the 1930 academic year her services were terminated as a result of the creation of the Atlanta University system. This system established Atlanta University as a graduate school and Morehouse and Spelman as institutions for undergraduates.

What happened next is unclear. Day may have taught at Howard University for a few years (Roses and Randolph 1993). At some point she moved to Durham, where her husband was an insurance executive with the North Carolina Mutual Life Insurance Company. Here Day went into semiretirement due to poor health. Although she had initially planned to work toward her doctorate, this objective was never realized. For many years Day had suffered from a heart condition, and this ailment may have impaired her graduate work. On May 5, 1948, Caroline Bond Day died from heart complications at the age of fifty-nine.

Day's Research

When Day began her work physical anthropologists were concerned with the identification and classification of human racial groups. Most scientists believed that biological traits were inherited through the blood. *Blood quantification* became the criterion by which an individual's race could be determined. "Full bloods" were of the pure racial type and would exhibit the typical physical features associated with it. "Mixed-bloods," on the other hand, contained blood of at least two racial types, so physical features were harder to predict. Mixed-bloods posed a particular problem for those who wanted a nice, orderly typological system. They fit the racial category of neither black nor white, but represented a mixing of physical traits from both groups.

This situation was intolerable for a society whose criteria for inclusion was based on physical appearances. Studies such as Day's were designed to document the results of miscegenation and to thereby create a typological category for mixed-blood individuals. The studies that proceeded Day's were also used to scientifically confirm the ill effects of race mixing. Day hoped her study would refute the myths and stereotypes concerning mulattos that had been generated by previous academic studies and perpetuated by popular opinion.

While Hooton had not initially considered a study of black-white crossings because access to the black community posed a major research obstacle, he was concerned "about the anthropological results of the race mixtures between Negroes and Whites" (Hooton 1930:767). He knew that access to the black community would require black researchers. In choosing Day, however, Hooton issued this warning: "This colored investigator had to be a person not only of scientific gifts and understanding, but also of such unquestioned honesty and impartiality as to guarantee the validity of his findings. And these, to be acceptable, should be checked rigorously by a disinterested white scientist" (1930:769). Hooton's comments reflected one of the most insidious realities of the scientific community at this time: Neither blacks nor women could be scientists because neither was considered capable of scientific or objective analysis. Anthropology offered few exceptions to this basic scientific premise, but some white anthropologists did use black researchers to collect data within the black community. Often these black researchers, like Day, were graduate students who hoped to one day become professional, practicing anthropologists. Many did not achieve this goal, and the few who did usually found that the larger anthropological community systematically dismissed or ignored their work (Drake 1978). Statements made by Hooton revealed his attitude toward Day and emphasized the conditions under which she worked. On several occasions Hooton wrote articles intended to generate interest and financial support for Day's study. He began one such article with the following passage:

> A Harvard instructor who teaches Radcliffe classes can select from his more promising pupils the most splendidly equipped and competent research assistants and super-secretaries to be found. These female aids are more patient, more conscientious, more accurate, and more loyal, than young men of comparable status are. They take better care of you and they do not immediately think that they know more than you do. . . . A perspicacious professor . . . can often manage to get these brainy Radcliffe graduates to do almost all of the harder work. Thereby he can enormously increase his scientific output. . . . I found such a rare individual in the class of '19 at Radcliffe College. (1930:768)

Although Hooton made it clear that he thought Day was the right person to have undertaken such an extensive research project, Day, like the other women scientists of her period, had to make do with short-term grants and fellowships to complete it (Rossiter 1982).

In *A Study of Some Negro-White Families in the United States* Day examines the biological and sociological characteristics of race crossing. The bulk of her study consists of the genealogies of several families, each of which originated in the mating of two "full-blooded individuals," one white and one black. Each genealogy includes photos, a brief discussion of morphological features, and possible inheritance patterns. Calculations of each person's racial ancestry are also given. Not all of the families and individuals Day measured are included in the published study. Shortage of research time and publication space caused her to limit the data she included to 45 of the 346 mixed-blood families studied (Day 1930, 1932).

Based on the data collected from these individuals, Day provides a typological system for classifying the offspring of mixed marriages. She furnishes descriptions of the corresponding morphological features, such as hair form, lip size, and nose width, that characterized each category. Her typological categories are visually clarified with photographs illustrating individuals who, in her opinion, represented the type specimen of each group. By using this process Day adhered to the accepted standards of this period for physical anthropology.

The classification system contains six categories defined by presumed heritage and physical features. Octoroons contain ⅛ Negro blood and ⅞ white blood. Quadroons have 2/8 Negro blood and 6/8 white blood. Those in the ⅝ white group have ⅜ Negro blood and ⅝ white blood. Mulattos, characterized as those who have ½ Negro and ½ white blood, are further divided into three categories based on their morphological traits: dominant mulattos have primarily white features; recessive mulattos have more Negroid than white features; and intermediate mulattos have a balance of both Negroid and white features (Hooton 1930; Day 1932).

A short chapter written by Hooton followed the genealogical material in the study. In "The Anthropometry of Some Small Samples of Negroes and Negroids" he statistically analyzes several standard measurements collected from a small portion of the sample. Hooton tests the anthropometric measurements against Day's typological categories to see if any correlation could be found. Skin color, hair form, hair texture, hair color, nasal size, and lip size are among the measurements presented. Also included are measurements such as the amount of tooth wear, sitting height, and leg length. Hooton's anthropometric findings substantiates that the offspring of mixed marriages exhibit physical features of white, Negro, or intermediate types based on the varying blood compositions.

In the final section of the publication Day provides sociological observations on family life, homes and possessions, occupations and salaries, religion, education, and special interests such as entertainment, social uplift, self-improvement, travel, drama, and music. Day includes this material to portray the similarities between the black and white middle class. Day attributes differences in lifestyle to racial segregation rather than to any innate biological differences.

At this point, the study abruptly ends. There is no discussion linking the biological and sociological findings, which leaves the reader to draw conclusions from the abundance of data presented. These problems were probably the result of the haste in which the final report was compiled, along with the fact that Hooton's goals differed from Day's. While they were united in their interest in race crossing, their objectives and motivations for undertaking the study were never the same. Day wished to stress the sociocultural similarities between a black middle-class population and a white middle-class population, while Hooton wished to stress the biological differences between these two populations.

Contemporary Attitudes on Race

Hooton was especially interested in the classification of racial types and the effects of hybridization. Unfortunately, his understanding of the inheritance process was limited by his Lamarckian views, according to which traits acquired by the parent were passed to the offspring (Barkan 1992). In his classic work *Up from the Ape,* which was not published until 1949, Hooton presented his theories of racial classification and inheritance. A large portion of the book was given over to descriptions of the racial categories of humans and their attributed racial characteristics. It is clear from this book that many of Hooton's ideas on race and inheritance were based on a pre-Mendelian understanding of genetics.

In the early 1900s, when Hooton and Day were working, scientists had a limited understanding of genetics and the process of inheritance. Genetic concepts such as genotype, phenotype, dominant traits, and recessive traits had been presented in the literature but were often misunderstood and misapplied by researchers who did not yet grasp the connections between inheritance and evolutionary theory. For example, Hooton uses terms such as *phenotype* and *genotype,* but the meanings he assigns them differ dramatically from the accepted genetic explanations. Day's understanding of these matters was most certainly influenced by Hooton's beliefs. In her monograph Day deliberately uses the terms *dominant* and *recessive* to identify types of mixed-blood individuals. Regarding this terminology, she wrote: "We are not using these terms in the usual Mendelian sense, but are employing the word *dominant* to refer to those persons who appear more European in type, and *recessive* to the more negroidal type, because of the fact that the white features do seem to predominate in general appearance" (1932:10).

Day's interest in race crossing was not surprising. As a mulatto she was quite aware of the stigma associated with mixed ancestry in the early decades of the twentieth century. Day approached the problem with the intention of disproving and dispelling racial myths. This vindicationist perspective characterized much of the work of early black anthropologists (Drake 1979). Unfortunately, she was trapped in the paradigm of scientific racism and by the attitudes of her society and her professor. The a priori assumption that races did exist as a biological reality limited the viability of her study to alter the status quo. Her use of blood quantification, application of typological classifications, and incorrect association of racial categories with class categories reinforced the system that she had hoped to change.

Scientific views on race mixing reflected society's attitudes. White Americans were more than willing to accept as truth that the races were unequal and that race mixing was degrading to the "superior" races. One of the more popular and ill-formed myths concerning miscegenation was the belief that two white people, one with African-American ancestry, or a white person and an African-American fair enough to be mistaken for white, could produce a black child.

The possibility that a "white" mother would produce a "dark" baby and the issue of African Americans passing for white were major social concerns of American society. The practice of passing also posed problems in the study of racial typology. Day writes about this problem in "Race-Crossings in the United States," which appears to be the summary lacking from the later published study. This article not just reveals Day's motivation for undertaking the study but also reviews some earlier literature on race mixture. On the issue of passing, Day stated: "Contrary to the popular idea that one must be a quadroon or an octoroon to 'pass' some persons of little more than one-half white blood . . . are frequently mistaken for Europeans, and are often addressed as Spaniards or Italians. This is a point on which the American public seems to be most stupid" (82).

This candor, along with her stated desire to disprove mulatto myths, are not reflected in the later study. Her association with Hooton may have precluded Day from openly stating these concerns there.

Reactions to Day's Research

Unfortunately, Day's stated intention to improve the image of African Americans was not appreciated and instead flamed the fires of antagonism between "full-bloods" and "mixed-bloods." The claim that by their white ancestry mulattos gained intellectual capacity over African Americans was often stressed in the literature as scientific fact, and Day neither substantiated nor refuted it. Her mixed comments on mulatto and "full-blood" intelligence were probably offensive to some, particularly those mulattos who would have liked to disassociate themselves from their white ancestry and by those "full-bloods" who were successful in spite of their economic and social circumstances.

In addition, many families who had cooperated with her were dissatisfied with the published study and many who had not participated were quite pleased that they had not. W. E. B. Du Bois, whose family was included in the study, noted its publication but offered no critical evaluation of it in *Crisis* (1932).

Furthermore, Day's study made little impact on the anthropological or scientific community. Hooton was the only physical anthropologist who called attention to Day's work, usually to raise financial support or to justify this type of research at a time when interest had declined (Hooton 1926, 1930; King 1981). No reviews appeared in the anthropological journals. Even Hooton's colleague, Aleš Hrdlička, editor of the *American Journal of Physical Anthropology,* made no reference to its publication. This omission is significant considering that Hrdlička routinely published reviews of Hooton's work and in some respects this study was Hooton's. By the time Day's study was published race-mixture studies were becoming increasingly unpopular, particularly among biologists, psychologists, and geneticists. The political climate of the 1930s, along with the advancement of scientific knowledge, had altered the trends of scientific research. Even anthropologists were beginning to question the legitimacy of racial topology. Still some researchers, like Hooton, maintained that the study of race mixture was an important topic in physical anthropology (Hooton 1935). Of course Hooton had his own agenda: He was involved in several projects on race mixture and Day's study was an integral part of his overall research program (Hooton 1926, 1930).

In succeeding years Day's study was occasionally cited in other anthropological studies about African Americans. In his classic sociological work *An American Dilemma,* Gunner Myrdal mentioned Day's work in his discussion about passing and in several lengthy footnotes (Myrdal 1944). For the most part, however, it was ignored and soon forgotten (Cobb 1942).

More recently it has been criticized by scholars for Day's inadequate methodology and classified as poor anthropology (Alexander 1993; Ross 1983). Although the criticism of unsophisticated methodology is understandable, it is not altogether accurate given the historical period in which Day worked. To call her work poor anthropology is to ignore the rapid changes that took place in physical anthropology in the years during and since her study. By the time Day published her study the battle lines had been drawn within the discipline between the adherents of racial typology, such as Hooton, and those who stood in agreement with the cultural relativists, such as Franz Boas. Other scholars, however, have drawn attention to her work for its genealogical implications. It is also used as an important source in historical discussions concerning scientific racism, miscegenation, and the study of African Americans (Davis 1991; Du Bois 1985; Williamson 1980).

Conclusions

Day's life and work represent several key issues in anthropology as well as the culture at large. Interest in her work declined primarily because views within the anthropological community changed drastically between the time she started her research and the time when it was published. Discrepancies in perspective between Day and Hooton and the eventual obsolescence of the blood quantification theory severely affected the impact of the study. Because of this change in scientific orientation, Day's work was not well received within either the anthropological community or the African-American community. Fortunately, Day's study has survived in the footnotes of anthropological and sociological studies. Her significance may ultimately lie in her challenge to the myths and stereotypes concerning the effects of race crossing.

Day's experience also illustrates the place of African Americans and women in early twentieth-century American scientific research. Being a black woman in a discipline of only white males was certainly no advantage. Her work in a profession chosen by few women and even fewer blacks deserves more recognition. Caroline Bond Day's 1932 master's degree in anthropology was no small accomplishment. Her study's importance as a first step toward a more accurate understanding of African-American biology should not be lost. Her task was a monumental one undertaken by a pioneer physical anthropologist who helped pave the way for future black researchers.

References Cited

Alexander, Adele Logan. 1993. "Caroline Stewart Bond Day." In *Black Women in America: An Historical Encyclopedia.* Ed. Darlene Clark Hine. 2 vols. Brooklyn, N.Y.: Carlson. 1:312.

Barkan, Elizabeth. 1992. *The Retreat of Scientific Racism.* Cambridge: Cambridge University Press.

Cobb, W. Montague. 1942. "Physical Anthropology of the American Negro." *American Journal of Physical Anthropology* 29:113–222.

Davis, F. James. 1991. *Who Is Black?* University Park: Pennsylvania State University Press.

Day, Caroline Bond. 1919. "A Fairy Story." *Crisis* 18 (Oct.): 290–91.

———. 1925. "What Shall We Play?" *Crisis* 30 (Sept.): 220–22.

———. 1926. "The Pink Hat." *Opportunity* 4 (Dec.): 378–80.

———. 1930. "Race-Crossings in the United States." *Crisis* 37 (1): 81–82, 103.

———. 1932. *A Study of Some Negro-White Families in the United States.* Cambridge, Mass.: Peabody Museum of Harvard University.

———. 1933. "Educational Fruit." *Opportunity* 11 (Aug.): 236.

Drake, St. Clair. 1978. "Reflections on Anthropology and the Black Experience." *Anthropology and Educational Quarterly* 9 (2): 85–109.

———. 1980. "Anthropology and the Black Experience." *Black Scholar* 11 (7): 2–31.

Du Bois, W. E. B. 1898. "The Study of Negro Problems." *Annals of the American Academy of Political and Social Science* 11 (Nov.): 1–23.

———. [1906] 1968. *The Health and Physique of the Negro American.* New York: Arno Press.

———. 1932. Review of *A Study of Some Negro-White Families in the United States. Crisis* 39 (2): 385.

———. 1985. *Against Racism.* Amherst: University of Massachusetts Press.

Gossett, Thomas F. 1963. *Race: The History of an Idea in America.* Dallas: Southern Methodist University Press.

Hooton, Earnest Albert. 1926. "Progress in the Study of Race Mixtures." *American Philosophical Society Proceedings* 65 (Apr.): 312–25.

———. 1930. "Radcliffe Investigates Race Mixture." *Harvard Bulletin* 3 (Apr.): 768–76.

———. 1935. "Development and Correlation of Research in Physical Anthropology at Harvard University." *American Philosophical Society Proceedings* 75 (6): 499–516.

———. 1949. *Up from the Ape*. New York: Macmillan.

King, James C. 1981. *The Biology of Race*. Berkeley: University of California Press.

Lange, Werner J. 1983. "W. E. B. Du Bois and the First Scientific Study of Afro-Americans." *Phylon* 44 (2): 135–46.

Myrdal, Gunnar. 1944. *An American Dilemma: The Negro Problem and Modern Democracy*. 2 vols. New York: Harper and Brothers.

Roses, Lorraine Elana, and Ruth Elizabeth Randolph. 1990. *Harlem: Renaissance and Beyond*. Boston: G. K. Hall.

Ross, Hubert. 1983. "Caroline Bond Day: Pioneer Black Female Anthropologist." Paper presented at the annual meeting of the American Anthropological Association. Chicago. Nov. 18.

Rossiter, Margaret W. 1982. *Women Scientists in America: Struggies and Strategies to 1940*. Baltimore: Johns Hopkins University Press.

Spencer, Frank. 1981. "The Rise of Academic Physical Anthropology in the United States, 1880–1980: A Historical Review." *American Journal of Physical Anthropology* 56 (4): 353–64.

———. 1982. *History of American Physical Anthropology*. Orlando: Academic Press.

Stephan, Nancy Leys, and Sander L. Gilman. 1991. "Appropriating the Idioms of Science: The Rejection of Scientific Racism." In *The Bounds of Race: Perspectives on Hegemony and Resistance*. Ed. Dominick Lacapra. Ithaca: Cornell University Press. 72–103.

Williamson, Joel. 1980. *New People: Miscegenation and Mulattos in the United States*. New York: Free Press.

2

Feminism and Black Culture in the Ethnography of Zora Neale Hurston

Gwendolyn Mikell

We seldom examine how Zora Neale Hurston's powerful images of black male-female relations and black culture may have been developed and sharpened by her anthropological research in Florida, Jamaica, and Haiti. Nor have we, until recently, analyzed the nature of the challenge that her approaches presented to the then-current portrayal of black males and females. This neglect is ironic given that since the 1960s anthropology has moved toward more reflexive and symbolic approaches to culture and Hurston's work offered an early and unique attempt at one. Hurston's views certainly reflected the influence of Franz Boas and Ruth Benedict at Columbia University, but they were also grounded in her relationship to black southern culture as well as her later relationship with Alain Locke and Howard University. Hurston was both a product of and a participant in the elaboration of the "New Negro" during the Harlem Renaissance, and these experiences provided the structure undergirding her literature as well as her anthropology. However, Hurston added a unique methodological tool.

Her portrayal of the potential of women and of black culture, using techniques that were controversial in the 1930s, reflect this synthesis of intellectual traditions. Her use of "horses" and "mules" as symbols for the complex and dialectical relationships within black culture and for the position of women within it must be seen as an outgrowth of her early

Zora Neale Hurston. (Courtesy of the Photographs and Prints Division, Schomburg Center for Research in Black Culture, New York Public Library, Astor, Lenox, and Tilden Foundations)

experiences as well as her later intellectual training and fieldwork. Because until recently many social scientists did not accept that there was logic within her methodology, Hurston was more widely proclaimed as a literary chronicler of black life and folklore than as an anthropologist, much less a black feminist anthropologist. Instead it is for her seven novels and countless short stories, articles, musicals, and plays that she remains famous. Why? That she was discovered and revived by writers such as Alice Walker and her literary biographer, Robert Hemenway, contributed to her literary reputation (see Walker 1979; Hemenway 1977; see also Trescott 1978). But Hurston's lack of recognition within anthropology also results from her insistence upon conducting ethnography her own way. As a consequence she had difficulty obtaining and keeping graduate fellowships and never successfully completed a graduate degree in anthropology. Although she was enrolled for graduate courses at Columbia under the supervision of Franz Boas and Melville Herskovits, she left academia in 1936 to pursue more research, folk literature, and theater. With her academic credentials incomplete, Hurston was eventually viewed as, and began to conceive of herself as, more artistic than scholarly.

In hindsight, we recognize Hurston's talent as an ethnographer and a writer and can debate the reasons for Hurston's plight within the discipline: Was it that her extreme financial dependence upon her white patron, Charlotte Osgood Mason, denied her full use of her own research materials?[1] Hurston as well as others, such as Langston Hughes, found Mason's support necessary, but limiting (Rampersad 1986). Was it Hurston's insistence upon participating in the "native" culture she studied and wrote about? Perhaps the most important question is whether it was because she had deliberately selected a framework that was contextual, literal, creatively symbolic, and participatory—what Roland Bush (1991) calls "ethnographic subjectivity." This framework encompassed everything anthropology avoided at that time. Even black social scientists of the period wondered how an anthropologist could become submersed in the creation of vulgar folklore and rituals as Hurston did—something that the wider American public of the day called "primitive." We have until recently tended to ignore these theoretical and methodological elements in Hurston's work and the social frameworks she created as she wrote.

It is my intention to examine Hurston's theoretical, methodological, and anthropological frameworks with respect to feminism and black women within black culture and to raise questions about the derivation of and change in these ideas. These features of her work are among her major contributions to anthropology and ethnography. My focus is on the years between 1918 and 1938 when Hurston was establishing herself as a bona fide folklorist and promising ethnographer. I am particularly interested in sorting out the intrinsically personal from the Howard University and Columbia University influences on Hurston's work and worldviews: her intuitive approach to black life and culture and how she portrays black women as fitting into this; how university mentoring and collegial relations contributed to her development; how formal fieldwork affected her written work and feminist perspectives; and how her later views of black women and culture differed from her early ones.

The Hurston who entered Howard University had already undergone experiences that helped shape her attitudes toward black male-female relations and black culture. Growing up in the black town of Eatonville, Florida, where her occasionally philandering Baptist minister father was also mayor, she participated in one of the most authentic arenas for black cultural styles—the church. Having a mother who was equally supportive and assertive as wife and mother provided her with positive and negative models of female behavior. Her mother's death when Hurston was nine began the chain of events leading to family instability, her father's remarriage, her departure from Eatonville in 1917, and the end of a gloomy phase in her life. While performing with a traveling theater company and during menial jobs she took before her employment in Baltimore, Maryland, she accumulated information on the contradictions of life in a race-stratified society.[2] Her enrollment at Howard University broadened her experiences far beyond as well as deeper into her southern roots and provided her with the beginnings of the process of ethnographic subjectivity—the desire for the "spy-glass of anthropology" about which she wrote in *Mules and Men* ([1935] 1970).

Hurston had grown up in Florida with almost "primordial" attachments to the nuances of black life in the church and community (Nathiri 1991). She understood and laughed at the intricacies of color differences, having become familiar with them from the controversies created by the marriage of her mother and father. She delighted in the spiritual sons, the biblical stories, and the institutions of the black community. In short, she had the ability to be "in culture while looking at culture" (Clifford 1988:93). But this was also a period of tremendous cultural-intellectual schisms for many black intellectuals. In the wider world the communist challenge to Western intellectual and political models was developing; in Washington, D.C., the black middle class was aggressively establishing itself in segregated neighborhoods; and in black intellectual circles the relevance of black culture, anchored in spiritual music and popular-lyrics-cum-slavery-texts, was hotly debated. Artists were beginning to discover the symbolism of African art but labeled it the creative genius of "primitive people" instead of giving Africans credit for artistic and philosophical traditions (see Torgovnick 1990; Mikell 1991a). Hurston rejected this metaphor of primitivity.

Her positions on black culture were evident even at this period when she voiced her resentment against Howard students whose attack on black culture and institutions she felt reflected a process of "bourgeoisification" (Hurston 1926). She considered Howard a bastion of legitimacy for black culture and black education and, as such, she felt that Howard "is to the Negro what Harvard is to the white" (Hurston 1924:372). Although Hurston had not yet actively translated her position into a methodology for investigating black culture, the articles she produced and published during the Howard years reflected the process of maturation toward this end.

Hurston's views on the roles of black women and on how skin color influenced women's life chances were already being formed, and they come through in fragmentary bits in her short stories. Rather early, Howard black women sorted themselves out based on their attributes and their aspirations—marriage and husband versus career. Hurston admired the women deans and administrators at Howard but appeared more ambivalent about the female students, from whom she was mostly aloof. Ophelia Settle Egypt reflected on her acquaintance with Hurston at Howard:

> There were these three sororities. The AKAs (who really could dress beautifully) . . . the Deltas (light skinned) . . . [and] the Zetas (it didn't matter how you looked as long as you had brains). I certainly wasn't light. I had enough brains to get into Zeta. Zora Neale Hurston was there and she was a Zeta. . . . I knew her. She was older than we were, I think. I know she wore these long dresses. . . . I don't know whether she was going full time. She must have been though, to be in the sorority . . . and she was majoring in Anthropology.[3] . . . And then she was sort of a loner. But she was brilliant, and she was writing even then. . . . But we always thought of her as a rather odd person. She was just too brainy for us. (Stinnette 1981–82:48–50; see also Clarke 1985)

These comments give an indication of Hurston's place in Howard society. Hurston considered herself bright, rather than especially gifted in feminine qualities or experienced in bourgeois manners, and she intended to rely upon her intellectual talents and brashness for success. There is no evidence that her female colleagues thought of her in any way other than as a talented but quirky intellectual with somewhat bohemian tastes. Nevertheless, there would remain an element of discord between her cultivated eccentricity of personality that set her apart from other educated black women, her aspirations for mobility in the literary and intellectual worlds, and her deep interest in the analysis of black culture.

Hurston's real development came through contact with her Howard University mentor and role model, Alain Locke, a black philosopher trained in European classics who was interested in African culture and archaeology and in developing new ways to understand black culture in the Western Hemisphere. Long before she entered anthropological training at Columbia, Locke's influences prepared her intellectually to create a unique methodological approach to understanding and presenting black culture. In opposition to many white sociologists who viewed black culture as crudely imitative of white culture but ravaged by slavery, Locke and his students asserted that there was valid cultural continuity and logic—not to mention historical depth—in black culture (Locke 1925:105–11).

Locke's legacy for Hurston's intellectual work was to pass onto her the insights that represented the culmination of an ongoing dialogue between white intellectuals such as Franz Boas, the father of anthropology at Columbia University, and black intellectuals such as W. E. B. Du Bois about the centrality of Africa and African people to world cultural development and the decline of racism. Both intellectuals argued for the significance of the cultures of oppressed peoples. Both had attended the World Conference of Races in 1911.[4]

A major contribution of these scholars was their conviction that a people must develop a literature that records their cultural realities and their triumphs. For example, Boas and others at Columbia were determined to understand the cultural life, not just the material artifacts, of the Native American cultures that were being destroyed before their eyes. They were convinced that important cultural knowledge resided in the styles people used to make and say things and that until anthropologists found the key to the cultural complexes that included the arts and music, they could never fully comprehend a people. One can debate the success white scholars had in truly understanding and comprehending Native American cultures, but Locke did help pass on to Hurston the sense of urgency that a similar energy be devoted to representing black culture.

What Locke and Howard University could not provide for Hurston was an adequate view of how black intellectual women fit into respected positions in urbane African-American life. Hurston had models only from working-class southern life. She gradually and decisively put aside the "New Negro" images of black women as idealized portrayals of primordial Africanity and of the value of black feminine beauty and motherhood to African men because they jarred with her memory of what black women had become in segregated cities, particularly in the South. Although the image of the tragic black woman appeared in Hurston's early literature, it would later be balanced by diverse views of black women and men that she acquired during her field experiences in the southern United States and in the Caribbean. Women in her work became broad-shouldered bearers of cultural burdens whose sense of humor and active participation saw them through any difficulties. Although Hurston could not rely on Locke for her view of black womanhood, she continued to rely on his opinions and his understanding of African-American and African culture in general. As she did research along the Florida coast, she fed Locke's interest in archaeology by sending him specimens of wood and rock from the area. She would frequently send him her own manuscripts, never seeming to get enough of his comments and suggestions (see her letters in the Alain Locke Papers).

Hurston was wholeheartedly involved with her anthropological training at Columbia, but her descriptions of this period reflect her initial uncertainties as well as the growing realization of the intellectual contributions that she alone could make. Her own natural interests as well as Boas's urgings prompted her to study Harlem lifestyles and take cranial measurements (all well-rounded analysts of culture change did that during this period). But she also sought the recognition of Boas and Ruth Benedict, even while moving Boas's eclectic approach and Benedict's psychological configurations in totally different directions. By the time she received her B.A. from Barnard in 1928, she had synthesized these influences with her black experiences and had rethought her original intuitive views on black culture. She demonstrated the complementarity of the sexes and their humorous manipulation of African cultural elements in defiance of racist domination within the American South. Hurston presented, rather than explicitly stated, her theoretical and methodological perspectives on field research in *Mules and Men.*

Ethnographic training heightened her inner tension about understanding the relationship of black women to American culture and academia. Since there were relatively few black women in white higher-educational institutions, she was an anomaly. She speaks generally favorably about her treatment from professors and contemporaries during her undergraduate training but expresses some awkwardness.[5] She was acquiring better academic credentials than most artistic and theatrical people she met in New York, but her goals differed from theirs. One major problem was class: her personality and life views made her reject the stereotypical retiring, middle-class, female role with which she was uncomfortable, but she had not yet been able to replace it with a more functional one. She felt she understood rural southern working-class women and could identify with them, but the question was how she could integrate her New York reality with this model. It was obvious that at Barnard Hurston had not yet found her niche. In fact, there was no real niche for black women intellectuals within American culture: America of the 1930s defined blacks as primitives, as bourgeois creoles, or as yet-to-be-defined "others" who were not capable of scholarly objectivity in the study of culture. Hurston was cast into the "other" category. The role of anthropologist allowed her to escape from some of these dilemmas, but in real life she had adopted the outrageous and showy, defensive reactive demeanor for which she became notorious among her black New York contemporaries, male and female. White patrons such as Mason seemingly encouraged such behavior in their efforts to collect the authentic black folklore and customs they so desired.

Fieldwork provided Hurston with an opportunity to test out her theoretical and methodological views as well as her notions about female roles. Fortunately, Hurston's initial orientation fit in with the eclectic and empiricist approaches that Boas espoused (Mikell 1983). Under Boas's tutelage, Hurston was prepared to be an astute observer and chronicler of black life without apparent imposition of an overarching paradigm except that of the legitimacy of culture. However, she, like Mead and Benedict before her, brought her own peculiar slant to Boas's eclecticism. In insisting that one give an authentic presentation of reality, she approached a methodology that later scholars would call "emic ethnography" and "reflexivity." As she became the instrument for recording and playing back the oral and visionary texts of black culture, she adopted what would later be called interpretive and symbolic styles, and she refused to translate culture for the benefit of outsiders.

She also gave far more attention to the role of women in the day-to-day play of culture than did other anthropologists except Mead and Benedict. Although her African-American work did not directly address the question of whether "culture can do anything," as did Mead and

Benedict, she outlined autonomous subgroups within dominant and oppressive cultures. Hurston saw black people, especially black women, struggling beneath the weight of racism and discrimination and laughing to keep from crying.

Although Hurston's techniques were in harmony with the salvage approach used by others of the Columbia school she saw the origins of her approach as being more varied and growing out of her dialogue with other black writers, such as Langston Hughes. She may have underestimated her own role in the movement toward combining ethnographic approaches to literature. In answer to her own question about how she should approach the collection of black data, Hurston told Locke: "I am using the vacuum cleaner method, grabbing everything I see. Langston is responsible for that to an extent. He writes and suggests new phases continually. I wish you would help me that way also" (Hurston to Locke, June 10, 1928, Locke Papers).

With good reason, Hurston approached her work with the assumption that the best researcher has a commonality with the people being studied. She did not often voice her belief that "white people could not be trusted to collect the lore of others" except to friends like Locke, with whom her ideas were in harmony (Hurston to Locke, June 10, 1928, Locke Papers). Although Boas's experiences with the Kwakuitl led him to understand Hurston's position, there is little evidence that he and other white researchers *really* sought a deep-level understanding as opposed to a superficial understanding of the cultures they were analyzing (Boas [1935] 1970).

In spite of Boas's endorsement, Hurston's acceptance as a researcher in the field remains in doubt. Evidence suggests that these field experiences were jolting, traumatic, and dramatically shaped the way she dealt with black material and with the intellectual world from that point forward. Hurston had observed the difficulty of male-female relationships in Eatonville but had emerged with optimism. Hurston's mother, although a dedicated housewife, was independent and held liberal ideas about freedom for girls. She envied her mother's ability to curb her strong husband, but as Hurston studied black culture more thoroughly she increasingly doubted her ability to achieve the same success (1984:30–34). Some of this insecurity surfaces in discussions in her autobiography about her two brief marriages, the struggles she had getting her partners to understand her need to be self-directed, and her failure to come to a compromise with herself on her role as intellectual and wife.

The hard-won successes of poor black women fascinated Hurston. She understood that black women in the Florida communities where she collected folklore were equally strong as men but their strength came in different ways—they were active participants in the "lies" that southerners told on their porches to wile away the time. The literary image she painted is seemingly supported by the ease of male-female co-participation in casual interaction within southern as well as northern ghetto communities. The images capture significant portions of life, but the limits on this male-female participation have not been well defined by Hurston in the southern folklore research and often present an illusory freedom for black southern women. Black men, unable to find work in the changing southern economy, often left black women as they migrated to find work. While Hurston must have become aware of the questions raised by other black sociologists, such as E. Franklin Frazier (1939), about traumatized male-female and family relations within such communities, this does not seem to have altered her goal of frankly presenting raw cultural life.

The feminine prototype that emerged from *Mules and Men* was of hardened, suggestive, vulgar, dice-rolling, and often knife-wielding women like Gold or Big Sweet, who held their own in verbal and physical combat with black men. Their morality was an obvious outgrowth of the difficult situations in which they found themselves, and it was a source of intrigue for Hurston. Witty and competitive, black women sometimes disintegrated into violence when other women threatened relationships with their men. Hurston admired but feared these women, as when she fled from them at the Polk County camp. However, underneath their tough rhetoric she saw "mules"—poor trapped women whose reality jolted her. Despite all, these prototypical women struggled to hold home, community, and culture together, and they bore the fierce repercussions.

Hurston's research in New Orleans revealed assertive female alternatives to the mule, but she seldom systematically pursued these relationships in her scholarly publications (an exception is Hurston 1931). In New Orleans culture was amazingly close to its African roots. Powerful voodoo and hoodoo queens held knowledge of the mysterious arts that tied them to the heart of the black community. The primordial black woman was continually manipulated, betrayed, and then abandoned by her man. Her angry score with her man was settled either through voodoo or through his death. The vulnerable brown or mulatto woman achieved revenge or a sense of justice through conjure. These women's strength was their reversion to their cultural roots—their final decision to use the secrets of culture to alter impossible situations. Hurston believed that white people would never be able to understand these ritual secrets because they were blind to the depths of black culture. For most of these prototypical women, their femaleness was their cross to bear, but they bore it with a regal sense of responsibility.

The centrality of black women to the culture was startlingly clear in Hurston's research and writings on the southern United States. Ethnographic research was developing in her a notion that because of women's roles culture adapted and refused to be crushed under the onslaught of racism. Probably, this was true of culture everywhere, so it had to be investigated in another context, with different types of colonialism and oppression, in other parts of the African diaspora.

By the time Hurston returned to Columbia to begin graduate work in 1935, she knew that she wanted to conduct research in the Caribbean and compare black culture in diverse places. An intellectual and methodological visionary, she created and used the oral and literary texts long before the anthropologists of the 1970s could generate the model as an alternative to materialist and Marxian analyses. But this approach had severe implications for her graduate career. She quickly became impatient with the normal course work and library research of graduate training and desired a more active approach. She enrolled for first-year courses under Boas as she set up work with Herskovits at Northwestern University in preparation for Haitian voodoo research. However, the intensive library work on cultures all over the world frustrated her, and the Rosenwald Foundation, which had awarded her a fellowship, would not agree to fund her fieldwork-based approach to graduate study.

In essence Hurston was refusing to allow graduate mentors to tamper with her methodology of ethnographic subjectivity. She redirected her attention to a quite successful collaboration in southern black folklore research with Alan Lomax. She drew up lists of informants and structured questions to elicit the information, but the Rosenwald Foundation withdrew the fellowship and Hurston left Columbia saying, "I have lost all my zest for the doctorate" (qtd. in Hemenway 1977:210). Although she continued research, she did so for its intrinsic appeal and for its contributions to black folklore, music, and theater, rather than for its contributions to academia. If anthropology as a discipline would not accept the lifestyle and research approaches necessary to produce the texts of black culture, she would abandon it.

Hurston's fieldwork in the South contributed to her thesis that male-female relations, rather than race, were central in the social interactions of black folk (Hurston to Locke, June 14, 1928, Locke Papers; Gates 1985).

Apparently she had internalized Locke's 1928 advice that she take care not to "open up too soon" to whites, because she never directly stated this thesis in her work (Locke to Hurston, June 2, 1928, Locke Papers). Instead, she turned to race, that public face cloaking the vulnerable layers beneath. Except for portrayals through folklore and literature, Hurston is amazingly silent in her early work about her views on the condition of women in the United States. Perhaps U.S. life held out the tantalizing but unattainable prospects of female assertiveness and male-female equality. Hurston was not prepared to accept this, as she demonstrated in her second novel, *Their Eyes Were Watching God* (1937). So she gave us Janie Starks, who had seen through the deceptiveness of female manipulation and had chosen for herself the kind of relationship *she* wanted and the type of man she wanted it with.[6] Janie's chosen husband was uneducated, hard-working, and genuine, and he may have reflected Hurston's view of male dignity among the black working class. This novel, written while she was in the Caribbean, was about female liberation within, not away from, black culture.

Hurston contented herself with letting her cultural texts-as-literature present her feminist perspectives until she embarked upon research in Jamaica, Barbados, and Haiti with a Guggenheim Fellowship in 1936. Many have accepted only her Haitian voodoo material as real anthropology and have shrugged off her observations in Jamaica and Barbados as impressionistic commentary and journalism because of her style of presentation (Hurston [1938] 1990:76–77). It is important, however, to take this work as the explicit continuation of the female consciousness reflected in *Their Eyes Were Watching God.* During her time in the Caribbean, the full reality of what black women faced within culture hit her, and she was taken aback. The fieldwork was both cathartic and threatening and made Hurston reflect upon the contradictions within her own life—the loneliness of the female intellectual and often the necessity of choosing between marriage and career (Hemenway 1977:5, 18, 93). Hence, she violated her rule of silence; she "opened up too soon" and perhaps too thoroughly, because the reaction to this book did much to destroy any future chances of positive responses from the anthropological community.

In Jamaica, Hurston was directly confronted with her own femaleness and the restrictions that men placed on women intellectuals because of their gender. It angered her to discover that black women were excluded from vast areas of culture because of their gender. Although the concept of the "mule" had been prevalent in her southern folklore, it was possible to interpret the mule as eternal black culture personified. However, her alternative interpretation of the mule is given full expression here in the Caribbean as she observed the difficulty of life for women. Even in common American parlance, mules are ambivalent entities. Mules are sterile; and although they are labeled as dumb, they are smart and strong enough to do incredible amounts of work and survive difficulties that horses could not. Hurston finally states her association of the mule with black women after observing women's plight in rural Jamaica: "Women get no bonus just for being female down there. She can do the same labors as a man or a mule and nobody thinks anything about it" ([1938] 1990:59). The only exceptions she noted were for mulatto and often middle-class females ([1938] 1990:59–60).

Despite her instinctive negative reaction to the treatment of women, she was intrigued to discover what it meant for her as a female researcher. She was warned by a Jamaican male that American females must learn to accept their proper function in life, and she is shown how rural females were introduced to the arts of lovemaking in preparation for their roles as wives. She was amazed to see no hint of the "mule" in these young Caribbean brides as they completed their socialization to feminine and wifely roles. However, when she was provided a rare opportunity to delve into men's activities through a "Curry Goat Feed" given in her honor, she was ecstatic. It is clear that her triumph comes because she has succeeded in grasping the richness of culture—a richness that transcends just maleness or just femaleness.

In Haiti, Hurston observed the ritualized antagonism and sexual complementarity of males and females in voodoo. In *Tell My Horse* ([1938] 1990) Hurston shows us how thoroughly integrated women are into ritual and religion, although she makes no explicit value judgment concerning what Haitian women are doing or thinking. Her observations on women and the voodoo cults and gods are excellent and detailed, and were received as such by the general public, but not by the scholarly community ("Zora" 1938). Through the work, we learned the intricacy of the voodoo cults and the role they played in the lives of ordinary Haitians. The voodoo hierarchy had males at the top and an abundance of female practitioners and worshipers at the bottom. However, the source of life and the ultimate relationship of male to female was shown to be at the center of the voodoo religion.

In capturing the Haitian parallels with that important sex-role element of Africanity, Hurston was returning full circle to her conclusions about the centrality of male-female relations in black American culture. She describes the high god Damballah and his female counterpart Eruzule as active and sexually symbolic, revealing truth about creation to all those who sought knowledge. That Eruzule is mulatto escapes her comment; nor does she remark on how the majority of the gods are males and the majority of "horses" through whom the voodoo gods speak are female. Despite this, we know that Hurston is cognizant of the impact of women on the voodoo structure, because she describes how the one entirely Haitian god, Guede, has all the hard arrogance and irrepressibility of the Haitian peasant woman and the domestic servant. "Gods always behave like the people who make them," she remarks ([1938] 1990:232).

Hurston consciously, and sometimes unconsciously, used her female "horses" and "mules" to represent the dialectical relationship between males and females in diaspora black culture. Black men and women were inextricably bound to each other for their total survival, and they created a unique cultural reality as they loved as well as abused and exploited each other under the pressure of life in whatever society they found themselves. Nevertheless, except for her verdict on Jamaican relationships, she was generally unwilling to address male dominance and female subordination except through literature and ritual. Just as Hurston fundamentally objected to the portrayal of black men and women as trapped and distorted by racial discrimination, she also demonstrated the aggressive and creative use of dialect and Africanisms in the often jarring relationships between the sexes in poor black communities. Her "horses" were proud and strong, even if ridden.

Public enthusiasm for her research was countered by scholarly ambivalence. Although her Barnard and Columbia colleagues had at first valued her folklore research and sought to use her contacts in the black communities of Florida and New Orleans as they pursued their own research, they soon were either ambivalent about her work, hostile to her methodology and research techniques, or scandalized by the depth of her participation in cultural practices.[7] Their explanation was that Hurston had rebelled against rigorous comparative training—to her own detriment. When they consciously compared her research to such work as Herskovits's *Life in a Haitian Valley* (1937) they found it wanting.[8] While her folklore work was ingenious, many felt it constituted preliminary rather than in-depth analysis. Particularly with *Tell My Horse,* Hurston was alternately accused of journalistic approaches or of entering too fully into the cultural experience of her informants (Mikell 1983).

Many of her black contemporaries were equally critical, but for more varied reasons (see Turner 1971). The descriptions she gave of the life and language of poor blacks in rural work camps and shanty towns were embarrassing to the black middle class. Hurston was accused of frequently ignoring the conditions of oppression under which blacks worked and the political structures that generated many of the cultural responses she documented. They resented that she commented only on the "communist" leanings of some black intellectuals and that she severely criticized poor black colleges as "Begging Joints" (Hurston 1945b). Her criticism of blacks who celebrated the desegregation of schools and other public places created considerable antagonism.

Many black intellectuals labeled Hurston bohemian and aggressive, and they found her lack of a conservative feminine style upsetting. When professional differences arose, as they did between Hurston and Langston Hughes over the authorship of *Mule Bone* (Hughes and Hurston 1991), men resorted to sexism by accusing her of being jealous or "restless and moody" (qtd. in Hemenway 1977:145).

In speaking about the response to Hurston's work the history professor John Henry Clarke, her acquaintance, offered some insight: "She was going from folklore into folk culture, and people didn't know what she was doing. . . . She was asking questions about to what extent this helped them to stay alive, to cope with life. It was brilliant, but she had gone beyond what most people could understand. . . . They were bothered by the whole thing. . . . People also reacted to women doing field research, and they thought only men were supposed to do that" (1985:3). Clarke also spoke about the personal response to Hurston and what he called the "misinterpretation of black women in history": "She loved controversy. She was a lot of fun, and she was outrageous. . . . People with Zora's ego thrive on attention, any kind of attention. People were scandalized that a woman was like that. . . . She used to think that if you didn't care enough about me to throw a few stones, I must not be worth much. . . . Other blacks couldn't deal with that strength" (1985:3).[9]

By 1938 Hurston's fieldwork seemed to have helped her resolve much of her own concern about the roles of black women—a concern that had become obvious from her first year at Howard University. Some of Hurston's major female characters in her literature had even begun mouthing her sentiments on the subject. Hurston became more confirmed in the outward, aggressive style she had chosen for herself and for which she was so ostracized. She continually affirmed the importance of women in the continuity of black religious and community traditions, whether as co-participants, leaders, or followers. Hurston had taken a position on male-female relations: she opted to celebrate the active female role despite ostracism and difficulty. Her post-1938 literature reflects this coming to terms, which freed her to take on new issues (see "Zora" 1955).

Although Hurston had parted company with formal anthropology in 1936, she never lost her appreciation for fieldwork and ethnography. During the 1920s and 1930s she was a member of the American Folklore Society to which Ruth Benedict was affiliated, the American Anthropological Association, and the New York Academy of Sciences. She never taught anthropology, although she did teach drama at North Carolina College for Negroes during the academic year 1939–40. She received an honorary doctorate from Morgan State University in 1939 and a Distinguished Alumni Award from Howard University in 1943. In 1947 Hurston made a last desperate attempt to get back to anthropology by proposing research in Honduras to find the ruins of a lost Mayan city, but her efforts were frustrated by the lack of funding. Instead, she wrote the last of her four novels in Honduras. The reviews of *Seraph on the Suwanee* (1948), however, were negative, and she encountered heightened professional difficulty after its publication.

Already intellectually misunderstood, Hurston soon became increasingly socially ostracized, sometimes through her own actions. Her public persona may have encouraged others to believe some of the more fantastic and unfounded accusations being made against her.[10] These rumors damaged her credibility, lost her public support, and encouraged her colleagues to believe that her work as well as her life was that of a dilettante. Such incidents also hardened her view of the world, turning her more politically conservative. She launched scathing indictments of the black middle class and black politics and of the eagerness with which blacks accepted desegregation and integration (see, for example, Hurston 1945a, 1945b). Since she wished to emphasize the legitimacy and wholeness of black cultural institutions, she was often resentful if others devalued them or if they stressed the benefits of white cultural contributions for black institutions. Soon these pressures crushed the subtle sensitivity that had made her such a unique participant observer until she was no longer capable of high quality ethnography (Mikell 1989).

Reexamination of Hurston's opinions about black cultural integrity, women, and black religion and ritual did not begin until after her death in 1960. A serious investigation of her contributions to anthropology, however, has not yet begun. Anthropologists need to view her work anew through the lenses provided by interpretive and feminist anthropologists as well as in light of the questions posed by world systems theorists and globalists. Stephen Tyler noted that "ethnography is a superordinate discourse to which all other discourses are relativized, and in which they find their meaning and justification" (1986:153). Hurston certainly understood that the discourses of politics, science, literature, and history were dependent upon the substance of culture to give them form. Why do we as anthropologists still hesitate to apply these new understandings to Hurston's ethnographic treatments of black women and culture?

Notes

1. See the original contract between Hurston and Mason in the Locke Papers.

2. In Baltimore she met friends who were instrumental in her attendance at Morgan Academy and her graduation in 1918. With encouragement from Mae Miller, Hurston went to Howard University in 1918. See Hurston (1984).

3. This association with anthropology might reflect hindsight, since the anthropology department at Howard was founded much later.

4. Du Bois had invited Boas to attend some of the Atlanta conferences, and he served with Boas on editorial boards of journals that dealt with the race issue, such as the *Journal of Race Development*. As Locke's reputation in philosophy and black education increased, he became part of this intellectual group of scholars and activists. See Aptheker (1973:77, 114, 131–32, 328, 352–53).

5. A sense of Hurston's insecurity comes through in the way she describes her adoption by the Barnard "social registry" and her employment as Fannie Hurst's secretary. Hurston does not appear to have had many female friends, although by 1942 she listed Fannie Hurst and Ethel Waters as two women whose friendship she valued highly (see Hurston 1984:165–73, 246–56).

6. Hurston claims that the impetus for this novel came from her own emotional difficulties after a failed romantic relationship prior to departing for the Caribbean (Hurston 1984).

7. Hurston was often in contact with Ruth Benedict to request comments about her work on *Mules and Men*. Later, Boas wrote to Hurston and recruited her to assist on Otto Klineberg's research project in New Orleans on the "special musical abilities of black people." See Hemenway (1978:128–29).

8. Herskovits was skeptical about whether black Americans could be objective enough to conduct field research in African and Caribbean areas. While Herskovits did have one or two black researchers, he opposed funding autonomous projects for blacks in African-based cultures, and he often refused to train them as graduate students (see Herskovits 1941).

9. Noteworthy is that Clarke demonstrates his own appreciation for the links between culture and his discipline. In his public talks and his writing, he is constantly going from culture to history and back to culture.

10. A 1948 morals charge brought against Hurston by a young boy was later proven unfounded. However, the damage had been done, and some of Hurston's former friends parted company with her (see Hemenway 1978). In his interview

John Henry Clarke stated that she was increasingly incommunicative with others before leaving New York.

References Cited

Aptheker, Herbert, ed. 1973. *The Correspondence of W. E. B. Du Bois.* Vol. 1. *Selections, 1877–1934.* Amherst: University of Massachusetts Press.

Boas, Franz. [1935] 1970. Preface to *Mules and Men* by Zora Neale Hurston. New York: Harper and Row. 16.

Bush, Roland. 1991. "Ethnographic Subjectivity and Zora Neale Hurston's *Tell My Horse." Zora Neale Hurston Forum* 5 (2): 11–18.

Clarke, John Henry. 1985. Interview with author. Philadelphia. Apr. 27. Transcript in Manuscripts Division, Moorland-Spingarn Research Center, Howard University, Washington, D.C.

Clifford, James. 1988. *The Predicament of Culture: Twentieth-Century Ethnography, Literature, and Art.* Cambridge, Mass.: Harvard University Press.

Frazier, E. Franklin. 1939. *The Negro Family in the United States.* Chicago: University of Chicago Press.

Gates, Henry Louis, Jr. 1985. "A Negro Way of Saying." *New York Times Book Review,* Apr. 21: 1, 43, 45.

Harris, Marvin. 1968. *The Rise of Anthropological Theory: A History of Theories of Culture.* New York: Thomas Y. Crowell.

Hemenway, Robert E. 1977. *Zora Neale Hurston: A Literary Biography.* Urbana: University of Illinois Press.

Herskovits, Melville J. 1937. *Life in a Haitian Valley.* New York: W. W. Norton.

———. 1941. *Myth of the Negro Past.* New York: Harper and Row.

Hughes, Langston, and Zora Neale Hurston. 1991. *Mule Bone.* Ed. George Houston Bass and Henry Louis Gates Jr. New York: HarperCollins.

Hurston, Zora Neale. 1924. "Drenched in Light." *Opportunity* 2 (Dec.): 371–74.

———. 1926. "The Hue and Cry about Howard University." *Messenger* 7 (Sept.): 315–19, 338.

———. 1931. "Barracoon." Alain Locke Papers, Manuscript Division, Moorland-Spingarn Research Center, Howard University, Washington, D.C.

———. [1935] 1970. *Mules and Men.* New York: Harper and Row.

———. 1937. *Their Eyes Were Watching God.* Philadelphia: J. B. Lippincott.

———. [1938] 1990. *Tell My Horse.* New York: Harper and Row.

———. 1945a. "Crazy for This Democracy." *Negro Digest* 4 (Dec.): 45–48.

———. 1945b. "The Rise of Begging Joints." *American Mercury* 60 (Mar.): 288–94.

———. 1948. *Seraph on the Suwanee.* New York: Scribner and Sons.

———. 1984. *Dust Tracks on a Road: An Autobiography.* 2d ed. Ed. Robert Hemenway. Urbana: University of Illinois Press.

Locke, Alain. Papers. Manuscript Division, Moorland-Spingarn Research Center, Howard University, Washington, D.C.

———, ed. 1925. *The New Negro: An Interpretation.* New York: Albert and Charles Boni.

Mikell, Gwendolyn. 1983. "The Anthropological Imagination of Zora Neale Hurston." *Western Journal of Black Studies* 7 (1): 27–35.

———. 1989. "Zora Neale Hurston." In *Women Anthropologists: Selected Biographies.* Ed. Ute Gacs, Aisha Khan, Jerrie McIntyre, and Ruth Weinberg. Urbana: University of Illinois Press. 160–66.

———. 1991a. "Western Longings: A Review of Torgovnick's *Gone Primitive.*" *Belles Lettres* 6 (2): 50–51.

———. 1991b. "When Horses Talk: Reflections on Zora Neale Hurston's Haitian Anthropology." *Zora Neale Hurston Forum* 5 (2): 1–9.

Nathiri, N. Y., ed. 1991. *Zora! Zora Neale Hurston: A Woman and Her Community.* Orlando: Sentinel Communications.

Rampersad, Arnold. 1986. *The Life of Langston Hughes.* Vol. 1. *1902–1941: I, Too, Sing America.* New York: Oxford University Press.

Stinnette, Eleanor Des Vessey. 1981–82. "An Oral Memoir of Mrs. Ophelia Settle Egypt." Manuscripts Division, Moorland-Spingarn Research Center, Howard University, Washington, D.C.

Torgovnick, Marianna. 1990. *Gone Primitive: Savage Intellectuals, Modern Lives.* Chicago: University of Chicago Press.

Trescott, Jacqueline. 1978. "The Fabulous Zora Neale Hurston." *Washington Post,* May 21: F1, F6.

Turner, Darwin. 1971. *In a Minor Chord: Three Afro-American Writers and Their Search for Identity.* Carbondale: Southern Illinois University Press.

Tyler, Stephen A. 1986. "Post Modern Ethnography: From Document of the Occult to Occult Document." In *Writing Culture: The Poetics and Politics of Ethnography.* Ed. James Clifford and George E. Marcus. Berkeley: University of California Press. 151–73.

Walker, Alice, ed. 1979. *I Love Myself when I Am Laughing: A Zora Neale Hurston Reader.* Old Westbury, N.Y.: Feminist Press.

"Zora Hurston's Tell My Horse a Good Book!" 1938. *Philadelphia Independent,* Dec. 18.

"Zora Neale Hurston Deplores Segregation Problem." 1955. *Atlanta Weekly Review,* Sept. 9. Copy at the Schomberg Library, New York.

3

Louis Eugene King, the Anthropologist Who Never Was

Ira E. Harrison

O! how wretched is that poor man that hangs on princes' favours!
. . . Had I but served my God with half the zeal
I served my king, he would not in mine age
Had left me naked to mine enemies.
—William Shakespeare, *King Henry VIII*

Full many a gem of purest ray serene
The dark, unfathomed caves of ocean bear:
Full many a flower is born to blush unseen
And waste its sweetness on the desert air.
—Thomas Gray, "Elegy Written in a Country Churchyard"

I first met Louis Eugene King in 1969 when I was a public health behavioral scientist with the Pennsylvania State Department of Health and project director of a migrant health project with the Pennsylvania Health Council. Marnel King, no kin to Louis, had mentioned him to me, but I argued that he must be a sociologist, not an anthropologist. This was in 1969, and I said that I doubted there were ten African Americans with Ph.D.'s in anthropology at that time. She insisted that King was an anthropologist with a Ph.D. from Columbia University. Later, she introduced him to me, and when I heard his story, I was shocked and angry, wondering how many other blacks who studied anthropology had been forgotten.

I promised King and his family that I would tell his story and try to situate him properly in the history of anthropology. After all, he was a graduate of both Howard University and Columbia University and a student of Ernest E. Just and Franz Boas. Had he received his doctorate in 1932 following his fieldwork, King would have been the first African

Louis Eugene King. (Official United States Navy Photograph)

American to receive a doctorate in anthropology from Columbia University. Unfortunately, he did not have funds to publish twenty-seven copies of his dissertation as required by the department of anthropology. Furthermore, the Great Depression was the worst time for a black graduate to seek employment in the new discipline of anthropology and King was in desperate need of work to support his growing family. Due to these circumstances, King was soon forgotten among anthropologists.

Background and Training

Louis Eugene King was born in Barbados in 1898, the last of nine children. King's parents died when he was a child, so he moved around and was partly raised by a sister and her husband. After arriving in New York on the ship *Maracus* in 1906, he attended public school, Dewitt Clinton High School, and Morgan College Academy. From 1918 to 1919 he attended Storres College in Harpers Ferry, West Virginia, majoring in pedagogy. He taught school for a year before attending Howard University from 1920 to 1924. At Howard King was an excellent debater and editor of the student newspaper, which he renamed *The Hilltop*. As president of the student body, he became the mouthpiece for Howard faculty such as Ernest E. Just, Kelly Miller, and Alain Locke in the push for a black man to become president at Howard.[1] His efforts were not rewarded until two years after he graduated, when Howard elected its first black president, Mordecai Johnson. Louis was voted the "deepest man" in his class and worked as laboratory assistant to Just. King was a general studies major, earning a bachelor of science degree, and was admitted to Howard's medical school in 1924. Due to increased family responsibilities, however, King dropped out of medical school and worked as a history instructor in Grafton, West Virginia, from 1924 to 1925, earning $1,350. At the suggestion of Just he decided to study anthropology at Columbia University in 1925. Just told him that anthropology was a promising discipline and thought that he would do well in it.

King at Columbia

During his first two years at Columbia University, King worked as a research assistant for Otto Klineberg and Melville Herskovits. Like most graduate students with a family, King had financial problems, but he was doing good research. On January 9, 1927, Ernest E. Just offered him some encouragement: "I know that everything will come out all right for you, if you stick on the job. . . . Do not allow the little troubles to obscure your vision. You have a big thing so go ahead and make good on your job" (Just to King, author's possession). Nevertheless, King felt compelled to write to the Laura Spelman Rockefeller Memorial on September 8, 1927: "Having received the Degree of Bachelor of Science from Howard University . . . in June 1924 I am now a student of Anthropology in Columbia University. I desire to continue my work to secure my Doctor's Degree in Anthropology. Last year my work was seriously handicapped due to financial difficulties. This year the situation has not improved and I find it necessary to seek aid from some source" (folder 993, box 98, Laura Spelman Rockefeller Memorial Archives; hereafter LSRMA). Among the people King suggested as references were Ernest E. Just, Franz Boas, and Frank A. Ross of Columbia University.

In his October 10 letter Boas deferred to Otto Klineberg and Heinrich Kluver, with whom King had also worked, for "information in regard to his personality and his method of work." Boas was, however, guardedly positive about King's abilities: "It seems to my mind that the opportunity for applying his knowledge is not unfavorable. I understand there is a good opportunity that he may be appointed at Howard University but I imagine that other Negro Universities will hardly be able to get along very long without some work in this line. I wish to repeat that I consider him well worthy of any support which may be given to him" (folder 993, box 98, LSRMA).

On October 14, 1927, Henry Garrett, assistant professor of psychology, wrote:

> Considering the fact that Mr King was beset by financial worries which made it necessary for him to do outside work, I believe that his performance was fairly satisfactory. Though he is not a brilliant student, King is ambitious, hardworking, and, I believe, deserving. Should his application receive the endorsement of Professor Boas, I should be very glad indeed to second it. Mr King intends eventually, I understand, to teach anthropology to members of his own race at Howard University, and any aid to that end seems to be very much worthwhile. (folder 933, box 98, LSRMA)

King maintained that Garrett was an avowed racist, and Garrett's evaluation appears typical of the period. Yolanda T. Moses notes that A. Irving Hollowell at the University of Pennsylvania did not consider Laurence Foster, the first black person to obtain a Ph.D. in anthropology, brilliant either (1983:37). When I discussed this with other African-American anthropologists, we could not recall any mention of a white person of this period calling a black person "brilliant."

Ernest E. Just, in his October 14 letter, was much more complimentary about King:

> It gives me great pleasure to recommend Mr. King to you in the highest terms. And this too when I try to be very careful in making recommendations.
>
> Mr. King was during four years a student in zoology here under me; during this time he showed initiative, capacity for individual work, and the possession of the spirit of inquiry to an unusual degree. As an undergraduate he showed leaning toward anthropology. . . . This is a field of the utmost importance for a Negro student today. The more science we can bring to bear on the Negro problem, the quicker will sentimentality and emotionalism vanish—to the good of both blacks and white[s] in this country. A sound man in anthropology can do a world of good. Mr. King is just the man for this. He has the capacity for development; and because he is teachable will go a long way. Mr. King on more than one occasion assisted me in the conduct of classes and once during my illness conducted my classes. He proved an excellent teacher, having had before then and since some experience in teaching. Should you give Mr. King the assistance which I know that he needs, I am sure that you will later have ample cause to congratulate yourself for having done so. (folder 993, box 98, LSRMA)

Frank Ross, of the faculty of political science, wrote on October 19:

> Last spring . . . Professor Boas suggested that I utilize King's services in experimenting with a questionnaire on Negro migration. I decided to do so on a part time arrangement. During the summer King very successfully, working without supervision, completed several hundred of these questionnaires. He showed real ability to grasp the implications of the problem, to weight the significance of its several features, and to "get the goods."
>
> I have had a number of interviews with King and believe that he is a man of real capacity, industry, and integrity. I found that others with whom he has been in close contact are of the same opinion.
>
> I believe that King has had a sound training in natural science. I am under the impression that his training in the social sciences has just begun. I can think of no greater need among the many that are pressing in the study of the Negro problem than a man, thoroughly trained in the scientific point of view, and equipped with social science research meth-

> ods, who is himself a Negro. With possibly one exception I know of no man who in my mind is more promising.
>
> I must admit that I am drawing my conclusions from scanty information. I do not wish to imply that I am certain in this connection. In the event that the Memorial sees fit to encourage King, I will consider it a most promising experiment and one that I would like to watch very closely. If there are further facts which you would like, I would be glad to furnish them as far as I am able. (folder 993, box 98, LSRMA)

Despite King's outstanding performance on the research project, Ross's conservatism kept the recommendation reserved.

King's Rockefeller grant was extended, but not before Just invited him back to Howard to teach physical anthropology. He would have a teaching position, but not a doctorate and perhaps not future employment. Together they decided that King should take the grant and finish his work.

African-American Communities Neglected

Prior to the 1960s, anthropologists neglected the serious study of American blacks. William S. Willis Jr. argued that cultural anthropologists were too occupied studying North American Indians (1970:33). Thomas Jefferson has borne the brunt of the blame for this neglect since he declared that blacks were ugly and inferior to whites and Native Americans and that Native Americans were talented, "primitive," intelligent, and interesting (Ruchames 1969:162–69; Fried 1972:69). Jefferson's motives were complicated by property ownership, of course. He may have pointed to Native Americans because they occupied land that he wanted to acquire, while blacks remained slaves, and thus were considered property. The Compromise of 1877 defining blacks as a southern problem freed the federal government and northern philanthropists from financing anthropological studies of southern blacks and from angering white southerners. Funds to study American Indians were more plentiful, especially since Native Americans were considered "primitive" and "savage," which were the preoccupations of anthropologists of the period (Willis 1970:36–37).

According to Ann Fischer, studying blacks was considered a poor fieldwork experience for anthropologists except during the 1930s, when funding for fieldwork overseas was scarce. Then "the Negro presented an inexpensive field experience" (1969:12). George L. Hicks and Mark J.

Handler observe that the tendency for anthropologists to concentrate on so-called primitive peoples and Native Americans combined with the sociologists' tendency to concentrate on industrial peoples and race relations left studies on blacks to sociologists until the late sixties (1978:2–62). They argue that even in the 1930s, when there was a shift in anthropology "from ethnographic salvage to studies of acculturation, and cultural purity ceased to be a fieldwork prerequisite, the 'acculturated' Negro was still largely ignored" (1978:314). It is against this tradition of avoidance and neglect that we must consider Louis King's work.

King was one of the first anthropologists—if not the first—black or white, to study black communities in the United States. King conducted fieldwork in West Virginia from 1927 to 1931 for Melville Herskovits, who was studying black body size (anthropometry), for Otto Klineberg, who was studying black intelligence, and for Frank Ross, who was studying black migration. This was before Hortense Powdermaker went to Mississippi in 1932, before Allison Davis studied blacks in Mississippi in 1935, and before William Bascom researched the Gullah in South Carolina in 1939. Whereas Arthur Huff Fauset, Laurence Foster, and Zora Neale Hurston were primarily collecting folklore in Canada, Guatemala, Mexico, Nova Scotia, and the United States in the 1920s and 1930s, King probably made the first anthropological community study of African-American life in the United States.

King's "Negro Life in a Rural Community" was an attempt to apply anthropological techniques to a modern society as well as an attempt to document objectively the daily experiences of black people in West Virginia—the most northern state considered part of the South. His ethnography focused on "family relationships, the securing of food and shelter, the acquisition of an education, religious experiences, group activities, mental attitudes, migration, and other related factors. . . . Emerging from a cultural background almost wholly influenced by slavery, Negro life in this area presents at this time a pattern similar to the life in the white community" (1951:1). King continues:

> This investigation reveals that there exists in the development of Negro life limited educational, economic, and social opportunities. These cultural limitations, in turn, created drastic psychological effects and inhibit full development of the Negro's potentialities. Under these circumstances it becomes a pertinent question whether any instrument can be devised that can determine accurately the relative superiority or inferiority of intelligence, without first securing an intimate and thorough knowledge

> of the background of those for whom the instrument is intended as a measure. (1951:2)

Here, King questions the validity of intelligence tests without a careful understanding of the cultural context of those to be tested. King also compares and contrasts his research with Thomas Jackson Woofter's study of St. Helena Island, *Black Yeomanry* (1930). King found that black lifeways in West Virginia were more like those of whites, while black lifeways in South Carolina, one of the most southern states, were unlike those of whites. King concludes:

> The differences found lead to the conclusion that although the two groups are racially similar, the pattern of life developed differently because of dissimilar cultural and environmental circumstances. . . . It appears that the more dissimilar the limitations placed upon the development of Negro life the more dissimilar the pattern between Negro and white groups become. The question shifts from that of a racial issue to that of cultural and environmental problems. Indeed the problem that confronts us today is how can the pattern of life be changed among those who are harassed and circumscribed by cultural limitations which tend to make the pattern of American life a patchwork of social inconsistencies. (1951:1–2)

Thus, King points to the environmental setting and the cultural context as a basis for understanding intelligence. As he observed, West Virginia blacks subsisted similarly to West Virginia whites because they were in greater proximity than were the South Carolina blacks and whites. Thus, association and opportunity to learn were more crucial for intelligence than just race.

Although King completed his dissertation in 1932, he could not publish his dissertation as required. Nor could he get a college teaching job without his Ph.D. in hand, despite Boas's advice and letters supporting his job applications: "I have written the letters for which you asked me. You do not need to hesitate to use your degree of Ph.D. because all is required is the printing of the thesis, which is a purely financial matter. Some of my students who took their Ph.D.s five years ago have not had their thesis printed yet" (July 24, 1933; author's possession).

King received no responses to his applications for positions at Howard University, West Virginia Institute, and Atlanta University. King believed that he was not hired because he did not have his doctorate, but perhaps the schools had no openings. He was particularly disappointed at not being able to return to his alma mater since he had been groomed to teach anthropology there. King had nowhere to go in black academia except to a school whose curriculum was extensive enough to include at least one course in anthropology. In 1932, however, black academia was in a depression and thus was probably restricting rather than expanding faculty numbers. The position Ernest E. Just had offered when King's funding was running out was not available, and Just was no longer at Howard.

The Great Depression, Anthropology, and King

According to May Ebihara, although anthropology was established in American academia by 1930, there were few centers of study and the number of faculty was small (1985:101–21). The Great Depression caused a decrease in funds for both fieldwork and museums, but established anthropologists were able to survive by affiliating with socialist and communist organizations or the government. "But graduate students who did not come from financially comfortable backgrounds often scrambled to support themselves as teaching assistants, instructors, waiters, janitors or whatever was available; and fresh Ph.D.s were faced with a paucity of academic openings" (1985:111). It is in this context that we must view King's decision to go to Gettysburg. Anthropology is still not well established in black academia, so a teaching position certainly was not a viable option in 1932 (Drake 1978; Harrison 1979, 1984; Harrison and Glenn 1980; Overbey 1991).

In 1934 King finally was hired as a junior historian at the Gettysburg National Military Park. As the *Gettysburg Times* announced, King became the first black historian at Gettysburg ("King" 1934). Although "there was a stir" among Pennsylvania politicians when he was appointed, "it soon died down [since] . . . he had a good record" (personal communication with park historical official, Oct. 12, 1983). His expertise in history and folklore was instrumental in the reconstruction and verification of events and monuments at the National Cemetery at Gettysburg. During World War II, however, there was a retrenchment at the military park and King, being the last hired, was fired.

King as a Federal Employee

In 1942, King was able to get a pick and shovel job at the Naval Supply Depot in Mechanicsburg, Pennsylvania. Desiring employment commensurate with his education and ability and seeing that he was being passed over for promotion, he tried to resign when the war ended. After reviewing his background, the commanding officer talked King into staying and created a position for him as a management analyst. The officer later noticed from his records that King had not officially received his doctorate even though he had completed the work. After he heard King's story, the officer contacted Columbia University and had a secretary type the three dissertation copies then required. King received his diploma in 1965, thirty-four years after the completion of his fieldwork.[2]

Ernest E. Just had died, and no one in anthropology encouraged him to seek employment, even with his Ph.D. in hand. King was still unable to get a job in academia or help establish anthropology at Howard. King finally became disillusioned and withdrew from the discipline. He mused: "I was very, very, very sore, and I became disgusted" (King 1979). Despite sending two daughters to Howard, King maintained, "I hadn't been back to Howard since my graduation in 1924" (King 1979).[3] Rather than quit the Naval Supply Depot, "I stayed there and put in the rest of my time and it really amounted to more than I would get anywhere else, even in college" (King 1979).

The commanding officer of the navy's largest inventory control point, with worldwide responsibility for the readiness and positioning of repair parts, ammunition, machine tools, electronics, and motor vehicles remembered Louis King:

> He was the lone humanist among 1500 technicians of one form or another. He knew the command, he knew the people, and he was not cursed (or obsessed) with the dogmas, doctrines, or professional prejudices that affected most of his fellow workers. I soon found him to be steady, loyal, and wise, and grew to respect and depend on his judgement and advice. He was no superman—there were things that he couldn't do. But he knew most of them and rarely started a task he didn't finish. If I had to pin down the characteristics that most typified Louis King, I would list honesty, simplicity, imagination, and a humble concern for the feelings of others—with his unusual (and almost amazing) imagination most prominent. (letter to author, Nov. 23, 1981, author's possession)

King's Significance

From King's life we can draw at least five main points of significance. First, as one of the few recipients of a Laura Spelman Rockefeller Memorial grant, King was being groomed by Melville Herskovits and Otto Klineberg to continue his anthropological research. Since important areas of black history and lifestyles were thought inaccessible to whites in the 1920s and 1930s, blacks were trained, through fieldwork, to get the information (King 1979; Stanfield 1985:78). King accomplished this work ably and thus was on his way to becoming an anthropologist in his own right.

But the Laura Spelman Rockefeller Memorial, according to John Stanfield,

> gave scholarships only to blacks admitted into a graduate program in one of the social sciences. Once they were admitted, they were at the mercy of white social scientists who used these scholarship programs to get blacks to do their research, often "dropping" their students after they had ceased to be useful. This was almost a routine practice among well known anthropologists and their black students. . . . In the late 1920s and early 1930s, there was a faddish interest in African and Afro-American cultures among American anthropologists, which created a demand for field-workers to collect ethnographic data on these cultures. During this period a number of blacks were recruited into the anthropology departments at Chicago, Columbia, and Harvard. But none of the memorial-sponsored black anthropology students finished their academic work, although most were competent researchers. (1985:84)

Thus King, like the other recipients, was merely a facilitator for another's career. Herskovits, in contrast, received his doctorate at Columbia University in anthropology in 1923, taught at Howard University in 1925, went to Northwestern University in 1927, and established the first African studies program in U.S. academia in 1960. Klineberg received his doctorate in psychology and anthropology in 1927 at Columbia University and was preoccupied with postdoctoral studies in Paris, Hamburg, and Rome from 1927 to 1929. He became the director of the International Center for Intergroup Relations of the International Social Science Council in Paris after a Guggenheim Fellowship in China in 1935–36.

Second, King's 1931 dissertation was a departure from the standard studies of the period and began a transition into community studies and fieldwork on blacks. Also, it sheds light on migration and intelligence, a prominent area of study in the 1920s and 1930s. During this time nature versus nurture theories predominated in the field. The thinking went that in any migration people with greater energy, stronger initiative, better potential for adaptation to a new environment, and therefore superior intelligence tended to leave, while those with inferior intelligence remained behind. This hypothesis of selective migration was used to explain why some blacks in the North scored higher on intelligence tests than either southern blacks or whites. Blacks in the North, then,

> would not represent an average group obtaining high scores because of the better environment (i.e., better schools, materials, and equipment in the North), but as a group they were superior to start with. If there has been a selective migration of the most intelligent Negroes, then the differences between North and South do not necessarily point to a definite environmental effect upon Negro intelligence test scores. However, if there has been no selective migration then the differences between Negroes North and South can be explained only in terms of such an environmental effect, indicating that Negro "intelligence" can markedly improve when there has been a corresponding improvement in the environment. (Klineberg 1935:4)

Of the 56 males and 54 females who had migrated to northern cities from rural West Virginia communities, King found that only 2 males and 4 females had obtained subsequent schooling. Eighty-six of these 110 migrants had definite connections with family or friends in the North. King discovered that the migrants' intelligence levels and social positions were not much different from those who stayed behind. King concluded that their departure was based on accidental and quite specific factors in their environment and not their innate intellectual abilities. King's contribution to the body of knowledge on blacks, migration, and intelligence was cited by Klineberg in his classic study *Negro Intelligence and Selective Migration* (1935).

Third, King points to the political nature of academic study. He was able to enter Columbia and anthropology in the 1920s primarily because policymakers needed information on southern black life. By the time King had collected the information, however, the sociopolitical climate in the country had changed and his work was no longer needed. The possible market for black anthropologists had collapsed, and King had nowhere to go and nothing to show for his fieldwork and study at Columbia. This was a fairly typical result according to Stanfield: "When elites resolve their racial crises of access to authority, or are disrupted by pressing national or international issues . . . the market for scholarship on blacks decreases along with the elite sponsorship of black entry into the social sciences" (1985:6).

Fourth, King reminds us of the importance of kinship obligations. With strength of character and resiliency King put aside his intellectual pursuits to support his family and educate his children.

Fifth, we can see the irony of history. King reentered anthropology long after he had renounced it. When he retired with thirty-two years of service for the federal government, he became a lecturer at Gettysburg College in 1969 and 1970, teaching introductory anthropology and courses on black life and culture. After teaching only two years, however, the effects of asthma and emphysema forced King to leave academia. He died August 13, 1981, in Gettysburg. King became more prominent in death, however, than he ever was in life. On February 13, 1986, Gettysburg College granted seven black students, five males and two females, Louis E. King Achievement Awards—a most fitting memorial to an important, but forgotten, scholar (Williams 1986).

Notes

This essay is a compilation of "Louis Eugene King, the Anthropologist Who Never Was" (1983) and "Louis E. King, Student, Federal Employee, Anthropologist" (1985). I thank Faye Jones Harrison, my former wife, for comments on an earlier version of this essay.

1. King told me that when he was president of the student body he told the president of the university, "Isn't it odd that your son can become president of Howard University, and I am a Negro, and my son can't become president of Howard?" (King 1979).

2. There is some disagreement about when King received his diploma. The dissertation is labeled 1951—the date the policy changed from twenty-seven to three copies required for graduation. The graduate school lists King's last date of matriculation as 1952. According to the *Gettysburg Times* King received his degree in 1965. King said he received his diploma about 1968 or 1969, even though he was able to teach at Gettysburg College in 1969.

3. King's youngest daughter, however, thinks that he may have returned once for a class reunion even though he never accompanied his daughters to Howard or visited them there.

References Cited

Bascom, William R. 1941. "Acculturation among the Gullah Negroes." *American Anthropologist* 43 (1): 43–50.

Davis, Allison, Burleigh B. Gardner, and Mary R. Gardner. 1941. *Deep South: A Social Anthropological Study of Caste and Class.* Chicago: University of Chicago Press.

Drake, St. Clair. 1978. "Reflections on Anthropology and the Black Experience." *Anthropology and Education Quarterly* 9 (2): 85–109.

Ebihara, May. 1985. "American Ethnology in the 1930s: Contexts and Currents." In *Social Contexts of American Ethnology, 1840–1984.* Ed. June Helm. Washington, D.C.: American Ethnological Society. 101–21.

Fischer, Ann. 1969. "The Personality and Subculture of Anthropologists and Their Study of the U.S. Negroes." In *Concepts and Assumptions in Contemporary Anthropology.* Southern Anthropological Society Proceedings, no. 3. Ed. Stephen A. Tyler. Athens, Ga.: Southern Anthropological Society. 12–17.

Fried, Morton. 1972. *The Study of Anthropology.* New York: Thomas Y. Crowell.

Harrison, Ira E. 1979. "Black Anthropologists in the Southern Region." *Anthropology and Education Quarterly* 10 (4): 269–75.

———. 1983. "Louis Eugene King, the Anthropologist Who Never Was." *Western Journal of Black Studies* 7 (1): 21–26.

———. 1984. "The Search for Anthropology at Hampton Institute." Paper presented at the 1984 National Endowment for the Humanities Summer Seminar for College Teachers, "History of Blacks in Higher Education, 1865–1984." Hampton Institute, Hampton, Va. July 3.

———. 1985. "Louis E. King, Student, Federal Employee, Anthropologist." Paper presented at the annual meeting of the American Anthropological Association. Washington, D.C. Dec. 6.

Harrison, Ira E., and Freda Glenn. 1980. "Afro-American Anthropologists in Southern Academia." *Notes from the ABA: A Publication of the Association of Black Anthropologists* 6 (1–2): 11–12.

Hicks, George L., and Mark J. Handler. 1978. "Ethnicity, Public Policy, and Anthropologists." In *Applied Anthropology in America: Past Contributions and Future Directions.* Ed. Elizabeth M. Eddy and William L. Partridge. New York: Holt, Rinehart, and Winston. 292–325.

King, Louis E. 1951. "Negro Life in a Rural Community." Ph.D. diss., Columbia University.

———. 1979. Interview with the author. Gettysburg, Pa. July 31.

"King Makes Plea for Colored Rights." 1934. *Gettysburg Times,* May 24.

Klineberg, Otto. 1935. *Negro Intelligence and Selective Migration.* New York: Columbia University Press.

Laura Spelman Rockefeller Memorial Archives. Rockefeller Archive Center, Rockefeller University, New York.

Moses, Yolanda. 1983. "Laurence Foster, a Black Anthropologist: His Life and Work." *Western Journal of Black Studies* 7 (1): 36–42.

Overbey, Peggy. 1991. "Committee on Anthropology in Predominantly Minority Institutions." *Anthropology Newsletter* 32 (8): 1, 7.

Powdermaker, Hortense. 1939. *After Freedom: A Cultural Study in the Deep South.* New York: Viking Press.

Ruchames, Louis. 1969. *Racial Thought in America.* Vol. 1. Amherst: University of Massachusetts Press.

Stanfield, John. 1985. *Philanthropy and Jim Crow in American Social Science.* Westport: Greenwood Press.

Williams, Janet M. 1986. "Seven Get King Awards." *Gettysburg Times* 84 (37): 1, 3.

Willis, William S., Jr. 1970. "Anthropology and Negroes on the Southern Colonial Frontier." In *The Black Experience in America: Selected Essays.* Ed. James C. Curtis and Lewis L. Gould. Austin: University of Texas Press. 33–50.

Woofter, Thomas Jackson. 1930. *Black Yeomanry.* New York: Henry Holt.

4

Laurence Foster: Anthropologist, Scholar, and Social Advocate

Yolanda Moses

Like many other social scientists of the depression era, Laurence Foster was an academic product of the best of times and the worst of times. It was the best of times because many anthropologists were redefining the discipline and questioning assumptions about whom they would study. It was easy for anthropologists to shift to the study of cultures of the United States during these lean years because, according to Elizabeth Colson, "anthropology was never primarily the study of exotic other peoples. It was about all of us and should apply to all of us equally. White or black middle class Americans and their customs and behaviors were as rightly a matter for comment as the customs and behaviors of anyone else" (1976:263). It was an interesting time for a black scholar like Laurence Foster, who studied some of the effects, both historical and contemporary, of institutional racism in American culture. But, I will argue this kind of research was not readily accepted as part of the study of American values. As a result, his scholarly work remained outside of the mainstream of anthropology.

Foster was not only a scholar and professor but also an applied social scientist. He advocated the use of knowledge of the truth about ourselves to make our society more democratic and humane. He was an idealist and a visionary who found out after thirty years of writing about truths that his work and his efforts were not enough to help change the condition of

Laurence Foster. (Courtesy of Lincoln University)

blacks in this country. He seems to have acknowledged this just a few years before his death in 1969 in a statement he made at a seminar on "The Negro Revolt" at Haverford, Pennsylvania, when he said, "The alienation of Negro intellectuals from the white world has gone far and bitterness against the white man has become intense" ("Foster" 1969).

Education

Laurence Foster was born on February 3, 1903, in Pensacola, Florida, where he grew up. He graduated from Millers Ferry Normal School in 1922. In 1926 he received a bachelor's degree from Lincoln University, an all-black school in Oxford, Pennsylvania. Some records also indicate that he received a degree from the Theological Seminary at Lincoln at about the same time. Foster was a part-time instructor in the philosophy department at the University of Pennsylvania from 1926 to 1928, which overlapped his enrollment in the graduate program in anthropology from 1927 to 1931.

Foster distinguished himself at the University of Pennsylvania. He was the class historian for several years, a student assistant in the Latin Department, winner of the Latin prize from 1927 through 1929, and recipient of a university scholarship in anthropology from 1927 to 1929. Foster received a grant from Columbia University for the 1927–28 academic year, during which time he conducted fieldwork in Canada, Mexico, and Guatemala for his dissertation. Records also indicate that he received a two-year National Research Council Fellowship, which he presumably used as a means of support while he wrote his thesis. In 1931 he became the first black to receive a Ph.D. in anthropology from the University of Pennsylvania.

Laurence Foster had the educational background for a brilliant career in anthropology: a distinguished educational record at the "right" university with the "right" graduate fellowships and fieldwork conducted outside the United States. Did these impeccable credentials confer on him the same advantages that would have been conferred on a white male counterpart? They did not. Foster was a victim of the institutional and cultural racism of his time. During the first part of the twentieth century, even anthropologists were caught up in the pervasive assumptions concerning the ability of blacks to perform as well as whites in academic settings. For example, in a letter of recommendation from Frank G. Speck at the University of Pennsylvania, we find Speck's need to refer to Foster's color twice: "Mr. Foster (a colored student) has shown himself to be a scrupulous and diligent man. His standing in his course with us is good, he is reliable, very ambitious and wonderfully persistent despite the obstacle of his color and poverty" (Aug. 10, 1929, University of Pennsylvania Placement Service records). Although most people in the United States circa 1929 were in dire financial straits, Speck probably would not have mentioned the skin color or economic conditions of any of his white graduate students.

In another letter of recommendation A. Irving Hallowell, then assistant professor of anthropology, comments on Foster's personal characteristics more than on his achievements in anthropology: "His record has been a good one without being brilliant and his interests seem more theoretical than concrete, a fact which might make him a good teacher of a general course in anthropology. Mr. Foster never pushes himself to the front unduly, is conservative (in the best sense) in his social relations, and altogether is to be recommended highly in his personal qualities" (Sept. 13, 1929, University of Pennsylvania Placement Service records). Hallowell seems to be sending several messages about Foster's abilities. First, the reference to his interests being "more theoretical than concrete" is undercut by Hallowell's judgment that Foster could be a good teacher of only a general anthropology course. Presumably this ability would be equally useful, if not more so, in upper-level undergraduate or graduate courses. Second, Hallowell describes Foster's record as good, but not "brilliant." This subjective statement does not specify what Foster had or had not done to earn the higher distinction. Third, Hallowell maintains that "Foster never pushes himself to the front unduly," but it is unclear whether this is meant as a negative or a positive statement. Graduate students are expected to be competitive, to vie for attention in seminars, to take the initiative to obtain department recognition and fellowship support. If this is a negative statement, then clearly Foster did not meet the expectations of his professor. But was Hallowell not aware, as other anthropologists of his time were, of the negative impact of racism on the behavior of blacks in all-white or potentially hostile situations (see Herskovits 1928, 1941)? Why did he not assume that Foster's actions were merely precautionary or protective? Like many blacks who have found themselves the only person of color in academic or employment situations, Foster may have chosen a more conservative stance to protect himself. If this was, on the other hand, a positive interpretation by Hallowell, it was positive only insofar as Foster's personality was concerned. Hallowell lauds Foster as being "conservative (in the best sense)" and recommends him highly on a personal level, not an educational or professional one.

These letters reflect the subtle forms of racism that were operative in higher education in general and in some departments of anthropology in particular during the 1920s and 1930s. In 1931 Foster graduated with a Ph.D. in anthropology, but he never taught in an anthropology department. Instead, his first position was as a professor of history at Stowe's Teachers College in St. Louis.

Formal Anthropological Training

Like many anthropologists of the early part of the twentieth century, Foster was more of a generalist than a specialist. He had training in Latin, philosophy, theology, and physical as well as cultural anthropology. It is not clear who Foster's mentor was at Columbia University, but since his study focused on blacks and Native Americans in the Southeast, it is reasonable to assume that Foster had at least some contact with Franz Boas and Ruth Benedict, both of whom dominated Native American studies.

Like Melville Herskovits, Foster wanted to document the cultural impact of blacks on other ethnic and racial groups in the Western Hemisphere, particularly Native Americans. He also wanted to point out how historians (white historians in particular) had totally disregarded blacks' influence when documenting the history of the Seminole Indians of the southeastern United States. Foster contended that if he studied both the cultural and physical characteristics of this group, he could show conclusively the extent that this admixture had taken place.

Foster began his thesis by showing how much blacks had culturally and physically altered the lives of Indians in the Caribbean, Mexico, Nicaragua, Panama, Peru, Venezuela, Paraguay, Ecuador, and Brazil (1931:10). The Bush Negroes of Dutch Guyana were of particular interest because their relationship to the Indians of Surinam in some ways paralleled black relations with the Seminoles: "The Bush Negroes have a great deal in common with the Seminole Negroes in Florida. The history of both begins with a similar motive, namely to escape from slavery. To do this, both sought the jungles. The Indians figured in the history of both groups" (10).

He was, however, quick to point out the differences between the two:

> The Bush Negroes were many thousands while the Seminole Negroes were only a few thousand, scarcely more than one-twelfth the number of the former. In addition Negroes of the Surinam had an extremely vast jungle, whereas the jungle of Florida was limited. In the latter case, the

> Indians were both enemies and allies; whereas in the case of the Negroes of the Surinam the Indians were enemies only. The Negroes of the Surinam preserved or reconstructed African culture in their jungle empire, while the Seminole Negroes, having been driven from the Florida jungle, are quickly losing both their African culture and their Indian culture and are rapidly becoming Euro-American. (10)

Foster concluded that throughout Latin America the interaction between blacks and Indians had been much more widespread than in the United States. According to his theory, Mediterranean Europeans who settled in Latin America procreated more freely and did not impose marriage restrictions. He added, tongue in cheek: "Yet those of us who know the Physical Anthropology of that large group of persons called Negroes who live in the United States can see that there is a vast difference between what is on the status and what actually exists in the physical make-up of the American Negro. In the final analysis it may be that the Anglo-Saxon is a bit more hypocritical than his Mediterranean brother" (11).

Using the work of such scholars as Melville Herskovits (1928, 1941), Caroline Bond Day (1930), Swan M. Burnett (1889), Carter G. Woodson (1918), and others, Foster sketched an overview of the history of black-Indian relationships throughout the United States but focused his fieldwork on the Southeast. His preliminary background research indicated that from the time the first slave settled in that area in the seventeenth century admixture between Indians and blacks was tremendous. He relied on Herskovits's figure of 27.3 percent of American blacks who possessed Native American blood, but no one had previously estimated the amount of African blood in the Native American groups of the region. Foster offered some suggestions: "It has been noted by many persons that there are tribes like those of New England and the five civilized tribes of Oklahoma who possess Negro blood. Many Indian tribes deny their Negro blood, so that the figures even recorded by our census bureau give an underestimation of the facts. The fact is, the disappearance of the identity of a very large number of Indian tribes is due to absorption by the Negro" (18).

Foster demonstrates that information on black-Indian relationships significantly altered the history of the Seminole Indians and blacks who fled to Florida from the slave states in the nineteenth century and eventually settled in Mexico, Texas, and Oklahoma. Not only does he document historical events that have been overlooked by other social scientists and researchers and posits reasons why but also he shows how the culturally ingrained racism of whites ultimately affected the Indian-black relationships over a century and how each of the three descendant groups developed distinctive values as a result of that racism.

Background

During the first half of the eighteenth century, both Native Americans and blacks fled south from the Carolinas and Georgia to what is now Florida. Since Florida was held by the Spanish and had not yet instituted slavery, many runaway slaves could become landowners and soon established friendly relationships with the local Creek and Kickapoo. In one of the first cultural exchanges the slaves taught the Native Americans how to improve their farming and how to select land and, in general, acted as their advisors (Foster 1931:207). These "runaways" coexisted with Native Americans somewhat peacefully in Florida until after the Revolutionary War, when the Continental Congress sent representatives to Georgia to settle a treaty dispute between the white settlers and the Creeks. In 1782 the newly formed federal government sent a representative to the territory of Florida to negotiate with the Spanish government for the return of the black exiles, who were living under the protection of the Spanish crown. The Spanish government refused to cooperate. During the two terms of George Washington little was done to get the exiles back. But in 1812 the United States went to war with Britain. The British established a fort along the Apalachicola River in Florida. When the British left the territory in 1815, they left the fort with all of its ammunition to the exiles who lived in the area under the leadership of a black man named Garcia (24).

The U.S. government, however, wanted the fort destroyed for several reasons. First, the black exiles could protect themselves and their fertile land from the white settlers who wanted to immigrate into the area. Second, they were amassing wealth in the form of land and cattle and were winning the respect and loyalty of the Indian groups around them, particularly the Seminoles. And third, "the fact that these Negroes were allowed to live in peace and enjoy their wealth endangered the institution of slavery and set a bad example for slaves living in the adjoining states" (25). It was no surprise when General Andrew Jackson, commander of the southern forces, wrote General Gaines that he believed the fort "had been established by villains for the purpose of rapine and plunder, that it should be blown up and destroyed, and these 'stolen Negroes' and their property returned to their owners" (24).

On July 27, 1816, the fort was finally blown up after several unsuccessful attempts. Of the 334 people in the fort, only 3 escaped unharmed, but they were quickly captured and killed. All the spoils went to the soldiers and the Creeks who assisted them. Twenty-two years after this massacre, the House of Representatives granted a large sum of money to the officers, soldiers, and sailors who participated as compensation for their gallant services to the United States. No one noticed the death of the exiles (27). In 1817, the black exiles and local Native Americans lost half of their population in a battle with General Jackson. In May 1818, Jackson wrote to the president that the war was over, withdrew his troops, and assumed his work was done.

Over the next twenty-five years, however, several battles, confrontations, and treaties eventually persuaded many of the Native Americans of Florida and the black exiles to migrate in 1842 to the part of Indian Territory that became Arkansas and Oklahoma, where they were assured of their freedom. Once there, however, the blacks realized they still were targets for the Creeks who had accompanied them because each black person captured and brought back into slavery was worth a bounty of one hundred dollars. So in 1849 about 300 blacks and Indians from various groups departed for Mexico, where they felt they would finally be safe. After some difficulty, this group reached Naciamento, Mexico, where Laurence Foster went in 1929–30 to study the cultural blending and the results of this interracial settlement.

Foster found not only that the Mexican settlement had persisted but also that other descendants of the early refugees were still living in the United States. One group had moved from Naciamento to Bracketville, Texas, in the 1880s and another was forcibly moved from Florida to the territory of Oklahoma by the U.S. government in 1860.

Study

Although Foster's fieldwork spanned four years, his intensive study was conducted between 1929 and 1930. When he collected data and lived with these three groups, he found different social patterns dependent upon not only their interactions with each other but also their direct association with European-American values and the ideology of racism. It is no surprise that the farther the descendants lived from European Americans, the less they were influenced by the prevailing cultural and institutionalized racist attitudes of the United States.

Data from Naciamento showed much intermarriage of the transplanted Floridians, black and Native American, with the Kickapoos and with Mexicans. Marriage to Mexicans was preferred to marriage to "Americans," black or white (Foster 1931:57). In 1930, twenty families still lived in Naciamento. Most spoke Spanish, but about 30 percent were bilingual in English and Spanish. This evidence of intermixture was further borne out by anthropometric tests.[1]

Data from Bracketville showed a slightly different social pattern. The laws of Texas forbade marriage between Native Americans and whites, but the transplanted Floridians frowned upon marriage to "Americans," black or white. Most were encouraged, instead, to choose marriage partners who had come from Naciamento. However, a number of marriages took place between the Floridians and "American" blacks. At the time Foster did his study, Spanish and English were spoken by the people of Bracketville. The transplanted Floridians of Bracketville professed to be Baptists, while the Floridians of Naciamento claimed Catholicism as well as the Protestant religion. In terms of physical anthropology, the Bracketville group showed a blending of the various older admixtures from Florida and Naciamento, but very little admixture with the Indians, blacks, or whites who lived in Texas (56).

The third group of black and Indian Floridians lived and farmed side by side from just after the Civil War until 1907, when Oklahoma was declared a state. Soon after that the legislature instituted segregation and "gave the [male] Indians the status of white men and prohibited marriage to any person having one drop of Negro blood," which essentially outlawed many social relationships that had already developed (67). As a result, old friendships between blacks and Native Americans were usually kept intact, but few new ones were formed. In 1930, Foster found that elderly Native Americans who had come from Florida expressed negative feelings toward blacks. Foster concluded that culturally they had become "more Indian and white," which was supported by his physical anthropological data demonstrating that their percentage of black ancestry was decreasing (67). The Floridian blacks, however, had become "more Negroid and white" with a more uniform, though smaller, percentage of Native American ancestry (67). Foster attributed this to blacks' view of themselves as Indians who thus did not encourage marriage with "American" blacks. Although some did marry "American" blacks, they usually did so for the educational and economic advantages thereby conferred.

Foster concluded his study by showing the close relationship between physical and social anthropology, especially when trying to reconstruct cultural linkages that are not reported in traditional historical literature:

"in the realm of Social Anthropology, the results of the Negro-Indian relationships are significant. We have indicated that the Negro has borrowed much of his material culture from the white man and has passed many of these cultural traits on to the Indians. In many instances, the Negro has learned much from the Indian, on the other hand, the whites have learned much from the Indian through their contacts with the Negro" (74).

He also used the anthropological method of the community study to show how what he calls the "race complex" has been responsible for the cultural separation of two groups that had historically been linked by their desire for the same thing—freedom. But because the Floridian Indians who associated with the Floridian blacks were perceived as criminals by law, the positive cultural interactions could not continue in the United States; in fact, quite the opposite occurred: "With determined propaganda, certain whites in the United States have worked persistently to change the attitude of the Indian of the United States from friendly lines to positive opposition to the Negro" (75).

Foster further postulates that this "racial complex" had also been detrimental to the institutions of religion, economics, education, and finance. He did not perceive this as a localized phenomenon but rather one that ordered the realities and shaped the worldviews of both blacks and whites: "In truth, it is a differentiating trait of the culture of the whole Southeast. The average Negro in the Southeast shapes his entire thinking and acting around this complex. His thoughts are either in anticipation of, or the consequence of, the race complex. The average White man in the Southeast is thus warped also, in that his thinking and acting center around the race complex. The complex takes up entirely too much of the time of both groups" (75).

Foster hoped that his anthropological approach to the study of this historical omission and the reasons why would provide some new insights into the study of institutionalized racism in the United States. There was little or no response to Foster's thesis from other anthropologists, however. His ideas and his findings remained as obscure in anthropology as did his name.

Other Published Works

After Foster received his Ph.D. in 1931, he became a professor of history at Stowe's Teachers College in St. Louis from 1929 until 1933. From 1933 to 1937 he was dean of instruction at Cheyney State College. During this time, he was not teaching anthropology or researching racism and culture, but was quite active in academia. He edited the series the History of Civilization, which included *A Short History of Greece, A History of Maya Civilization, A Short History of the Civilization of India,* and his contribution, *The History of Education* (1936b). As editor he garnered some local recognition: he was asked to become a research associate of the University of Pennsylvania Museum as well as to serve on various civic committees.

In 1936, he published another book, *The Functions of a Graduate School in a Democratic Society.* Although this was not an anthropological study, he used many ideas and methodologies gleaned from anthropology to compile his data, which were based on the examination and ranking of forty of America's leading graduate schools. Foster insisted that the main function of any graduate school should be to produce leaders, but the leading American graduate universities failed to do so. Foster explained: "the fundamental hypothesis is that the immediate end of research is the discovery of truth and that its ultimate end is the application of this truth to the benefit of mankind" (1936a:2). He was advocating the application of knowledge to solving problems, echoing Herskovits's applied approach to knowledge. This publication received some heated criticism, particularly from the universities that did not rank high on his final list. His astute analysis of the shortcomings of graduate schools in 1936 and his recommendations to improve them are quite applicable today, when we are facing similar financial constraints in higher education. His recommendations included cooperation between graduate schools when it is of mutual benefit; the use of the facilities of many cultural and noncultural institutions and foundations with purposes similar to those of graduate schools; cooperation with commercial institutions; cooperation with branches of municipal, county, state, and federal governments; international cooperation; and "the formation of centers for advanced study and research in which representation and support from each type of agency listed above is pooled to work toward the common goals of all, without hindering the cause of any one agency represented" (56).

At this time Foster was a philosopher and an idealist. He believed that if you discovered the truth and presented it, the truth would stand on its own merits. He worked very hard in all that he did. He gave academia and society his best ideas, and felt that should be enough. He believed that academia was the answer to the problems of racism, bigotry, and prejudice. In 1936, he was full of hope.

The Lincoln Years

Laurence Foster was a faculty member at Lincoln University from 1937 until he died in 1969. During his years there he contributed to the growth and development of the university's educational excellence by focusing on improving its programs, developing a link with Africa, and tying it to a global community.

Foster can best be described as an activist, regardless of the particular endeavor in which he was involved. From the moment he arrived at Lincoln University in 1937, he constantly looked for ways to improve his students' experience. Foster addressed the improvement of the seminary curriculum (1943); the improvement of the liberal arts curriculum (in 1941 and in 1960); the establishment of a medical college (1963); and the establishment of an academic program called Learning How to Learn (1969).

Foster's educational philosophy for Lincoln University was "prepare students to enter leading graduate schools of arts and sciences as well as graduate professional schools" (1944). In 1944, Foster wrote a 144-page report outlining lower-division as well as upper-division aims for excellence in the liberal arts. Many of his proposals and suggestions were adopted by the university and became a part of the Lincoln University curriculum. He revised his program in 1960. Foster had also begun to develop a medical curriculum when the university president dashed his hopes by telling him it would not be feasible for such a small university to have a medical school.

In an interview Frank Wilson, retired professor, administrator, and longtime colleague of Foster, reiterated Foster's commitment to excellence in teaching and scholarship and his pursuit of excellence for himself and for his students: "He was a very effusive person. He had so many ideas. He was unafraid to expose his ideas; he was not afraid to test them, even at the expense of ridicule. For example, Foster had a dream for a medical school and for a graduate program in African studies. There was little chance for those things to happen at Lincoln in those days, but he pushed for them anyway" (1986).

Frank Robinson, now an administrator at a large western university, said of Foster: "That man made a lasting impression on me. He was not concerned about material possessions, or what kind of image he was supposed to have as chair of the Division of Social Sciences. All he cared about were ideas, and how to make us excited about them. I remember how, very often, his lectures would not focus on the topic in the syllabus, but would focus on whatever idea had caught Dr. Foster's fancy that day. Looking back on it, it was quite an exciting class" (1986).

At Lincoln he held many titles, including chair of the department of sociology, chair of the Division of Social Sciences, faculty member on the board of trustees, and member of "innumerable committees dealing with the curriculum, the seminary, premedical education, housing, and the like. He was interested in student and faculty activities, whether they involved the development of a new course or program, chapel exercises, or efforts in the field of equal employment" (Stevens 1969). During his tenure at Lincoln Foster was also the coeditor of several books and readers: *Introduction to Sociology* (1954), *Selected Readings in Sociology* (1954), *Introduction to American Government* (1952), *Readings on the American Way* (1953), and *Analysis of Social Problems* (1954).

Foster's concern for the application of knowledge to the solving of social problems led to a public activism that spanned over thirty years. Foster was the director of the Research Council for the National Protestant Council on Higher Education in 1953; a fellow in the American Folklore Society; a member of the Executive Committee of the International Academy of Physical Anthropology; president of the Stearns Housing Corporation; chairman of the board for the Model Cities Foundation in Philadelphia and in New York; and executive director for the Pennsylvania State Temporary Commission on Conditions of the Urban Colored Population, for which he wrote a preliminary report.

When one colleague was asked whether Foster taught anthropology at Lincoln University, he answered: "He never taught anthropology at Lincoln University; he taught in sociology only. But he did have a strong concern for cross-cultural issues, especially toward people of the West Indies and of West Africa. He even began to get involved in East Africa and in Kenya in the late 1960s." Cross-cultural studies were so important to Foster that he encouraged his children to participate: "His daughter went to Italy and France. She learned to speak Italian and studied abroad" (Robinson 1986).

Lincoln University has long had ties with Africa; hundreds of Africans call Lincoln University their alma mater, including Nnamdi Azikiwe, prime minister of the eastern region of Nigeria, and Kwame Nkrumah, prime minister of Ghana. Foster deliberately sought out African students to incorporate their culture and experiences into the curriculum and campus life. As early as 1949 Foster demonstrated his enthusiasm for this project to Horace Mann Bond, then president of the university: "It would be well for us to consider ways in which these students can make some contributions to our collection or to have them begin making dictionaries or to record folk tales. It would be a pity for those intelligent men to come here year after year without our helping both them and ourselves in an effort to develop their culture through such well-established media as I have suggested" (Sept. 28, 1949, Langston Hughes Library, Lincoln University, Oxford, Pa.).

By 1955 Foster urged President Bond to establish an institute of African affairs at Lincoln: "I wish to call to your attention that the Underhill Collection (African Material Culture) already contains enough material for us to integrate it into our curriculum. Moreover, I am certain that Dr. Underhill would work toward the enlargement of this collection if we utilized it more. Further, we have on the faculty Dr. Hubert B. Ross, an anthropologist specializing in Africa area studies, with both the artistic appreciation and ethnological knowledge of African material culture to make the proper educational use of this material" (Apr. 15, 1955, Langston Hughes Library, Lincoln University, Oxford, Pa.). Foster argued that establishing the institute would cost the university no additional funds, which was enough to convince the administration.

By 1957 Foster had proposed another international link with Africa—a graduate school of African studies. In a letter to the president he requested permission to begin work on the curriculum, which he had developed with Kwame Nkrumah, and offered partial support for the program from the profits of a business venture that he had embarked upon in the Gold Coast (Robinson 1986). Although the university offered a few courses, a master's degree program was not implemented. But Foster continued to develop international contacts with colleagues in the West Indies, Europe, and Asia. He focused on international alumni, partly through an alumni newsletter, so wherever they were in the world, they would remember Lincoln University and offer financial support.

Foster's activism outside of the university is most noted in his tireless efforts to educate people about civil and human rights. Frank Robinson, his colleague, discussed his loyalty to Lincoln University and the surrounding community, which is still quite rural and white: "Dr. Foster was always concerned about the relationship between Lincoln and the town of Oxford very nearby. The black population was only 10–12 percent of Oxford then. He was very helpful in the 1950s to get that town opened up to our students" (Robinson and Frankowsky 1986).

Foster spent thirty-six years at Lincoln University as a student, instructor, and administrator and became a legend at the school. As the Reverend Samuel G. Stevens, chaplain of Lincoln University and longtime friend and colleague, proclaimed in his eulogy: "Generations of Lincoln men and women and those whose life Laurence Foster has touched, wish to join all of us here in expressing our thanks that Laurence Foster came our way and contributed to the fullness of our lives and to the accomplishments of Lincoln University" (1969).

Notes

Special thanks go the following people at Lincoln University for their assistance with this project: Joseph Wimbish, director of the Langston Hughes Library; Sophie Cornwell, director of research and publications of the Langston Hughes Library; Grace Frankowsky, executive secretary to the president, Lincoln University; and Frank Wilson. Special thanks also to the National Endowment for the Humanities for travel funds.

1. Foster used the anthropometric techniques of Herskovits (1930). Foster included such measurements as standing height, entire length of arm, greatest breadth of head, interocular breadth, nasal height, nasal depth, maximum ear length, lip height, length of left foot, and pigmentation.

References Cited

Burnett, Swan M. 1889. "A Note on the Melungeons." *American Anthropologist* 2 (4): 347–49.

Caldwell, Morris G., and Laurence Foster, eds. 1954. *Analysis of Social Problems.* Harrisburg, Pa.: Stackpole.

Colson, Elizabeth. 1976. "Culture and Progress." *American Anthropologist* 78 (2): 261–70.

Day, Caroline Bond. 1930. "Race-Crossings in the United States." *Crisis* 37 (1): 81–82, 103.

Foster, Laurence. 1931. "Negro-Indian Relations in the Southeast." Ph.D. diss., University of Pennsylvania.

———. 1936a. *The Functions of a Graduate School in a Democratic Society.* New York: Huxley House.

———. 1936b. *The History of Education.* New York: Huxley House.

———. 1944. "A Preliminary Report on the Proposed Program for the Liberal Arts at Lincoln University."

Foster, Laurence, Warner E. Gettys, Walter Firey, and C. W. McKee, eds. 1954. *Selected Readings in Sociology.* Harrisburg, Pa.: Stackpole.

Foster, Laurence, Paul S. Jacobson, and C. W. McKee. 1952. *Introduction to American Government.* Philadelphia: Foundation for the Advancement of Social Science.

Foster, Laurence, Walter A. Lunden, and Lloyd V. Ballard, eds. 1954. *Introduction to Sociology.* Harrisburg, Pa.: Stackpole.

Foster, Laurence, Sidney G. Morse, and John B. Rae, eds. 1953. *Readings on the American Way.* Harrisburg, Pa.: Stackpole.

"Foster, Laurence P." 1969. *New York Times,* Aug. 18.

Herskovits, Melville. 1928. *The American Negro: A Study in Racial Crossing.* New York: Alfred A. Knopf.

———. 1941. *The Myth of the Negro Past.* New York: Harper and Row.

Robinson, Frank. 1986. Interview with the author. Lincoln University, Lincoln, Pa. Dec. 9.

Robinson, Frank, and Grace Frankowsky. 1986. Interview with the author. Lincoln University, Lincoln, Pa. Dec. 9. Transcript.

Stevens, Samuel G. 1969. Transcript of eulogy of Laurence Foster delivered at funeral services in the Mary Dodd Brown Memorial Chapel, Lincoln University, Lincoln, Pa. Aug.

Wilson, Frank. 1986. Interview with the author. Lincoln University, Lincoln, Pa. Dec. 9.

Woodson, Carter G. 1918. "The Beginning of Miscegenation." *Journal of Negro History* 3 (4): 335–53.

5

W. Montague Cobb: Physical Anthropologist, Anatomist, and Activist

Lesley M. Rankin-Hill and Michael L. Blakey

> Not many men are able to prove, by their own example, that, despite the wisdom of the Good Book, a prophet can sometimes be "not without honour—even in his own country." . . . To fewer still is it possible to . . . [be] named as "one of the most influential Negroes in the United States." . . . Montague Cobb built up a collection of over 600 documented skeletons and a comparative anatomy museum in the gross anatomy laboratory. His anatomical researches have dealt with collections of human materials in American institutions, cadaver demography, comparative dental anatomy, ageing changes in the bones of the human skeleton and the physical anthropology of the American Negro . . . and indeed he is, recognized as the principal historian of the American Negro in medicine.
> —Phillip Tobias 1977

W. Montague Cobb's career from its inception paralleled nearly the entire history of professional physical anthropology in the United States. As a leading activist scholar in the African-American community and the only black physical anthropologist with a Ph.D. before the Korean War, Cobb was the sole representative of black perspectives in physical anthropology for many years. W. Montague Cobb exemplified the orientation of the physical anthropologist of the 1930s. Grounded in anatomy and medicine prior to the maturing of a separate bioanthropological curriculum, Cobb was part of a generation that linked the founders of American physical anthropology to all of its succeeding generations. Yet, he is unique not only for being the only professional African-American physical anthropologist in the early years of the discipline, but also for pioneering approaches and accomplishments in human biology and health. Cobb characterized himself as "marching to the beat of a different drummer."

W. Montague Cobb. (Courtesy of the Cobb family)

W. Montague Cobb, A.B., M.D., Ph.D., became the first distinguished professor of anatomy at Howard University in 1969. He was distinguished professor emeritus from 1973 until his death in 1990. In 1980 he received the Henry Gray Award, conferred by the American Association of Anatomists for outstanding contributions to the field of anatomy. He accrued over one hundred other honors and citations, including many of paramount distinction. He served as president of the NAACP (1976–82), the American Association of Physical Anthropologists (1957–59), and the Anthropological Society of Washington (1949–51). He also served as editor of the *Journal of the National Medical Association* for twenty-eight years (1949–77). Cobb chaired the department of anatomy of Howard University College of Medicine from 1947 to 1969. He was the author of 1,100 publications on diverse topics and taught over 6,000 anatomy students. His influence as an organizer and advocate for health improvements and civil rights was felt and acknowledged by leaders in government, the military, the world of letters, law, medicine, and the general public.

As an extraordinary man of wit and energy, the sum of his work assures his place among the greatest American scholars. We provide a primary accounting of key aspects of his rich career as a pioneer black anthropologist based on the edited transcripts of six hours of formal interviews, bibliographic research, and literature reviews of selected publications. Interviews were conducted at his home in 1985. Interview questions were submitted in advance and structured the initial interviews. Important issues and questions were pursued in subsequent interviews. The interviews were transcribed and then edited by the authors; the transcripts are now archived at the Moorland-Spingarn Research Center at Howard University in Washington, D.C., with other Cobb documents, and will be referred to as "CPRHBI or CPRHBII 1985." Bibliographic research included a search for Cobb's publications, many provided by Cobb himself and others located at diverse libraries throughout the Washington, D.C., area. This search was based on a preliminary draft of Cobb's composite vita, including publications, formal presentations, awards, and offices. The literature review focused primarily on publications that were distinctly physical anthropological and clearly applications of physical anthropology/anatomy to civil rights, social inequality, and education. Many discussions with Cobb as teacher, colleague, and friend have also influenced our understanding of the "Cobbian" worldview.

The analysis of Cobb's influences and contributions in this essay is preliminary; a far more extensive text would be required to bring so complex and prolific a scholar into focus. We present Cobb's recollections integrated with our descriptions of the historic context of his education and scientific career, highlighting what we believe to be key aspects of the history of physical anthropology in America.

We started out with the goals of collecting Cobb's views on physical anthropology within a historical setting and attempting to have him recreate for us the personalities, interactions, and issues of the emerging discipline during his early years. In most instances, it is the events, people, and issues Cobb himself considered most important that we have selected. We will also examine the corpus of Cobb's work as it represents an African-American genre of anthropology, much of which remains forward thinking and current.

Our specific emphases include Cobb's participation in the early history of American physical anthropology and his relationship to its founding fathers and his teachers T. Wingate Todd and Aleš Hrdlička; his views on the relationship between physical anthropology and anatomy and anatomy as a key to understanding his universe; his roles in professional associations and civil rights programs; his early approaches to applied anthropology and its relationship to his theoretical and methodological approaches; and his utilization of both the African-American and European-American professional and political organizations within which he worked for social change.

Physical Anthropology: Historical Background

W. Montague Cobb entered graduate school during the very same year that physical anthropology was founded as an autonomous profession in the United States. The field had come far in some ways; it had been infused by Darwinian theory, mounting hominid fossil evidence, the discovery of blood groups and Mendelian genetics, and government support for anthropometric surveys. However, the tremendous emphasis placed on craniometric studies (which sought to determine phylogenetic and mental differences in racial, subracial, and institutionalized groups) had not changed much since Samuel Morton's studies in the 1830s. Morton's original work and compendium, published posthumously by Josiah C. Nott and George R. Gliddon (1854), served to legitimize slavery by claiming innate differences in African and European mental capacities. Its support for the South's "peculiar institution" was substantial enough for it to have been hailed by the *Charleston Medical*

Journal (Gould 1981) and to have brought forth a lengthy counterresponse from Frederick Douglass ([1854] 1950).

Following a lull in American studies during the Reconstruction (Hrdlička 1918), craniology became popular again at the turn of the twentieth century and served anew to justify class, racial, and subracial (immigrant versus American-born whites) inequalities. Thus, the continuity of interest in the size and shape of the head was influenced by social inequality, albeit transformed from a means of legitimating slavery on its last legs to the inequities of urban-industrial monopoly capitalism in its nascency.

Aleš Hrdlička (1869–1943), the leading American physical anthropologist during these early years (1910–30), was the first curator in physical anthropology at the Bureau of American Ethnology in the U.S. National Museum of the Smithsonian Institution. Hrdlička, a medical doctor who received training in anthropology at the École d'Anthropologie de Paris and the Laboratoire d'Anthropologie ("Broca's Institute," as Hrdlička referred to it [Spencer 1979]), firmly believed in the innate superiority of academicians (Hrdlička 1941), men (Hrdlička 1925b), and "native" or "old American" whites (Hrdlička 1925a). Although his craniometric methodology was deeply flawed by a priori biodeterministic assumptions, such results captured the popular and scientific imagination of the time (see Blakey 1987).

Nevertheless, material support for physical anthropology remained modest, especially when compared to that of the eugenics movement (applied social Darwinism), which was making the same biodeterministic claims but which was more highly politicized and popular in elite philanthropic circles. Indeed, the rapid growth of the field of genetics was dependent on the movement's support (Allen 1975). Although often at odds with the eugenics leadership, Hrdlička supported its most virulently racist spokesmen, Charles B. Davenport (1886–1944) and Madison Grant (1865–1937), when influencing the formation of the Anthropology Committee of the National Research Council (NRC). The NRC had been established by President Woodrow Wilson in 1916 to foster the development of the sciences that could aid in World War I. The NRC was a natural vehicle for Hrdlička's efforts to advance the credibility and support for his field. Hrdlička's goals at the time were to have physical anthropology recognized as a distinct discipline and area of research, to establish an American journal of physical anthropology, and to establish a national institute of physical anthropology. In 1918 he founded the *American Journal of Physi-*

cal Anthropology, which served as organ for the NRC committee. The first issues of the journal contained sections devoted to war anthropology and eugenics, with Davenport on its editorial board and Hrdlička in editorial control (Blakey 1987; Spencer 1979).

In contrast to this mainstream, Franz Boas at Columbia University was publishing antiracist studies that stressed the developmental plasticity of body and mind. The conflicts that arose in the scientific literature are no less revealing of the political differences between the "Boasian school" and the "Washington-Harvard axis" (of which Hrdlička and Earnest Hooton [1887–1954] are representative) than were their battles to block or oust each other from major committees of the NRC and the National Academy of Sciences (Spencer 1979; Stocking 1968). Although Boasian liberalism would capture the public imagination and institutional support in the years surrounding World War II, the mainstream scientific racism that emanated from Washington and Harvard would dominate the scene during these early years.

Hrdlička dreamed of establishing an anthropological institute in the United States like that in France. He showed himself to be an institution builder of "missionary zeal" (Montagu 1944). Hrdlička had outlined the scope and aims of physical anthropology in 1918 and 1921. He felt the need to branch out from medicine and anatomy, where physical anthropology had its first academic base, and to attract the best medical students to the new career. Physical anthropology, he wrote, was intended to have practical application through racial eugenics, directed at engineering the biology and social "progress" of American society (Hrdlička 1918; also see Blakey 1987). These are the same general concepts that would form the ideological underpinnings of racial segregation, the Ku Klux Klan, and European fascism (Patterson [1951] 1970).

At the American Association for the Advancement of Science's Section H meetings (Anthropology) in 1928, Hrdlička urged the creation of a new and separate association and an American institute of physical anthropology in Washington, D.C. A resolution to this end was adopted and a committee was formed. Committee members included Fay Cooper-Cole (1881–1961), Davenport, George A. Dorsey (1868–1931), William King Gregory (1876–1970), Earnest Hooton (1887–1954), and Robert J. Terry (1870–1966), with Hrdlička as chairman and Dudly Morton (1884–?) as secretary (Spencer 1979:745–48). Morton assembled a list of fifty-eight prospective members for the new association. The highly regarded T. Wingate Todd (1885–1938), who would never have favored instituting a professional separation between physical anthropology and anatomy, was conspicuously absent from the list. The American Association of Physical Anthropologists was founded in November 1929, and Hrdlička's *American Journal of Physical Anthropology* was unanimously adopted as its official organ. This event marks the birth of professional physical anthropology in the United States. Hrdlička never got his institute, but he continued to campaign for it until his death in 1943 (Spencer 1979:745–48).

During this very same autumn of 1929, a young African-American physician, W. Montague Cobb, arrived at Western Reserve University to study anatomy and physical anthropology under T. Wingate Todd. The circumstances and events that brought him to venture into the study of humankind at this place and time were as much circumscribed by the social realities and historical moment as was the development of the field.

Becoming an Anthropologist

William Montague Cobb was born at 1326 T Street in the northwest quadrant of Washington, D.C., on October 12, 1904. His mother, Alexzine Montague Cobb, was descended from an old Massachusetts family that recognized a partly Native American ancestry. His father, William Elmer Cobb, was a native of Selma, Alabama, who had come to Washington, D.C., in the late nineteenth century and was well known as the "one-horse operator" of an important printing business for the black community. The young "Monty" grew up in this secure but less than affluent family.

When he was still too young to read, Cobb became fascinated by pictures of human variation in his grandfather's book on the animal kingdom (Goodrich 1868). He recalls that it was the question of race that led him to anthropology. The book's drawings of racial types in traditional dress represented each race (as Cobb describes it) "with equal dignity" (CPRHBII 1985:7). He would never cease to be fascinated by the pedagogical utility of drawing, whether in his anatomy classroom or in cave drawings as a means of instruction by the Paleolithic hunter.

As Cobb matured, he encountered directly the institutions of racism and segregation. When the time came to enter primary school, he was perplexed that he could not go to the nearest school, which he had often watched in anticipation. Over the coming years he would learn that, in his own society, the rich variation in human anatomy that had so pleased him was the basis for differentiating human worth, opportunity, and life experiences. This interested, perhaps angered, and certainly motivated Cobb to set his life on a course to expose and destroy racism and replace it with a more sophisticated understanding of human biology. As importantly, Cobb was impressed in childhood by the fact that doctors could make people well, which, he recalled, struck him simply "as a good thing." His perception of the status of the physician in his community, furthermore, fueled his aspirations to a medical career.

Cobb received a diploma from Dunbar High School, the summit of African-American secondary education, "possibly the best high school in the world," in 1921. During this period there were few colleges where blacks could teach, and many outstanding teachers with higher degrees came to Dunbar. Because it was an academic high school in the tradition of W. E. B. Du Bois, its alumni read like a social register of the so-called talented tenth. Among these was a hefty proportion of the few who were chosen (partly by Dunbar's faculty) to attend the best black colleges and white colleges that would admit blacks. Some returned to recruit and share the news, and Cobb was particularly impressed by the Amherst men, such as his life-long friend and fellow Dunbar graduate Charles Drew. Cobb received the A.B. degree from Amherst College in 1925.

While at Amherst, Cobb took advantage of a broad curriculum of classical scholarship and training in European arts, languages, literature, philosophy, and history, as well as in the sciences, which were then only in the process of taking on their modern forms. He also won three championships as a cross-country runner and two in boxing. His eclecticism was by no means new. He had developed skills as a violinist and a boxer in his youth (he had taught himself boxing from a manual at Dunbar as the need arose from caste-class conflict in the neighborhood). In many respects, which can only be touched on here, Cobb made the most of every opportunity to achieve the rich intellectual, activist, and humanitarian qualities of his heroes and kindred spirits of both the European and Harlem renaissances.[1]

On graduation from Amherst College, Cobb received the Blodgett Scholarship for proficiency in biology at the prestigious Woods Hole Marine Biology Laboratory in Massachusetts, where he was able to pursue his interest in embryology. There he found his way to the distinguished Howard University biologist Ernest E. Just (see Manning 1983 for a discussion of Just's contributions to biology). Cobb's meticulous notes and drawings of the fertilization and development of a broad spectrum of marine species show an excellent grasp of biology, artistic talent, attention to detail, and joy in learning. There he recorded, by the hour and minute, each phase of development from zygote to embryo as he had observed them microscopically.

Cobb recalled an experiment in 1925 in which the young Just and a twenty-one-year-old, somewhat talkative Cobb stood squatting in the Woods Hole lagoon, awaiting the habitual approach of spawning sea worms (*Nereis limbata*) in the middle of the night. As Cobb recounted their work, the experienced Just noted the first signs of the worms' approach and quietly motioned to Cobb. Within moments the moon-glazed water's edge became thick with the swarm. The researchers rapidly identified males and females, netted them before they could mate, and deposited them into separate sample jars. No sooner had they completed their collection than the remaining swarm became frenzied with mating; the swirling mass released their gametes, suddenly making the water around them milky white. Of this occasion Cobb remarked, with characteristic drama, as Shakespeare spoke of Romeo and Juliet, "violent delights have violent ends, and in their triumph, die"—as, in fact, *Nereis limbata* do after spawning. Just, Cobb, and other students would then spend a vigilant night in the laboratory, observing and recording the development of the sea worms from the moment of fertilization.

The following summer, Cobb helped pay for his medical education by working as a waiter on a Great Lakes steamship. A racial division of labor existed on board ship in which there were black waiters, Chinese cooks, Irish deckhands, Scots-Irish engineers, French-Canadian stewards, and English-Canadian officers. This scene (as recounted to us), with its almost surrealistic moments of group conflict and cooperation, represented for Cobb a deliberate and exacting divide-and-rule policy. Later that summer, he traveled to Saskatchewan, where he signed on to a crew of grain harvesters and earned wages on the rugged and sometimes volatile Canadian frontier.

From Howard University Medical School, to which he would later devote his entire professional career, Cobb earned an M.D. in 1929. His work was so outstanding that he was given an instructorship in embryology during his last year of medical study. In 1927, immediately following the completion of the new medical building, Howard Medical School was at the nexus of a dramatic transformation. Mordecai Johnson, the first African-American president of the university, recognized that the often patronizing, white-dominated, part-time faculty retarded the medical school from reaching its full potential. Johnson was committed to transforming the institution into one in which African-American physicians acceded to full responsibility in the medical school's operation and development. The newly appointed dean of the school, Numa P. G. Adams, was assigned the task of reorganization. He set out to recruit the best-trained black faculty in the country. While there were few African-American Ph.D.'s in medical fields, the college had a number of outstanding students who, if opportunities for graduate study could be secured, were potentially the kind of faculty the college needed (Cobb 1951b).

Three were chosen for the development of the department of anatomy; R. L. McKinney received special training in microscopic anatomy at Chicago, M. W. Young was trained in neuroanatomy at Michigan, and Cobb was sent to Western Reserve University with a fellowship from the General Education Board to receive training in gross anatomy and the then-nascent physical anthropology. Adams, who had been instrumental in nurturing the young Cobb's interest for physical anthropology, made arrangements for him to receive his training under T. Wingate Todd, one of the most prominent members of the first generation of physical anthropologists in the United States. Todd was distinctively progressive for this period. In his October 28, 1930, address to the Association for the Study of Negro Life and History he remarks, "Anthropology can be hammered into an instrument for solving our most pressing problems of population, race or social status. But if it is not hammered with the greatest care and skill it may turn out to be a dangerous weapon wounding alike him who wields it and the victims on whom it is applied" (Todd 1931).

Todd's studies showed that there were no "racial" differences in the development of the black brain and the white brain, but that "a misadventure due to defective growth in childhood induced by unsatisfactory circumstances of life" producing laggard growth in the braincase of some black children had been misinterpreted and generalized (Todd 1931). He was a strong critic of the racial determinism among colleagues, such as Hrdlička, and lent his anthropological studies to the support of racial equality: "Our researches carried on over a large amount of material, demonstrate that what happens in the White happens in the Negro and at the same time, so that we come to realize there is but one humanity, one experiment of nature, whatever the color of the result" (Todd 1931). Cobb recollected:

> I came into the field through Dr. [Numa] P. G. Adams, the first Black Dean of an approved medical school. And I was getting ready to open my office for private practice here in Washington, having passed the state board, when Dr. Adams, newly appointed, asked me if I would be interested in a full-time academic career. And I said, "yes if I could pick my field." He said, "What do you want?" I said, "Anatomy." (CPRHBI 1985:1)

A place for advanced training was sought which would afford sound work in gross anatomy and its expansion into physical anthropology. It first appeared that there was no institution in the United States where this kind of training could be obtained by a Howard man. Then Dr. Adams remembered that he had met a man in Cleveland, a very busy man, of compelling personality. . . .

It was a great joy to discover that Dr. Todd was already so advanced in his thinking and had amply demonstrated by his published work that prevalent American concepts in respect to race and human potential had no place in his laboratory. More than three decades ago Wingate Todd in word and deed lived the principles which underlie the great social changes of our time and foreshadow those yet to come. Two decades after his passing he is still the embodiment of the anatomist, the physical anthropologist, the medical educator, and the physician of the future. (Cobb 1959:237)

[These] proved to be the two most rewarding and exciting years of my life. I would major in physical anthropology, [with] a minor in neuroanatomy and a minor in dental anatomy [and also served as an apprentice in gross anatomy]. (CPRHBI 1985:12, CPRHBII 1985:18)

And one of the most remarkable things about Todd, was he did so much in such a short time. . . . And I can say from this perspective, only now, are the fruits of Todd's work being realized. Because assessing age and race in a skeleton are always difficult things, and the critics abounded then. But he had a set of skulls that he called the Humiliators . . . they looked like one thing, but he had photographs and documents to show what they were. And he would have the experts look at these skulls and say what they were, and prove them wrong. . . . The Todd laboratory was way ahead. It was interdisciplinary already. Of course now they [physical anthropologists] are coming around to it. (CPRHBI 1985:2, 22)

The Hamann museum was a working laboratory where the student of medicine and human biology in its broader aspects could explore the biological processes which produced clinical conditions. Structure portrayed function on the dissecting table, under the microscope and in the successful adaptations for survival represented by various orders of mammals and primitive man. The United States had a modern anatomical laboratory which was carrying forward to new expression the Hunterian spirit and principles. (Cobb 1959:235)

Today the Hamann-Todd Collection is housed at the Cleveland Museum of Natural History, which is associated with Case Western Reserve University. This collection is one of the two largest skeletal populations available for study, along with the Terry Collection at the Smithsonian Institution.

Cobb's dissertation, a massive survey of anthropological materials and methods of documentation, processing, and preservation, could not have been better chosen for one whose mission was to establish a laboratory of anatomy and physical anthropology at Howard University (Cobb 1936a, 1951b, 1959). He believed such a laboratory would allow each African-American scholar to make his or her own "contribution not defense" (Cobb 1936a:10) in the debates on racial biology.

He began work on his laboratory immediately when he returned to Howard in 1932. He also continued his research in Todd's laboratory on human craniofacial union (suture closure) and began another survey of skeletal collections at the U.S. National Museum (Smithsonian Institution) under Hrdlička. "After receiving the Ph.D. in 1932, I returned to Reserve for a portion of each summer [for six years] for further studies on the Hamann-Todd collection, under appointments as a Fellow or an Associate in Anatomy. My papers on the cranio-facial union were completed in this way. . . . And I think two of my best papers are 'The Cranio-Facial Union and the Maxillary Tuber in Mammals' [1943a] and 'Cranio-Facial Union in Man' [1940]. Race is not involved in it and you can do that on simple anatomy" (CPRHBI 1985:1; CPRHBII 1985:8).

"The Cranio-Facial Union in Man" (1940) and its companion, "Cranio-Facial Union and the Maxillary Tuber in Mammals" (1943a) established Cobb as a functional anatomist. These publications were based on a comprehensive study of 1,100 mammalian crania and several hundred human crania from the Hamann mammalian collection and the Hamann-Todd human skeletal collection. The basis of this research was the morphological and functional examination of the "cranio-facial hefting area" of the skull. This area is where the "cerebral" cranium (braincase) and the "visceral" cranium (face and jaw) are joined. Cobb described these as two parts of the cranium with different functions and patterns of growth that came together in structural unity. The braincase grew rapidly and remained fairly stable after postnatal development, while the face and jaw grew slowly and could be modified throughout life by environmental factors. Cobb considered the morphology and function of this anatomical feature as significant in evolutionary terms. This area of anatomical research had been given little consideration at the time. In the human article, he establishes the different patterns between humans and other mammalia; other mammalian orders exhibit the pneumatization (expansion of internal air passages and sinuses) of the crania and the development of bony external reinforcements (i.e., crests). He then systematically explores the craniofacial union in humans and its developmental changes throughout the growth process. The mammalian article compares the functional morphology of the cranial-facial union in eleven orders, including several primate suborders.

As in much of Cobb's writing, these articles are elegant in their clear and poetic style and tightly packed substantive content. These papers give an analysis of the functional, developmental, and evolutionary interrelationships of the definition and bones of the face and cranium. Cobb's enthusiasm for learning is apparent in his close attention to detail and fascination with the integration of ontogenetic, phylogenetic, structural, and functional aspects of craniofacial anatomy. We were unable to identify a more comprehensive study on the subject. Craniofacial growth and development remains a significant area of research in contemporary physical anthropology (i.e., Kolar 1987; Rightmeier 1987). However, perhaps in part because the majority of these contemporary studies focus on craniofacial developmental pathology, referencing of Cobb's contributions remains obscure.

Cobb continued his work on critical issues in skeletal biology, utilizing the scarce but vital resources of skeletal collections. Cobb recalled,

> I enjoyed the cordial relationship with Dr. Todd's successor, Dr. Norman Hoerr, a histochemist, as I had with Dr. Todd. . . . At the time of Dr. Todd's passing in 1938 [Cobb 1939c], the human collection at Reserve numbered over 3300 individuals. I embarked on a comprehensive study of suture closure. . . . After completing the Reserve skulls, I went to St. Louis to do the same on the 1500 skulls in the collections at Washington University assembled by Dr. Robert J. Terry [now curated at the Smithsonian Institution in Washington, D.C.]. I enjoyed fine relationships there with Dr. Terry, Dr. Edmund Cowdry and Dr. Mildred Trotter, as well as Dr. George D. Williams and Dr. Seib. (CPRHBII 1985:10)
>
> Preliminary reports on these studies were made at the meetings of the International Gerontological Congresses in London and Merano, Italy. This is the only study of which I am aware which assembled data on all skulls in both collections for a single project. (CPRHBII 1985:11)

In one preliminary report, "Suture Closure as a Biological Phenomenon" (1957b), Cobb presented an analysis of a sample consisting of 2,351 crania of males and females of white and "American Negro stock." The analysis was based on 104 separate observations of 22 sutures. Although it is only a short paper, Cobb clearly establishes that utilizing suture closure as a method of age estimation was unreliable because of specific biological factors. These factors are based on basic principles of bone growth, the functional morphology of the crania, the functional significance of suture closure, and the overall process of human growth. These studies were significant contributions and some of his colleagues continue to reference this research in lectures (i.e., J. Lawrence Angel's forensic anthropology classes) and publications (i.e., St. Hoyme and Iscan 1989).

Emerging with Anthropology

This was no ordinary stage on which Cobb began his career. He entered the field when it first emerged as a recognized profession. Yet, having studied principally under Todd (who opposed the professional separation of physical anthropology from anatomy) contributed to Cobb's continuing belief that physical anthropology should be a subdiscipline of anatomy, and the latter should form the core of physical anthropological training.

Cobb encountered fundamental differences between Todd and Hrdlička in their racial perspectives as well: "At that time I didn't know all the inner workings of these personalities. Hrdlička had wanted a Survey of Human Materials in American Institutions Available for Study. Todd was the chairman of that committee. I didn't know then that Todd was familiar with Hrdlička's attitudes. But he put the load on Hrdlička by assigning me to do the work of that committee" (CPRHBI 1985:20; CPRHBII 1985:11). While reflecting on his early career, Cobb stated:

> now I have just understood in the last couple of years or so why Todd gave me the job of the committee of which he was chairman. He turned that over to me because I was right down here near Hrdlička. But he also wanted to see how Hrdlička would treat me. . . . So, I went down to see the great man. And he said in his thick German accent "well, you have been up there with the Professor Todd, a brilliant man, with far too many radical ideas. Now if you will come down and talk with me, I will show you the way." Alright, well I did not really know all that [that Hrdlička knew "the way" versus Todd], but he never did anything unfair, see? (CPRHBI 1985:20)

"Hrdlička's attitudes" are exemplified in a lecture given at American University in the spring of 1921, in which he claimed that "there is no question that there are today already retarded peoples, retarded races, and that there are advanced races, and that the differences between them tend rather to increase than to decrease. . . . And there is no acceptable possibility . . . that would make the white man wait upon the Japanese or Chinaman who is only a little bit behind, or the Negro who is a long way behind" (1921:12–14).

When assigned to review the literature on the Negro by the NRC, Hrdlička concluded that "the real problem of the American Negro lies in his brain" (1927:208–9). Little wonder that, when conducting his study of the "full-blood American Negro" at Howard University, Hrdlička received less cooperation from his subjects, whom he described as "semi-civilized, suspicious, scattered free laborers and servants" than "among the pliant, trusting savage" (1928:15).

Historians will agree that, once having reached a conclusion, Hrdlička's thinking would never be altered (Schultz 1945; Spencer 1979). His intransigence extended from his view that North America was populated no earlier than the Archaic period, to the Victorian clothing he wore long after it was fashionable. Cobb attributed the peculiarity of Hrdlička's attire to his shopping habits: "Hrdlička with his formal collars would walk down Pennsylvania Avenue shopping where he could get the cheapest things" (CPRHBI 1985:21). "Then one day I said 'Dr. Hrdlička, you accept me alright, why do you have these restrictive ideas about so called pure Negroes?' [i.e., Hrdlička 1927, 1928]. 'Well the Negro is alright when he's had the hardships the white man has had. You have the vigor of the hybrid,' he said. Well anytime you see anything you cannot explain, you invent an explanation" (CPRHBI 1985:21).

Hrdlička would publish much of Cobb's dissertation, "Human Archives" (1932), in the *American Journal of Physical Anthropology* in 1933 ("Human Materials in American Institutions Available for Anthropological Study"). Perhaps, as suggested above, the fact of Cobb's obvious admixture and his association with Todd made it easier for Hrdlička to accept Cobb and his work, which was a much needed survey of skeletal materials that today remains unparalleled in its comprehensiveness.

In 1939 Cobb profiled the biology and demography of the African-American population of the 1930s and showed the historical and social processes that led to its composition (1939b). "Negroes" are described as Afro-Euro-Indian hybrids who, since the end of slavery, had become an intrabreeding group. Cobb argues that the selective bottleneck of slavery enhanced (if anything) their physical strength and mental ability, and he even goes so far as to pose a biodeterministic argument for "special aptitudes" for music and dance. He explains the socioeconomic and demographic factors that have *enhanced* African-American fertility. Rather than suggesting inferiority, the intellectual achievements of African Americans seem extraordinary in light of the barriers to social and economic achievements that are described. Ultimately, the African-American population is shown to be highly adaptable. In contrast, Cobb questions the humaneness and efficiency of a western European civilization predicated on oppression, exploitation, and repeated wars of conquest. "The Negro as a Biological Element of the American Population" was designed to counter arguments that American blacks had not been exposed to European civilization sufficiently to gain "competence in management of the complexities of modern life" (1939b:344). Finally, he predicted that African Americans will increase as a percentage of the population and that the American population will become increasingly mixed as immigration is restricted and attempts to eliminate minorities remain futile. Despite not foreseeing the changes in American immigration policies, his predictions clearly represent the demographic profile of contemporary America.

Associations and Meetings in the Early Years

The first meeting Cobb attended of the American Association of Physical Anthropologists (AAPA) was the association's second meeting in December 1930, which was held at Western Reserve Medical School during Cobb's tenure (the meeting was held at the time of the American Association for the Advancement of Science [AAAS] meetings and in special collaboration with Section H-Anthropology). Hrdlička gave a public lecture concerning "children who run on all fours." Cobb regularly attended these and other professional meetings after that. His recollections of these early meetings provided a means of reconstructing some of the issues, contexts, personalities, and interpersonal dynamics of the period. In addition, these recollections provide a window on Cobb's own perspectives on the actors involved and reveal a distinctly African-American view of the problems and issues current at that time.

> Now there were no separate groups. The sessions were all one and everybody participated. So that if a concept of being a close knit group exists, that was a natural result of everybody being there. . . . However, there was always mutual respect in the original group of physical anthropologists; to describe them as close knit, I do not know that that ap-

plies. . . . Now, those were always very rewarding sessions. And, I would say that they were always clean cut, they were not taking any crusading attitudes on race or anything like that. (CPRHBI 1985:6–8)

Now, Boas never had any sense of humor, and . . . neither did Hrdlička you see. [What was] entertaining as well as rewarding was to see a debate between Hrdlička and Boas. [For example], Hrdlička was for standardizing all measurements so that all measurements would be comparable. . . . He put out a book on that called *Anthropometry*. . . . And Boas said that you determine the measurement by what you want to discover. And they had it out. Boas had had his stroke by that time and that was a little sad. So Hrdlička began to show how Davenport and Love did their Army Anthropometry series "those measurements were no good" [he said]. . . . So, it got very heated there for a while. But Raymond Pearl . . . a mathematician who really had a superior mind, would pour oil on the waters by saying, "that if you had enough measurements, the volume of the measurements and the errors would cancel each other out." But on that one, I would say it was a draw. Because if you want to study the dermatoglyphics of the palm and the major lines there is no need for some standardized measurements. You put down what you want to find out and devise a measurement to take that. (CPRHBI 1985:6–7)

It was at these meetings that Cobb would begin many lifelong friendships. There were, of course, his close neighbors and friends at the Smithsonian, J. Lawrence Angel (1915–86) and T. Dale Stewart. Angel worked as an adjunct member of the department of anatomy at Howard Medical School for several years, in addition to his museum curatorship. They each became members of the Cosmos Club, where Cobb often took his meals and entertained guests. His regard for Stewart was high, also partly because he was "a very gifted artist" (CPRHBI 1985:5) who chose to do what he enjoyed rather than pursue wealth, either as an artist or as a physician (Stewart had earned an M.D. from Johns Hopkins before he came to work at the Smithsonian under Hrdlička).

Cobb's admiration of the artist/scientist was equally evident in his fascination with the works of Vesalius and Leonardo da Vinci (Cobb 1943b, 1944) as with that of his contemporaries. "Now Adolph Schultz was a preeminent anatomist at Johns Hopkins. He was a gifted artist and did all of his own illustrations. He's got [drawings of] chimpanzees that will talk!" (CPRHBI 1985:5). For his own part, Cobb would help "perfect the standard color plate of the anatomy of the heart" (Morais 1978:2).

Many of his associations, however, were not so gratifying.

"When I applied to the 'Anatomists' a man held me up one year. And later apologized for it and said it was not on account of the racist stuff, I don't know. But that stuff was all around, however, in the physical anthropologists." (CPRHBI 1985:14)

Charles B. Davenport was the weakest of the lot. . . . He went to Jamaica and wrote a book on race crossing [Davenport and Steggerda 1929]. . . . He came out with a thesis that those who were more white could do more complex problems, and Blacks could do simpler problems. But the mulattoes were seen to have a little difficulty, getting mixed up, and all that [expletive deleted]. (CPRHBI 1985:5; CPRHBII 1985:10)

Gregory was a superb paleontologist. . . . [He] didn't show his true colors until . . . the blood program came out and the Red Cross planned to segregate blood [after World War II], the physical anthropologists passed a resolution [against the Red Cross]. And Bill Greulich and Bill Howells very strongly supported it. But when they appointed a committee to draft a resolution . . . William K. Gregory, who I believe was then president, did not put me on the committee. [This was after Cobb had been vice president of AAPA, and the issue was well within his expertise.] . . . I went to see him at the American Museum. . . . He explained by saying "I just didn't." However, I later learned that he was a realist as a politician and you just do not put somebody in a position where they can be effective. And Gregory did not like the brother [African Americans]. . . . That's William King Gregory, a superb paleontologist. . . . His volume on comparative dentition will stand today. But he had that other side. I don't recall any of the older fellows who were bigots. And the man at Harvard . . . Coon, Carlton Coon. He redid Ripley's *Races of Mankind*. But when he came up for nomination, I supported him. (CPRHBI 1985:5, 9–10; CPRHBII 1985:5)

In 1953, I was placed on the council of AAAS. And, I brought it up [the segregation issue] at their meeting in Boston. And when I said that they should not meet in Atlanta in '55, some of the big shots said "what's he talking about?" And then it was explained that they could not change the segregation laws of Atlanta. . . . Well, a deal was cooked up. All Blacks would stay at Atlanta University and they would be admitted to the meetings at the hotels but they could not stay there. Gabriel Lasker was then Secretary of Section H. Gabe said he would not prepare the program if they went there. And I said I would not attend. . . . So Section H had no program and at that meeting the unexpected came in! Detley Bronk [President of Rockefeller University] wrote a resolution stating that "the AAAS should meet only in places where there will be free association among scientists within and without the places of meeting." . . . So they

> had to go by mail vote, which came out overwhelmingly for the adoption of the resolution. (CPRHBII 1985:26–27)
>
> Incidentally, I have formed a fairly low opinion of Margaret Mead. She had been elected to the board of AAAS and the ASW [Anthropological Society of Washington] sat us side by side at a dinner in her honor, and she said to me, "Dr. Cobb, not all Negro leaders are in agreement with your position [on integrated meeting places]." I said, "Who for example?" She said, "Dr. Channing Tobias." I said, "Dr. Tobias? That seems very strange, because we are good friends and he's the Chairman of the Board of the NAACP, I cannot imagine him saying [that]." . . . What she had done was mix up Tobias with Al Maron, at Hampton. . . . But this lady is another one of those who apparently does not know many brethren [blacks] and they all look alike to her." (CPRHBI 1985:30; CPRHBII 1985:27)

The Cobbian Perspective

In the 1930s, physical anthropology was torn between at least two major approaches. The "Boasian" approach stressed developmental plasticity, environmental effects, and racial equality. The mainstream evolutionary approaches emphasized racial comparison, biological determinism, and—in its usual form—the racial "inferiority" of blacks. The Boasian trend was only beginning to take hold of the public interest in the years approaching World War II when his students, prominently including Margaret Mead, utilized and publicized its perspective (Drake 1980; Harris 1968; Stocking 1968, 1976). W. E. B. Du Bois, like other "vindicationist" African-American scholars, had accepted and used Boas's work since the turn of the century (Drake 1980).

Cobb, on the other hand, had been trained within the mainstream by the fair-minded Todd. Cobb claimed no intellectual roots in the so-called Boasian school and showed little interest in sociocultural anthropology, in particular, or the four-field approach, in general. There is, nonetheless, biocultural integration in his work that focuses on biological or medical relationships in the history and structure of his own industrial society, or biomedical connections with artistic aesthetics and philosophical generalities.

Yet, there was substantial agreement between Cobb and the Boasians in contradiction to mainstream racial-deterministic ideas. Both Cobb and Boas emphasized an appreciation of human diversity, equality, flexibility, and creativity. In this vein, Cobb's article on the significance (or insignificance) of race in athletics (1936b) remains one of the most poignant counterarguments to biological determinism as an explanation of athletic abilities. "Race and Runners" was written during the furor over the Olympic triumph of Jesse Owens, in response to the view that the emergent Olympic dominance of African-American sprinters and broad jumpers between 1920 and 1936 was somehow due to racial characteristics. For some, this might have seemed a convenient example of black superiority flying in the face of Nazi claims to the contrary.

Cobb, however, applied the methodology of physical anthropology to the problem. He tested the hypothesis that there were basic anatomical characteristics associated with race that would determine the type of athletic abilities in question. His methodological approach to testing the hypothesis included taking anthropometric measurements of living individuals (Jesse Owens, other athletes, and males of similar age and size); utilizing anthropometric standards established by Todd and Lindala (1928) for the Hamann-Todd specimens as a comparative database of black and white leg, foot, and heel lengths; radiographic assessment; interobserver testing, providing a series of radiographs (including Jesse Owens's) to another anatomist to attempt identifying black and white "anatomical" characteristics of the leg; an analysis of human calf muscle anatomy; biomechanical assessment of the morphology and function of the leg; the incorporation of fledgling research on nerve fibers and their role in neuromuscular coordination; and personal histories of sprinters and broad jumpers available at the time.

Cobb demonstrated that the average differences (such as the lever function of heel and foot) were too small or contradictory to support racial determinism. Cobb personally examined Jesse Owens's anatomy to determine that the longer calf muscles most commonly associated with the Caucasian physique were present in Owens, while a European Olympic track star whom he had examined had a short-bellied calf associated with Negroids. Relative to the standards (average measurements) of blacks and whites in the Hamann-Todd Collection, Owens's anatomy compared closest to "Caucasoids" in some dimensions, yet measured closest to "Negroids" in others. Here was an example of the discordance of "racial" traits that makes extrapolation from race to behavior dubious.

Furthermore, the improvement in performance, marked by the setting of new world records with each Olympiad, clearly suggested to Cobb that training was far more important in athletic performance than racial or genetic endowment. Cobb's own experiences as a collegiate runner and boxer doubtlessly influenced him to undertake such an in-depth study. The symbolism of athletics as a general index of human capacities was as profound in the twentieth century as Cobb knew the Olympics to have been in ancient Greece. The implications of Cobb's paper were not exclusive to the sports arena but extended to the broader society and the discipline.

We can only begin to explore the unique combination of influences by which Cobb found his way to the scientific support for human equality and how he proceeded from this understanding to engage in political activism. The seeds of his perspective began growing from the social realities of his childhood. These views were partly molded by the experience of being raised in a well-developed African-American community within a deeply racist and segregated society. Having experienced firsthand both black and white society, Cobb also knew by observation the fallacy of black inferiority. The "radical ideas" of T. Wingate Todd complemented, reinforced, and gave anatomical structure to Cobb's antiracism and appreciation of humankind. Cobb's appreciation for the arts, humanities, and athletics was often integrated to give social meaning to anatomical form, and vice versa.

The following partly characterize the Cobbian tradition that is a particularly humane and humanitarian concept of physical anthropology and its applications:

1. An emphasis on African Americans (the "Negro") in their biological diversity, with a discarding of Hrdlička's principal focus on the study of a pure race (e.g., Cobb 1941, 1942a, 1942b).
2. A heightened emphasis on the social and historical factors, relative to evolutionary factors, as major forces affecting human biology (e.g., Cobb 1935, 1939b).
3. A thorough demonstration of human equality, not only by presenting the positive attributes of African Americans and their plasticity as Boas had done but uniquely balancing his argument by recognizing weaknesses that were simultaneously present in European society: "The defects of modern European civilization are so obvious, particularly in respect to its dependence on exploration and periodic slaughter and its failure to adjust population size and caliber to resources, that while its material achievements excite amazement, its social organization hardly evokes excessive admiration" (Cobb 1939b).
4. Cobb developed in his research and teaching a rich integration of art, literature, philosophy, history, physical anthropology, and anatomy

that has been unusual among physical anthropologists. Throughout the history of physical anthropology, its practitioners have been more concerned with the natural sciences than with the social sciences, or, least of all, the humanities. Without questioning its integration with the natural sciences, Cobb uses anatomy to explore beauty. Other examples are illustrated in his published teaching methods—"Graphic Approach" (1945), "Artistic Canons" (1944), and "Master Keys" (1943b)—that integrate anatomy with art, history, archaeology, preventive medicine, and clinical medicine. As a college instructor, he was known to recite poetry and play the violin to demonstrate points he wanted to make regarding anatomy.

Applied Anthropology

> Now I started out doing the things that had to be done in the area of the Negro, but I was careful always to do something that did not have to do with race [also]. . . . But because we had to get a little room, I began to be offensive to some people. [Sometimes I would] "have to swing a baseball bat to get a little room."
>
> —W. Montague Cobb 1985

Cobb was one of the first, if not the first, physical anthropologist to undertake a sophisticated demographic analysis that would point to noneugenical, biomedical applications. His demographic analysis exposed and documented the toll racism was exacting on the African-American population. He also illustrated the high cost of these conditions to the broader society. Therefore, racism, segregation, and poverty were problems the nation had to confront to ensure its own health and survival (Cobb 1939b). He determined that the racial integration of hospital patients and their "Negro Medical Men" would go far to remedy national health problems. Critical to this integration was the concomitant desegregation of medical education. Indeed, the integration of the society as a whole would be required to improve the health status of African Americans (Cobb 1947). Integration policy thereby becomes a program of applied physical anthropology.

He identified racial discrimination in four principal areas of health care: professional education, professional societies, hospital facilities, and prepayment medical plans (Cobb 1953). The main focus would be to obtain access to adequate medical facilities for African Americans. To this end he developed an effective multifaceted strategy for the elimination of the health effects of racial segregation and discrimination (Cobb 1942b, 1951a, 1953).

His masterminding effort and implementation of the Imhotep National Conferences on Hospital Integration was a major achievement. The Imhotep conferences were sponsored jointly by the National Medical Association's Council on Medical Education and Hospitals, the NAACP's National Health Committee, and the Medico-Chirurgical Society of the District of Columbia. Established in 1957, the conference met annually for seven years (1957–63), until one of its major goals was met with the passage of the 1964 Civil Rights Act.

"Imhotep," the Egyptian demigod of medicine, "was chosen for the conference for two reasons. First, as a reminder that a dark skin was associated with distinction in medicine before that of any other color, this served to emphasize the dignity of the approach to the problem. Second, because the name meant, 'He who comes in peace,' that sponsoring organization came in peace in a time of emotional tension" (Cobb 1962).

The Imhotep conferences served to compile and disseminate otherwise scant information on African-American health through their surveys, conferences, and publications. These conferences were also a forum for long-range planning and lobbying at the national and local levels (Cobb 1957a, 1962, 1963, 1964a, 1964b, 1964c). Lyndon B. Johnson attended one meeting, the first American president to do so. Although national health insurance was one of the conference goals, Cobb would not be invited to the presidential signing of the legislation introducing Medicare (the 1965 Medicare Bill) that his efforts had helped to bring about (see also Cobb's Senate testimony in support of H.R. 6675 in Morais 1978:269–71).

The Public Intellectual: Getting the Word Out

Central to his remarkable effectiveness was Cobb's keen knowledge of and energetic activity within both the African-American and European-American worlds of the time. One could say that he understood the kind of "dualism" explicated by Leon Damas and Du Bois, so characteristic of the African, Caribbean, and African-American intelligentsia. Therefore, he approached the fight for desegregation from a dual perspective; he disseminated information and generated action, in both arenas, from a growing position of strength.

Within the African-American world, he used the existing institutions, organizations, publications, and personal networks to launch his campaigns. As mentioned, he took on responsibilities of leadership in directing the national agenda for the desegregation of hospitals and educational institutions from within the medical and civil rights organizations. He created the *Bulletin of the Medico-Chirurgical Society of the District of Columbia;* edited and upgraded the *Journal of the National Medical Association,* in which he published prolifically; and published manuscripts through his own means (including his father's printing shop in the early years) when appropriate organs for his views were unavailable to him.

Cobb published information on health and race not only in "Negro" journals and magazines (*Journal of Negro Education, Negro History Bulletin, Crisis,* and so forth) but also in popular African-American magazines and newspapers. The latter included *Copper Romance, Negro Digest,* the *Pittsburgh Courier,* and *Ebony Magazine.*

He was involved in a close network of leading African Americans from diverse fields, including William Hastie (judge), Charles Drew (medical scientist), Ralph Bunche (United Nations representative), Carter G. Woodson (historian), Constance Baker Motley (judge), W. E. B. Du Bois (sociologist), Ernest E. Just (biologist), Percy Julian (chemist), and others (like Arthur P. Davis [1987:26], with whom he "has had a decades-long battle . . . over who is more handsome").

Cobb became a respected active member in professional and scientific associations of the European-American world and he ascended to leadership in many of them (see table 1). In addition to positions mentioned previously, he served as vice president of the AAAS and spent eleven vigilant years on the board of directors of the American Eugenics Society.

His publications in European American–controlled journals are diverse and numerous, including the *American Journal of Physical Anthropology, Scientific Monthly, Journal of Gerontology,* and *American Journal of Anatomy.* Topically, his articles range from skeletal aging techniques (1952) and comparative functional morphology (1940, 1943a) to general articles on "Negroes" for the *Encyclopedia Britannica* (1961), and from philosophy of the nature of humankind (1978, 1980, 1981b) to biography and medical education (1939a and 1981a).

The Laboratory of Anatomy and Physical Anthropology at Howard University: A Material Legacy

Between 1932 and 1936 Cobb established the Laboratory of Anatomy and Physical Anthropology at the Howard University Medical School. The facility was physically impressive and well equipped (Cobb 1936a), but

Table 5.1. Selected Professional Affiliations in Anthropology, Science, Medicine, and Civil Rights

Association/Committee	Position	Years
American Association of Physical Anthropologists	President	1957–59
	Vice President	1948–50
		1954–56
	Associate Editor	1944–48
Anthropological Society of Washington	President	1949–51
	Vice President	1941–47
	Board of Managers	1944–48
American Association for the Advancement of Science	Vice President	1955–56
Section H (Anthropology)	Chairman	1955–56
American Eugenics Society	Board of Directors	1957–68
National Association for the Advancement of Colored People	President	1976–82
National Medical Committee	Chairman	1950–52
National Health Committee	Chairman	1953–77
Imhotep National Conference on Hospital Integration	Executive Director	1957–63
	Organizer	1957
Medico-Chirurgical Society of the District of Columbia	President	1945–47
		1954–56
	Bulletin Founder/ Editor	1941–86
National Medical Association	President	1964–65
	Editor	1949–77
	Emeritus Editor	1978–90
Council of Medical Education and Hospitals	Chairman	1948–52
		1953–63

little support was forthcoming for additional personnel to help with teaching and research in physical anthropology. He, nonetheless, pushed forward with an advanced anthropology course and integrated anthropological concepts into other areas of teaching. He also began to systematically collect and prepare the skeletons of cadavers from the anatomy dissecting room, along with detailed anatomical, demographic, and medical records. This farsighted and painstaking effort (1932–69) resulted in a human biology research collection of anatomical records on 987 individuals and the preservation of more than 700 documented skeletons. Cobb's laboratory was the first to prepare an African-American institution to enter authoritatively into the lively and highly politicized discussion of differences in "racial" biology, as well as basic biological and medical research on the skeleton.

Raymond Pearl states in his review of Cobb's monograph *The Laboratory of Anatomy and Physical Anthropology of Howard University* (1936a):

> This account is withal so straightforward, so modest, so unselfish, and so intelligent as to win instant sympathy and admiration for its author's clear-headedness and philosophical soundness. . . . It recognizes that the Negro group in America presents unparalleled opportunities, taking into account all the circumstances historical and present, for the investigation of some of the most fundamental problems of human biology—problems of variation, development, and growth with different degrees of hybridization and under definable environmental conditions. It also recognizes that these opportunities have not hitherto been adequately taken advantage of, and that for Howard University it should be not merely a privilege, but a duty to do so. . . . Dr. Cobb's research program is sensible, modest, and scientifically sound. It should be encouraged and supported both from within and without the institution in which he labors. (1936: 447–48)

A recent assessment of the W. Montague Cobb Human Skeletal Collection (Blakey 1988) has shown it to be comparable to the Terry and Hamann-Todd collections (the world's most frequently studied human skeletal collections) in the quality of data that can be derived from it. The Cobb Collection is also unique as a sample of the eastern urban population of the United States. The collection provides an irreplaceable biological record of the development and pathology of the poorest Washingtonians, from the years of the Great Depression until 1969. In 1992 a working physical anthropology laboratory housing the Cobb Collection was established in the College of Arts and Sciences at Howard University with the assistance of the National Science Foundation.

The Elder Philosopher

In 1969 Cobb took leave from Howard University for a one-year visiting professorship at Stanford University. His departure occurred in the wake of a student protest that targeted Cobb as a symbol of a university establishment (some considered him to be the most prominent scholar in the medical school) that students considered to be inadequate, paternalistic, archaic, and politically compromised from the perspective of the Black Power movement. Within this context, Cobb came under fire by an organization of first-year medical students who had little regard for the humanistic aspects of his curriculum, preferring a more strictly clinical education focusing on the requirements of the national board examinations. These students boycotted Cobb's classes, forcing him from the chairmanship of the department of anatomy, a post he had held since

1947. Meanwhile, fifty-eight faculty members of the medical school petitioned for Cobb's reinstatement. By the end of that year he was appointed Howard University's first distinguished professor by a new university president. He achieved emeritus status in 1973.

On November 10 of that year, the two former students (then members of the faculty) to whom he felt closest (LaSalle D. Leffall Jr. and Charles H. Epps) organized a testimonial dinner in his honor. Five hundred people attended the testimonial, including many of those who had joined the boycott of 1969. According to Epps, "When many in that class became seniors they realized how unfair they had been to Cobb. . . . By then they had a chance to become familiar with and reflect on what the man had accomplished under very difficult circumstances and at great financial sacrifice. . . . So it was gratifying to see that some in that class realized that they had mistreated him and made efforts to make amends" (Scarupa 1988:13–17). Despite a nagging sense of disappointment for several years following what he called "the mess in '69," Cobb remained undaunted. He had for some time taken to heart the saying "Illegitimati[s] non carborundum."[2]

During the last two decades of his life, Cobb's work took on a more philosophical bent. Among his philosophical works, those framing the concepts of "*Homo sanguinis*" and "man the slow learner" stand out. An article entitled "Human Variation: Informing the Public" (1988), first presented as a paper at the 1987 meeting of the American Anthropological Association in Chicago, reviews these theses and applies them to current events. This would be his last presentation of a professional paper. Here one finds Cobb's own perspective of his philosophical theses articulated during the two previous decades (1974, 1978, 1980, 1981b). "[The] problem of hate resulted from Man's dual nature as Homo sanguinis or Man, the Bloody, vs. Homo sapiens or Man, the Wise. Man has been a bloody predatory primate always given to the overkill for over a million years, but only during the last 3,000 years or so has he developed anything like ethical systems. At the present time it would seem that Homo sanguinis has the upper hand. Can sapiens win? One hopeful sign is that the concept of human rights seems to have taken hold internationally" (Cobb 1988:674).

The turning point for this "new high in cultural evolution" came in 1948 when the United Nations adopted its Declaration of Human Rights, which exceeded "the more limited concept of civil rights." He asserted, furthermore, that the implementation of civil rights laws in the United States has made the "entrenched racial hatred of the American population" more apparent, making it ever clearer where additional efforts need be directed. But for Cobb, the struggle against racism was not limited to national boundaries: "Before my first visit to South Africa in 1977, I told my friends that I did not need to learn anything about apartheid, because all of my early life had been lived under apartheid in the capital city of the great nation declaimed as the Land of the Free and Home of the Brave" (1988:674).

His high regard for the courage of blacks and whites rallying against apartheid in South Africa was often expressed in our discussions with him. There seemed to be no one whom Cobb respected more than his friend Phillip Tobias. A physical anthropologist, Tobias was dean of the Medical School at the University of the Witwatersrand, whose faculty denounced the "whitewash" that the S.A. Medical and Dental Councils had made of Steven Biko's murder in detention (Cobb 1988:672). As human actors struggle against racism for human rights, *Homo sapiens* contends with *Homo sanguinis.*

Furthermore, in "Human Variation: Informing the Public" (1988) Cobb uses biological metaphors for the problems and prospects of accelerated social change at the end of the twentieth century. In summary, he argues that the more rapid the rate of development, the more precision is required to coordinate interrelated structures and processes in a developing organism (or other system). Small errors during the accelerated early stages of an individual's development (as with the aging process toward a life's end) often lead to exaggerated, irreversible, and disastrous effects. "Just as an embryological defect cannot be corrected, so our mammoth construction programs can be wrong, which is not obvious until it is too late." Flexibility is allowed during the more stable middle years of life, during which time "tremendous variability among individuals" occurs without the same risk of structural damage.

> Let us hope that Homo sapiens will prevail over Homo sanguinis, and that we may use reason more in the solution of our problems. Otherwise, we may eliminate our species, along with many others, and ruin our planet in the process. (1988:675)

> In contemplating the potential future of humankind, it is necessary to recognize that the genus Homo is a slow learner. The paleolithic paintings, drawings, and sculpture in over 100 caves in Europe and others in southern Africa and Australia show that our Old Stone Age ancestors were good artists and that their principal subject was anatomy. . . . Why did it take 35,000 years, until 1543, when Vesalius published Fabrica, for

> an accurate atlas of human anatomy to appear? Many complexities are involved that we cannot go into here. [Often cited prominently among these complexities is the obstructive role of dogma.] Nonetheless, the strife that besets our planet today indicates that Homo is still a slow learner. (1988:674)

Physical Anthropology Today

We were very interested in Cobb's overview of changes that have taken place in his field and in his recommendations for future anthropologists.

> The contrast of what you call a close knit group of physical anthropologists when I got into it, to the multi-ring circus you have today at meetings is enormous. It's over specialized. Not that that is damaging. But it is the loss of the integrative habit. . . . I think they ought to be more grounded in the medical field, pathology, anatomy, gross and microscopic. You can move then to any field. And you don't have to move into sociology to do it. (CPRHBI 1985:23–24, 26)

> But the changes that I have witnessed have been more in the direction of ultra-specialization. I do not think there is anyone I know in anthropology who was as broadly trained as the people I grew up with in the Association [AAPA]. . . . The young folk today don't know the other fellow's field, which is unusual. (CPRHBII 1985:23)

> The emphasis should always be on getting a generalized beginning. . . . Unless you have your eye on everything from super-galaxies to quarks you don't know where to fit things. . . . So my theme is to be "in tune to the universe." (CPRHBII 1985:23)

In many respects W. Montague Cobb exemplifies the physical anthropologist of his day—anatomist, physician, and physical anthropologist—grounded in anatomy and profoundly interested in human variation. Yet, he clearly did "march to the beat of a different drummer" in several ways. His research and publication agendas in physical anthropology were carefully planned. While we can find no reason to doubt the sincerity of his interest in everything he did, he seemed to be aware that some of his research was strategically important for giving him "credibility" as a physical anthropologist in keeping with the field's most conservative standards. Such "simple anatomy" publications were devoid of social and racial issues. Yet, even for this sizable body of work, his study of cranial suture closure and human aging is the only one of his 1,100 publications we have seen cited in the physical anthropological literature.

His works on African Americans and on race do not appear to have been responded to or utilized by the otherwise European-American field of physical anthropology. He took on the physical anthropology of the "Negro" because, as a physical anthropologist, he wanted to challenge the discipline's erroneous principles and change the basic approaches and assumptions of anthropology. These changes were fundamentally concerned with refocusing the field from racial description and causation (with its attendant racism) to human variation, adaptation, and evolution, where all humans were treated "with equal dignity." These were not necessarily new ideas; clearly his association with T. Wingate Todd played a significant role in shaping his view of physical anthropology. Cobb's views were not all equally liberal or forward thinking. But he was, in the black parlance of his time, always a "Race Man," conscious that his own people held him accountable and taking meaning from that service. Cobb used his membership on professional committees to realize his agenda whenever possible.

When it came to applying anthropology, Cobb was not limited by the traditional parameters of professional concern. He chose activism, an applied anthropology directed against the effects of social inequality and discrimination. There simply was no biological evidence for black inferiority, an apparent fact that Cobb sought to communicate in the most compelling of scientific terms, although journals in human biology seem, paradoxically enough, not to have been the place where Cobb could make that point clearly. It was in the African-American organs—especially the *Journal of the National Medical Association,* which he edited—that Cobb could address the integration of biology and medicine with history and social policy.

Cobb saw education, also, as a means of effectuating social change. He was a consummate educator whose emphases on illustration and playfulness stand out as distinctive pedagogical methods. Through educating scholars (his colleagues), students, government officials, and the general public, he could correct biological misinformation and thereby help eliminate the scientific seeds of racism, hoping to wear away the foundations of social inequality. These were (and are) big, institutionalized problems requiring solutions in public policy. Civil rights organizations and legislative efforts promised solutions of comparable scale. It was in areas related to health that the civil rights movement most benefited from his credentials.

By making a commitment to Howard University Medical School, Cobb was unable to pass on a legacy through students of anthropology as he would have had he taught in a department of anthropology or even a medical institution with an affiliated anthropology program (as many of his colleagues did). For the bulk of his career, black faculty were barred from white institutions in which American anthropologists were employed, and there has never been a graduate program or department of anthropology in an African-American college or university. Instead he achieved distinction in civil rights activism and produced several generations of primarily African-American physicians and dentists, many of whom have made significant contributions to their fields. We do not think, however, that these factors adequately explain the dearth of citation and professional attention given his writings beyond the borders of the "black world" in which he was renowned.

W. Montague Cobb did leave an important legacy to anthropology; clearly his diverse and unparalleled number of publications and his extensive documented skeletal collection are primary contributions. But most importantly his legacy is one of admonishment and a call for social responsibility and scholar activism: an admonishment to understand the historical roots of the discipline, to rectify the misinformation of the past, and to be careful with the information we put forth today; an admonishment that racism and racist interpretation are often subtle, insidious, and potentially anywhere in our work. Cobb's history is that of one who believed that anthropologists must take responsibility not only for their own thoughts and actions but also for their own society—and that these thoughts and actions make a difference. The key, he often said, is to "do what one enjoys." To enjoy the responsibilities of a life of struggle represents one of the most fundamental African-American values.

Epilogue

We consider ourselves extremely fortunate to have had the opportunity of knowing W. Montague Cobb. This essay began as a short professional meeting paper. We thought it would be appropriate to interview Cobb, since we all lived in the District of Columbia at the time. It became a significant learning experience and a turning point in our professional lives as physical anthropologists. We forged an enduring friendship and mentor relationship with Cobb that we consider a precious gift.

This essay represents only selected highlights of Cobb's accomplishments and contributions. Yet, after reviewing an early version of this manuscript, Cobb was pleased.

W. Montague Cobb passed away on November 20, 1990. His death has left a void in our lives but his lessons, admonitions, and inspiration remain with us.

Notes

Reprinted by permission of the American Anthropological Association from *American Anthropologist* 96 (1), March 1994. Not for further reproduction.

We would like to thank Kim Boyd (Howard University) and Glenis McKie (University of the District of Columbia) for dedicated, efficient research and abstraction; Heather York (University of Oklahoma) for physical anthropological biographic research; and Amelia Marie Adams for bibliographic research. In particular, we would like to thank Ellen Tolliver for the professional transcription of interview tapes. We are grateful to the late W. Montague Cobb for his patience, time for interviews, reprints, and personal photographs and to Carolyn Cobb Wilkinson and Amelia Cobb Gray, his daughters, for their encouragement.

1. The Harlem Renaissance is a term for a prominent creative period in American history; Harlem in the 1920s developed and attracted the major African-American authors, poets, performers, and artists of the day.

2. "Don't let the bastards get you down." This popular term is not formal Latin. We show Cobb's, and colloquial, usage and correct the grammar.

References Cited

Allen, Garland E. 1975. "Genetics, Eugenics, and Class Struggle." *Genetics* 79 (supp.): 29–45.

Blakey, Michael L. 1987. "Skull Doctors: Intrinsic Social and Political Bias in the History of American Physical Anthropology, with Special Reference to the Work of Aleš Hrdlička." *Critique of Anthropology* 7 (2): 7–35.

———. 1988. "The W. Montague Cobb Skeletal Collection Curatorial Project." First Report.

Cobb, W. Montague. 1932. "Human Archives." Ph.D. diss., Western Reserve University.

———. 1933. "Human Materials in American Institutions Available for Anthropological Study." *American Journal of Physical Anthropology* 17 (supp.): 1–49.

———. 1935. "Municipal History from Anatomical Records." *Scientific Monthly* 40 (2): 157–62.

———. 1936a. *The Laboratory of Anatomy and Physical Anthropology of Howard University*. Washington, D.C.: W. M. Cobb.

———. 1936b. "Race and Runners." *Journal of Health and Physical Education* 7 (1): 1–9.

———. 1939a. *The First Negro Medical Society: A History of the Medico-Chirurgical Society of the District of Columbia, 1884–1939*. Washington, D.C.: Associated Publishers.

———. 1939b. "The Negro as a Biological Element in the American Population." *Journal of Negro Education* 8 (3): 336–48.

———. 1939c. "Thomas Wingate Todd: An Appreciation." *American Journal of Physical Anthropology* 25 (supp.): 1–3.

———. 1940. "The Cranio-Facial Union in Man." *American Journal of Physical Anthropology* 26:87–111.

———. 1941. "Problems in Physical Anthropology." Proceedings of a conference on negro slavery, Mar. 29, 1941, Washington, D.C. *American Council of Learned Societies Bulletin* 32:90–100.

———. 1942a. "Physical Anthropology and the Negro in the Present Crisis." *Journal of the National Medical Association* 34 (5): 181–87.

———. 1942b. "Physical Anthropology of the American Negro." *American Journal of Physical Anthropology* 29 (2): 113–222.

———. 1943a. "The Cranio-Facial Union and the Maxillary Tuber in Mammals." *American Journal of Anatomy* 72 (1): 39–111.

———. 1943b. "Master Keys to Anatomy: Preliminary Notes." *Journal of the National Medical Association* 35 (3): 75–86.

———. 1944. "The Artistic Canons in the Teaching of Anatomy." *Journal of the National Medical Association* 36 (1): 3–14.

———. 1945. "A Graphic Approach to a Complete Anatomy." *Journal of the National Medical Association* 38 (3): 155–63.

———. 1947. "Medical Care and the Plight of the Negro in Medicine." *Crisis* 54 (7): 201–11.

———. 1951a. "Medical Care for Minority Group." *Annals of the American Academy of Political and Social Science* 273:169–75.

———. 1951b. "Numa P. G. Adams, MD, 1885–1940." *Journal of the National Medical Association* 43 (1): 43–52.

———. 1952. "Skeleton." In *Cowdry's Problems of Aging*. Ed. A. I. Lansing. Baltimore: Williams and Wilkins. 791–856.

———. 1953. "The National Health Program of the N.A.A.C.P." *Journal of the National Medical Association* 45 (5): 333–39.

———. 1957a. "The Imhotep National Conference on Hospital Integration." *Journal of the National Medical Association* 49 (1): 54–61.

———. 1957b. "Suture Closure as a Biological Phenomenon." In *Estratto dal Volume degli Atti*. Fourth Congress of the International Association of Gerontology. Fidenza, Italy: Tito Mattioli. 1–6.

———. 1959. "Thomas Wingate Todd, M.B., Ch.B., ERCS (Eng), 1885–1938." *Journal of the National Medical Association* 51 (3): 233–46.

———. 1961. S.v. "Negro." *Junior Encyclopedia Britannica*. Chicago: Encyclopedia Brittanica.

———. 1962. "History of the Imhotep National Conference on Hospital Integration." *Journal of the National Medical Association* 54 (1): 116–19.

———. 1963. "Statement to John F. Kennedy on Behalf of the National Medical Association." *Journal of the National Medical Association* 55 (5): 437–40.

———. 1964a. "H.E.W. Conference on the Elimination of Hospital Discrimination—The 'Eighth Imhotep Conference.'" *Journal of the National Medical Association* 56 (5): 226–29.

———. 1964b. "Past Gains and New Challenges." *Journal of the National Medical Association* 56 (4): 347–48.

———. 1964c. "Statement to Lyndon Baines Johnson." *Journal of the National Medical Association* 56 (4): 463.

———. 1974. "An Anatomist's View of Human Relations: Homo sanguinis versus Homo sapiens, Mankind's Present Dilemma." *Georgetown Medical Bulletin* 28 (1): 12–22.

———. 1978. "Human Rights—A New Fight in Cultural Evolution." *Crisis* 85 (2): 67–68.

———. 1980. "Love Is the Greatest Power—The Struggle for Survival Today." *Crisis* 87 (8): 304–6.

———. 1981a. "The Black American in Medicine." *Journal of the National Medical Association* 73 (supp.): 1185–1244.

———. 1981b. "Man, the Slow Learner." *Journal of the National Medical Association* 73 (10): 973–86.

———. 1988. "Human Variation: Informing the Public." *Journal of the National Medical Association* 80 (6): 671–75.

CPRHBI and CPRHBII. 1985. Rankin-Hill and Blakey Interview Transcripts, Cobb Papers, Moorland-Spingarn Research Center, Howard University, Washington, D.C.

Davenport, Charles B., and M. Steggerda. 1929. *Race Crossing in Jamaica.* Washington, D.C.: Carnegie Institution.

Davis, Arthur P., as told to Jill Nelson. 1987. "A Washington Life: An Eighty-Two-Year-Old Howard University Professor Looks Back on a Turbulent Century." *Washington Post Magazine,* July 5: 26–29.

Douglass, Frederick. [1854] 1950. "The Claims of the Negro Ethnographically Considered." In *The Life and Writings of Frederick Douglass.* Ed. Philip S. Foner. New York: International Publishers. 289–309.

Drake, St. Clair. 1980. "Anthropology and the Black Experience." *Black Scholar* 11 (2): 2–31.

Goodrich, Samuel Griswold. 1868. *Johnson's History, Comprehensive, Scientific, Popular, Illustrating, and Describing the Animal Kingdom.* New York: A. J. Johnson.

Gould, Stephen Jay. 1981. *The Mismeasure of Man.* New York: W. W. Norton.

Harris, Marvin. 1968. *The Rise of Anthropological Theory: A History of Theories of Culture.* New York: Thomas Y. Crowell.

Hrdlička, Aleš. 1918. "Physical Anthropology. Its Scope and Aims; Its History and Present Status in America." *American Journal of Physical Anthropology* 1 (1): 3–34.

———. 1921. Lecture no. 27, American University, Washington, D.C., May 21, 1921. National Anthropological Archives, National Museum of Natural History, Smithsonian Institution, NMNH—Hrdlička Papers.

———. 1925a. *The Old Americans.* Baltimore: Williams and Wilkins.

———. 1925b. "Relation of the Size of the Head and Skull to Capacity in the Two Sexes." *American Journal of Physical Anthropology* 8 (3): 249–50.

———. 1927. "Anthropology of the American Negro: Historical Notes." *American Journal of Physical Anthropology* 10 (2): 205–35.

———. 1928. "The Full-Blood American Negro." *American Journal of Physical Anthropology* 12 (1): 15–30.

———. 1941. "Observations and Measurements on the Members of the National Academy of Sciences." *Memoirs of the National Academy of Sciences* 23 (3): 1–108.

Kolar, J. C. 1987. "Symposium on Quantitative Methods in the Diagnosis and Treatment of Cranio-facial Anomalies: Preface." *American Journal of Physical Anthropology* 74 (4): 439–40.

Manning, Kenneth R. 1983. *Black Apollo of Science: The Life of Ernest Everett Just.* New York: Oxford University Press.

Montagu, M. F. Ashley. 1944. "Aleš Hrdlička, 1869–1943." *American Anthropologist* 46 (1): 113–17.

Morais, Herbert M. 1978. *The History of the Afro-American in Medicine.* International Library of Afro-American Life and History. Corwells Heights, Pa.: Publishers Agency.

Nott, Josiah C., and George R. Gliddon. 1854. *Types of Mankind.* Philadelphia: Lippincott, Grambo, and Co.

Patterson, William L. [1951] 1970. *We Charge Genocide: The Historic Petition to the United Nations for Relief from a Crime of the United States Government against the Negro People.* New York: International Publishers.

Pearl, Raymond. 1936. Review of *The Laboratory of Anatomy and Physical Anthropology of Howard University* by W. Montague Cobb. *Journal of Negro History* 21 (4): 447–49.

Rightmeier, Joan T. 1987. "Comparative Study of Normal, Crouzon, and Apert Craniofacial Morphology Using Finite Element Scaling Analysis." *American Journal of Physical Anthropology* 74 (4): 473–93.

Scarupa, Harriet J. 1988. "W. Montague Cobb: His Long, Storied, Battle-Scarred Life." *New Direction* 15 (2): 6–17.

Schultz, Adolph. 1945. "Biographical Memoir of Aleš Hrdlička, 1869–1943." *National Academy of Sciences, Biographical Memoirs* 23:305–38.

Spencer, Frank. 1979. "Aleš Hrdlička, M.D. 1869–1943: A Chronicle of the Life and Work of an American Anthropologist." Ph.D. diss., University of Michigan.

St. Hoyme, Lucille E., and Mehmet Y. Iscan. 1989. "Determination of Sex and Race: Accuracy and Assumption." In *Reconstruction of Life from the Skeleton.* Ed. Mehmet Y. Iscan and Kenneth A. R. Kennedy. New York: Alan R. Liss. 53–93.

Stocking, George W., Jr., ed. 1968. *Race, Culture, and Evolution: Essays in the History of Anthropology.* New York: Free Press.

———. 1976. "Ideas and Institutions in American Anthropology: Toward a History of the Interwar Period." In *Selected Papers from the American Anthropologist.* Ed. Robert F. Murphy. Washington, D.C.: American Anthropological Association. 1–54.

Tobias, Phillip. 1977. Speech delivered upon conferral of the honorary degree of Doctor of Laws. University of Witwatersrand, Johannesburg, South Africa. Apr. 20.

Todd, T. Wingate. 1931. "An Anthropological Study of Negro Life." *Journal of Negro History* 16 (1): 36–42.

Todd, T. Wingate, and A. Lindala. 1928. "Dimensions of the Body: Whites and American Negroes of Both Sexes." *American Journal of Physical Anthropology* 12 (1): 35–119.

6

Katherine Dunham: Anthropologist, Artist, Humanist

Joyce Aschenbrenner

The description of Katherine Dunham's lifework is an awesome and complex task. In the interest of clarity, this treatment is divided into three parts. The first part is a discussion of her background and education and is primarily based on her autobiographical works, *A Touch of Innocence* ([1959b] 1994) and *Island Possessed* ([1959a] 1969). In part 2 I treat Dunham's fieldwork as described in *Journey to Accompong* ([1946] 1971), *Dances of Haiti* ([1947] 1983), and *Island Possessed* and its relationship to her professional career as a dancer and choreographer, as well as to her contributions to anthropological knowledge. In the last section I describe Dunham's view of both dance and anthropology as a way of life, the development of her professional and personal ethical views, and her efforts and successes in changing the lives of many with whom she has come into contact.

Background and Education

Katherine Dunham's early life was a preparation for her dual career in dance and anthropology—a career that has exemplified an intensive level of teaching, research, and service, both within and without the academic world. She also became a superb artist, a role that she has never separated from her identity as an anthropologist; and she created a prototype

Katherine Dunham. (Courtesy of the Katherine Dunham Museum)

and a standard of African-American dance performance. The many aspects of her career render even more critical the attempt to grasp something of the whole person, the originator and catalyst of these many ideas, movements, and expressions, an endeavor made possible by her autobiographical works.

Katherine Dunham was born in Chicago in 1909, the second child of Fanny June Taylor Dunham, of French Canadian, Indian, and African ancestry, and of Albert Millard Dunham, a descendant of slaves from Madagascar and West Africa. As a child in Glen Ellyn, a white suburb of Chicago, Dunham mentally recorded vivid glimpses of her birth mother—her cultural and intellectual accomplishments (she was an assistant school principal) and her status as a property owner. Both parents were trained musicians: her mother played the piano and her father played the guitar. He had met and courted his wife while performing with a group at Chicago's Palmer House. Dunham was acutely aware of her mixed ancestry and of the social disparity between her mother's and her father's relatives due to skin color and economic status. Conflicts relating to class, first within her own family, were to recur throughout her career.

Dunham's mother died when she and her older brother, Albert Jr., were young. In the tenement on Chicago's South Side they shared with their father's relatives, Dunham was introduced to the underground black theater. She witnessed basement rehearsals by stage-struck relatives of never-to-be-produced programs and joined her cousin in sneaking out to attend vaudeville shows at the Monogram and Grand Theaters. She also observed the influx of southerners into south Chicago and the economic repercussions on the older residents. Her aunt, who was a beautician, lost her white clientele as a result of backlash against the immigration.

When their father married Annette Poindexter, a schoolteacher, the children moved to Joliet, Illinois, where their father owned and operated a dry-cleaning establishment. Their stepmother was a conscientious parent but was no match for their father, who was strict to the point of abuse with his children, especially his son. Brother and sister became strong allies against paternal oppression. Dunham came to forgive her father in later years, as she understood how ambition and frustration had embittered him, but her primary sympathies remained with her brother, whom she believed had never been allowed to fulfill his early promise.

Dunham's penchant for dance first became evident when, as a young girl, she organized a cabaret for a church social, performed a Russian dance, and enjoyed the heady applause for her personal creation. In high school she was active in athletics, particularly track, and joined the Terpsichorean Club. She continued her studies at the junior college in Joliet.

At the same time her brother was studying philosophy at the University of Chicago with George Herbert Mead and Alfred North Whitehead, who adopted him as a protégé. With her brother's encouragement, Dunham applied for admission to the University of Chicago and passed the entrance examination. Albert had a meager scholarship and could not help her much financially; she worked in a library and gave dance lessons to survive. She studied ballet with Ludmilla Speranzeva, formerly of the Russian Kamerny Theater. This was a fortunate affiliation; Speranzeva's training was in the Chauve Souris school, which eschewed "pure ballet"; acting, mime, and story lines were integrated in dance performance, providing for social and cultural context.

The experimental Cube theater, founded by her brother and some of his associates, led Dunham to expand her interest in theater. Albert's commitment to the project was activated in part by his concern and interest in her progress: he recognized that she was not a scholar and wanted her to meet cultured and accomplished people. At the Cube theater, she met black actors, artists, and writers such as Langston Hughes, Ruth Attaway, Bill Attaway, Canada Lee, Alain Locke, Arna Bontemps, Charles White, Charles Sebree, and W. C. Handy, as well as the anthropologist St. Clair Drake. The white "Bohemian elite" who participated in the productions included James T. Farrell, Meyer Levin, and Ben Hecht. She also met Mark Turbyfill of the Chicago Civic Opera, who had a studio nearby, and Ruth Page, dance director of the Ravinia Festival and prima ballerina of the opera. Dunham's ongoing involvement in theater provided a medium in which she later projected her understanding of cultures through setting, drama, and performance (Aschenbrenner 1981).

Dunham's artistic growth was stimulated by her introduction to the field of anthropology and to Robert Redfield, whose appreciation of art and ritual and of the role of dance in African societies stimulated and expanded her own interest. Redfield greatly influenced Dunham with his view of folk society as exhibiting cohesive social organization and a sacred worldview; these ideas helped her later to see the sacred dance of the *voudun* in Haiti as an intrinsic part of peasant social and cultural life (Aschenbrenner 1991).

Electing to study anthropology, Dunham was mentally stimulated and expanded in what was becoming the most influential department at the time. A. R. Radcliffe-Brown impelled her to look at the social aspects of dance and ritual; Fay Cooper-Cole attuned her to rhythm and percussion as components of cultural communication. Others who made appearances as visiting lecturers in the department—Margaret Mead and Bronislaw Malinowski—challenged her and stirred her imagination. Her intellectual growth was fostered in the context of Robert Maynard Hutchin's leadership at the university, under which the philosophy of humanism flourished, and creativity and independence of mind overshadowed narrow academic "requirements."

In the meantime, Dunham persevered in her dance lessons, working with Turbyfill and Speranzeva, as well as taking occasional lessons with many of the artists who came to Chicago—Vera Mirova (Balinese, Javanese, East Indian), La Argentina and her partner Escudero, and members of the Ballet Russe de Monte Carlo, including choreographers Léonide Massine and Michel Fokine. She organized an all-black dance troupe but had difficulty obtaining practice rooms in a highly segregated social and artistic environment until Speranzeva, Turbyfill, and Ruth Page assisted her. The group danced at the Chicago Beaux Arts Ball in 1931 and Dunham was invited by Page to replace her as star in *La Guiablesse,* based on Martinique folklore, at the Chicago Civic Opera Theater in 1934. In commenting on Dunham's performance, Page noted "she remembered every detail" (1978:126). The dancers also performed at the Chicago World's Fair in 1934.

Dunham's growing interest in dance of the African diaspora and the influence of her mentors in anthropology—especially Redfield and Malinowski—instilled in her a desire to study dance firsthand in the Caribbean. Erich Fromm and the sociologist Charles Johnson took an interest in the dynamic and talented Dunham and recommended her to the Julius Rosenwald Foundation as a candidate for a fellowship as a young artist. She presented her proposal to study dance and society in the West Indies to the startled committee by performing the dance styles of different cultures. She was granted the support and later received a Guggenheim Award, both of which enabled her to study the dance forms of Haiti, Jamaica, Martinique, and Trinidad.

Melville Herskovits at Northwestern University, noted for his work on African continuities in Caribbean and U.S. societies, prepared Dunham for life in the tropics, gave her valuable direction in conducting fieldwork, and provided letters of introduction to political leaders and scholars, including a president, a former president, and the anthropologist Jean Price-Mars of Haiti.

The elements of Dunham's career were now in place: her drive to express herself through dance and theater, her skills as a teacher and performer, and her fascination with cultural differences and the social contexts of art and ritual. Then a critical experience transformed a promising career into a brilliant one: "The Great Experience," as she referred to her fieldwork (1969). Her mentors had inspired her, introduced her to cultural concepts, instructed her on research techniques, and made her field objectives accessible. She brought an immediate and profound recognition and understanding of cultural forms and skills in recording and interpreting them—both in compelling descriptions and in her personal dance idiom—to audiences throughout the world.

Fieldwork and Its Fruits

Katherine Dunham's first field trip to the West Indies—especially her stay in Haiti—laid the groundwork for her phenomenal career in dance. In turn, her dancer's eye—her ability to pick up nonverbal cues, social relationships, and personality traits through movement—enhanced her anthropological search for the social and spiritual significance in ritual. Franz Boas, whom she met in New York on her way to the West Indies, anticipated her advantage in field studies, remarking that because she was a dancer she should be more successful than other anthropologists in penetrating the forms and rituals of a culture (Dunham n.d.).

Malinowski's description of his field experiences in New Guinea had stirred Dunham, who was ready to become immersed in Caribbean social and cultural life. As Stocking has pointed out, Malinowski set the precedent of the "mythic charter" of anthropology, of the ethnographer as hero, and of the "ethnographer's magic" in translating inexplicable actions into meaningful behavior through a process of identification that can only come with complete involvement in an alien culture (Stocking 1983). True, the anthropologist as hero has been subsequently exposed as having clay feet; yet the ideal and principle remain as goals, and the young Katherine Dunham, like most aspiring anthropologists, was enticed by the glamor of adventure and cultural heroism. This theme is especially pronounced in *Journey to Accompong,* her first field account available to the general public. Dunham self-consciously reports her dealings with the Maroons, recognizing her subordinate role as petitioner and learner, but stressing the excitement and thrill of fieldwork.

In the introduction to *Journey to Accompong,* Ralph Linton wrote: "While Miss Dunham's observation is that of a trained anthropologist, her method of approach was that of a sympathetic participant. . . . While many ethnologists go to a primitive group seeking proof for previously conceived theories, Miss Dunham seems to have been completely open-minded. . . . Much of her own excitement and her youthful response to the romance of the tropics color her story without, however, destroying the accuracy of her observations" (1946:viii).

In *Journey to Accompong* we are presented with a clue to why Dunham was able to fulfill Malinowski's "mythic charter" more completely than many anthropologists, perhaps including Malinowski himself. In Accompong, the Maroons identified her as one of the "lost people of 'Nan Guinée" and revealed their secrets to her so that she could inform her people about their ancestry. In contrast to many fictions that anthropologists employ to gain the confidence of informants or that informants use to justify or explain their own cooperation, this structure was actualized in a way and to a degree that neither party could envision at the time.

In *Island Possessed* (1969), her more mature work, Dunham continued to share the process of gaining admittance and insight into another culture as she detailed a long-term study commitment to her culture area. We see through her personal experiences and observations passions and growing understanding that add meaning to her earlier work. Instead of decreasing the aura of mystery, such exposure increases it; we witness the transformation of an initiate into a seer, one who sees and understands that about which we have little comprehension. Seeing through her eyes, we can only *know* what she imparts but are intrigued by what she implies by her feelings, actions, and metaphors.

Nowhere is this mystical element more present than in the description of Dunham's initiation into the *voudun,* which exemplified participant-observation in its most intense expression. The ceremony (*lavé tête*) introduces and celebrates powers over which participants have little control, but which they can contact and influence through ritual. She described the paraphernalia, costumes, colors, smells, rhythms, movements of the *lavé tête* and its psychological and social contexts. During the ritual, the initiates' individual powers were expanded through intense sharing of experiences with each other, lying "spoon-fashioned" in the inner sanctum of the *hounfort,* or temple compound, for three days. It is as though Dunham absorbed the perspectives and energies of those with whom she shared the initiation, whom she characterized in detail. She was enlarged by an experience encompassing the psychic fields of her co-initiates, and her personal power was heightened. Speaking of her participation in the public dance in the outer courtyard afterward, she stated: "I felt weightless like Nietzsche's dancer, but unlike that dancer, weighted, transparent but solid, belonging to myself but a part of everyone else. This must have been the 'ecstatic union of one mind' of Indian philosophy, but with the fixed solidarity to the earth that all African dancing returns to, whether in assault upon the forces of nature or submission to gods" (1969:136).

As a result of her intensive and extensive fieldwork Dunham was later enabled to relate to international audiences effectively through her art. For example, a member of her company described the scream of recognition by a postwar London audience to a presentation of *Shango,* a dance expressing the essence of the god of thunder and war. Dunham recalled people coming to her dressing room after a performance with tears in their eyes and psychiatrists sending patients to her performances (Aschenbrenner 1981). It was her abilities to empathize and to penetrate to the heart of conflicts, suffering, and joys of the people she studied that revealed the artist; her ability to see the universal in cultures, as well as to capture the unique and distinctive, that reflected the anthropologist as well as the artist.

Claude Lévi-Strauss, who in the 1940s attended the Boule Blanche parties at Dunham's dance school in New York, appreciated her presentation of the dances and culture of Martinique, where he had worked. In his foreword to the French edition of *Dances of Haiti* ([1957] 1983) he commented on the emotional richness and social cohesiveness in *voudun* rituals, comparing this with the restrictions on such expression in European civilization. In this work Dunham classified Haitian dance forms, particularly sacred dance. She discussed its social and political significance, analyzed the organization of dance groups, and described the material aspects, musicians and their instruments. The last sections are devoted to her views concerning the functions of dance and the relationships between dance forms and social and psychological functions. Following Herskovits (1966), she noted that the release of energy and emotions is a critical function of Haitian dance; for the African, the release of energy is an important part of therapy, since holding in feelings can make one ill. She applied this principle later in her work with youth, encouraging them to vent frustration constructively in energetic, disciplined movements expressing aggression (Aschenbrenner and Carr 1989).

When Dunham returned to the University of Chicago from intensive fieldwork in Haiti in 1935 and 1936, she received her bachelor's degree and planned to begin graduate work. She received a Rockefeller grant to continue her studies with Herskovits, but soon discovered she would be required to attend Northwestern University. Unwilling to leave the

University of Chicago, she discussed her dilemma with Redfield, who encouraged her to continue in both dance and anthropology, whether inside or outside academia. Professional dance opportunities ultimately led her to forgo her academic work, although she continued to maintain contact with academia throughout her career.

Dunham soon reestablished her black dance troupe and began developing her own dance technique through study, performance, and consultation with Uday Shankar, who encouraged a systemization of dance movements similar to that in Hindu classical dance. Dunham's technique is based on African movement as well as ballet, with the release of the knees and flexible movement of spine and pelvis differentiating it from classical ballet. It is expressed through a series of dance progressions, but as Dunham and her company members were exposed to the dances of countries through which they toured and in which they taught and studied, they added variations. Thus, she constantly conducted fieldwork, taught and motivated her students and company members to emulate her anthropological orientation, and transmitted her knowledge to both academics and nonacademics.

The group first appeared at the Young Men's Hebrew Association in Manhattan in 1937. In 1938 the dancers performed *L'Ag'Ya*, based on her research in Martinique, in Chicago. She supported these early productions through the New Deal writers' and theater projects, which also enabled her to conduct research on cult groups, including the Temple of Islam in Chicago. Through her work with the Federal Theater Project she met John Pratt, a costume and set designer; they married in 1941 and formed a lifetime artistic partnership.

The Katherine Dunham Dance Company formed in 1939. Dunham soon collaborated with George Balanchine on the choreography for *Cabin in the Sky*, but he deferred to her mastery of African-American movement. Dunham's troupe performed *Cabin in the Sky* on Broadway at the Windsor Theater in New York in 1940 and 1941 and then toured with the production. During subsequent years, the company appeared in movies, toured the United States in Sol Hurok's *Tropical Review*, and between 1946 and 1961 performed to widespread acclaim in Europe, Mexico, South America, Australia, New Zealand, Japan, North Africa, Canada, and the United States with no government sponsorship.

The last production of the Dunham company was *Bamboche* (1962), which also employed the Royal Troupe of Morocco, recruited by Dunham during a visit to the king. When the show closed on Broadway—largely because of poor publicity caused by a newspaper strike and upstaging by the Cuban missile crisis—it was moved to the Apollo Theater in Harlem. Members of the company regrouped in 1963 for a performance of *Aida*, for which Dunham choreographed authentic African movements. Some critics were dismayed by the intrusion of African rhythms and movements into an Italian opera, but the audiences were entranced.

Durham also focused on the social and cultural contexts of dance by founding a series of schools. In New York in 1943 the Katherine Dunham School of Arts and Research opened with an international faculty of dance, language, music, drama, and theater instructors as well as philosophers, psychologists, and anthropologists who held M.A. and Ph.D degrees from such universities as Columbia, Cambridge, and Fordham. Lee Strasberg and Susan Strasberg taught acting and Margaret Mead was an occasional visiting lecturer. Columbia University accepted credits from the school, and veterans were able to finance their studies with the G.I. Bill. The roster would soon list the names of many future stars: Marlon Brando, Geoffrey Holder, Shelley Winters, Ava Gardner, James Dean, Doris Duke, Butterfly McQueen, Jennifer Jones, Arthur Mitchell, Louis Johnson, Eartha Kitt, Chita Rivera, José Ferrer, and Jerome Robbins.

Dunham's academic pursuits have not been limited to her own school. She has lectured on dance at the Royal Anthropological Institute of London, the Anthropological Society of Paris, the Anthropological Society of Rio de Janeiro, the University of Chicago, and Yale. Responding to Dunham's lecture-demonstration at Yale Donald Horton, department chairman, wrote: "Few of us have been so deeply stirred by any dancing as we were by this return to simple, universal human experience" (Jan. 22, 1941, Dunham Papers, box 1/10). Geoffrey Gorer (Jan. 20, 1941, Dunham Papers, box 1/10) called the presentation "revolutionary," and George Murdock (Jan. 20, 1941, Dunham Papers, box 1/10) wrote that he found the presentation "pleasant and profitable" and a genuine treat."

Dunham has also been visiting professor at Case Western Reserve University, artist in residence at Southern Illinois University at Carbondale and at the University of California at Berkeley, and university professor and professor emerita at Southern Illinois University at Edwardsville. For her achievement she has been granted numerous honorary degrees and has received many awards, including a Professional Achievement Award from the University of Chicago Alumni (1968); the Albert Schweitzer Music Award (1979); the Kennedy Center Honors (1983); the prestigious Scripps Dance Award (1989); the Presidential Arts

Medal sponsored by the National Endowment for the Arts (1989); the Distinguished Service Award of the American Anthropological Association (1986); Circle of Dance Award (1996); medals and citations from the governments of France, Brazil, and Haiti; and many local and regional awards.

Legacy for Anthropology

Dunham's importance for anthropology consists in her detailed ethnographic descriptions and her skill in communicating profound cultural insights through artistic expression. It is this latter gift that involves Katherine Dunham the artist, the *voudun* initiate, the woman of "indefinable glamour" ("Dance" 1969) and mystery, whose theatrical persona is briefly glimpsed in films such as *Stormy Weather* and *Carnival of Rhythm.* It is this genius transmitted through her ability to command a class, a group of disaffected youths, or a large audience with her soft-spoken, now tentative, now assured tones that has inspired many African Americans and others to adopt a new way of being. Her teaching grips the imagination as well as the mind, and she lives the lessons she teaches.

Not all of her lessons are taught in a formal setting, however. Dunham credits her association with Dumarsais Estimé, who later became president of Haiti (1946–50), with awakening her political consciousness (1969). Although she was aware of the cultural exploitation inherent in much fieldwork, she has shown an ongoing commitment to Haiti and its people, sharing Estimé's goals. Despite her social and economic advantages, she closely identified with the peasant class, thus defying conventions to pursue her commitment to the African cultural influences that were suppressed by the elite. She has tirelessly worked for the economic and social betterment of the Haitian poor, including a forty-seven-day fast in protest of the treatment of Haitian immigrants by the United States in 1991–92. During the fast, she demanded that President Bush and members of Congress change governmental policies and was visited in her East St. Louis home by then-exiled President Jean-Bertrand Aristide and Jesse Jackson.

She has received considerable recognition for her humanitarian work; the completion of her fast was celebrated on her eighty-third birthday at a party given by Jonathan Demme and his brother, a Presbyterian minister who works in depressed communities in New York City; Mayor David Dinkins presented her with a key to the city. Afterward, she was honored at a Maroon celebration held in Washington, D.C.

In 1994 two major exhibitions opened at the Caribbean Cultural Center in New York City: "The Worldview of Katherine Dunham" and "Katherine Dunham in Cuba, 1947." Photographs celebrated her role in recognizing Caribbean cultures among the world's richest expressions. Dunham has interpreted Haitian worship and dance to the world as an organized, sophisticated religious ritual whose priests are astute psychologists possessing wisdom and authority. She established a *hounfort* in her residence in Haiti so that she could support and observe the ritual activities of the *voudun*. Specifically, she has pursued the universal in the rhythms of the *voudun*, noting that visitors to the *hounfort* exhibit trance-like behavior triggered by a drum beat they had never heard before (personal communications with Dunham and Jeanelle Stovall, 1980–86).

In her eyes one of her most lasting contributions to social welfare was integrating dance companies and audiences. In 1944 she announced she would not return to Louisville until the audience was integrated; she also protested segregation at army camps where the company performed. Working with the NAACP and other civil rights groups, she fought restrictive codes in public accommodations because in city after city she had difficulty securing rooms and practice space for her dancers. When she was denied lodging by a hotel in Brazil, the resulting publicity forced the country to adopt an antidiscrimination code for public accommodations (personal communications with Dunham and Jeanelle Stovall, 1980–86).

The worldwide success of her dance company helped to open opportunities for other black dancers, encouraged black choreographers, and stimulated the formation of new companies. When African-American dancers began to be perceived as competent in ballet as well as in other dance forms, they were hired by major dance companies. Still, as Dunham has pointed out, the progress is not as great as it should be.

Unfortunately Dunham has been the victim of cultural appropriation despite the recognition of her work as pioneering by George Balanchine, Agnes De Mille, Arthur Mitchell, and Alvin Ailey, among others. Ailey called the Dunham technique "the closest thing to a unified Afro-American dance existing" (Terry 1969). Despite this acclaim, much of Dunham's choreography has been bowdlerized and popularized in the media, particularly since laws against plagiarism are difficult to enforce in dance.

To Dunham, the culmination of her career came in changing the lives of African-American youths in East St. Louis, Illinois, a city torn apart by riots in the 1960s. She regarded it as a special challenge to educate the young people in such a depressed environment to strive for and attain their highest potential. Dunham felt that much of her success throughout her career lay in her attention to the social and psychological functions of dance: "I was living through my needs and the community's needs. By putting this process into theater we were creating a powerful experience with deep authenticity" (personal communication with Dunham, Aug. 10, 1986).

Katherine Dunham's cultural and social programs have been, characteristically and somewhat paradoxically, conceived on a grand scale but anchored by down-to-earth concerns for people's needs. Dunham began working for change in East St. Louis, Illinois, a city troubled by active youth gangs and restless young people. Her association with the city grew out of an invitation to become artist in residence by DeLyte Morris, chancellor of Southern Illinois University, who had attended a performance of *Aida*. On her return from choreographing pieces for the National Ballet of Senegal for the Festival of Black Arts in Dakar, she was arrested and spent a night in jail in East St. Louis for inquiring about a student's arrest. Worldwide publicity was immediate, and she was soon released. The arrest gave her even greater determination to pursue social and cultural goals in East St. Louis and a feeling of identification with those whom she wished to help. According to the poet Eugene Redmond, who worked closely with her at this time, this event gave her an entree into the local culture that nothing else could have (personal communication, Jan. 20, 1995). Characteristically, she pushed her advantage to provide horizon-expanding experiences to East St. Louis youth. She took a group of gang members to New York to visit her friend Erich Fromm, who talked to them about alternatives to destructive violence. In 1970, Dunham took sixty-six children, ages four to twelve, to a White House conference, where they danced, sang, played instruments, and performed martial arts.

Dunham was instrumental in developing the Experiment in Higher Education, Southern Illinois University's program in East St. Louis to bring anthropologists, sociologists, educational specialists, scientists, writers, musicians, and theater people together to create a liberal arts curriculum that would be a foundation for further college work. The Performing Arts Training Center, directed by Dunham, was extremely active from 1969 to 1974. Many former members of her company came from around the world to teach at the center, and the center's dance group toured regionally as well as in the South and East. In 1972 the center's dancers premiered Scott Joplin's *Treemonisha* in Atlanta and later performed it at Wolftrap and in Carbondale, Illinois.

The vision of changing the face of East St. Louis was not limited to educational programs. In 1966 and 1967 Dunham collaborated with Buckminster Fuller on a comprehensive proposal for a cultural arts center in East St. Louis that included housing and economic centers. One of Fuller's energy-conserving geodesic domes was projected as part of a riverfront development on the east side of the Mississippi. The project was never completed but offered impetus to other developments.

In 1975 the Dunham Foundation purchased several buildings in East St. Louis, including the former YWCA, to house the art objects, artifacts, musical instruments, costumes, and paintings from her research and world tours for the Katherine Dunham Museum. The museum opened in 1977 and hosted an international opening in 1978. In 1982 a grant from the Columbia Broadcasting System made possible the conversion of the carriage house behind the museum to a studio and a year-long cultural arts program for children that has grown into the Katherine Dunham Children's Workshop. The children's workshop has continued the tradition of imparting cultural knowledge, skills, and professionalism to the young and of presenting dance and cultural programs throughout the region.

The children's workshop is presently the only dance group authorized to present Dunham choreography and recreate Dunham costumes. The children learn languages (French, Creole, and Wolof), folk songs, stories, dance, and music as well as other cultural knowledge. They acquire discipline and a sense of responsibility as they learn to teach each other, monitor younger children, and maintain cleanliness and order in the studio. Parents lend moral as well as practical support by making costumes, raising money for tours, helping with refreshments, and attending classes.

Thanks in part to the international reputation of the children's workshop, many East St. Louis residents, who at first were suspicious of a multicultural approach to education, now claim Dunham programs with pride. City signs herald the museum and one announces, "Welcome to East St. Louis, the home of the Katherine Dunham Museum." Dunham's technique has become an essential ingredient of public ritual, including dedications, school programs, Martin Luther King's birthday celebrations, and recognition of Black History Month (Aschenbrenner and Carr 1989).

While Dunham's programs have increased knowledge of and pride in African ancestry and ethnic identity, they have also injected a cosmopolitan flavor into East St. Louis. Visitors from Haiti, Brazil, France, Italy,

Japan, Senegal, and Barbados as well as from all over the United States have contributed to the educational experiences at the Dunham studios and at public events. Thus, children from economically depressed backgrounds are exposed to knowledge often available only to the affluent, given the opportunity to develop and display their skills, and become leaders in interpreting them to the community. Dunham firmly believes that dance is a social act, not merely a technique to be learned, and thus should return to its roots in communal living (1968).

Unfortunately, many of Dunham's dreams for East St. Louis remain unfulfilled. The riverfront project has been recently revived but remains stalemated because of partisan politics and economic difficulties. The Experiment in Higher Education no longer exists, and the Katherine Dunham Performing Arts Training Center carries her name but has not benefited from her direction since her retirement in 1982. Dunham's dancing also continues through annual technique seminars, at which former company members, students, colleagues, and participants join in an intensive community of artistic work and social celebration. The museum, envisioned as one of the keystones of the cultural center, is suffering from lack of financial support. Still, the children's workshop continues under the tutelage of her former students. Graduate students from the University of Illinois urban planning department have been working on community projects and assisting in efforts to put the Dunham centers on a sound financial basis.

Through her dancing and teaching of it, Dunham goes beyond academic anthropology by treating cultural studies as a way of life, not an exercise. Dunham dancers are exposed to a wide variety of cultural experiences and encouraged to participate in the skills and aesthetic expressions of those cultures, thus they are trained as anthropologists. Never satisfied with a simple reconstruction of folk art, Dunham desired to communicate the meaning and contexts of art through her theater productions. Yet she has consistently displayed respect and gratitude for the traditions of academia, particularly those of anthropology. She celebrates tradition—the repository of past creative efforts—by adding her own interpretations to received knowledge.

Katherine Dunham has provided intensely personal accounts of fieldwork and a multidisciplinary approach to her subject, incorporating insights from psychology, African-based religions, art, and philosophy. Perhaps more importantly, she has attained an identification with her human subjects and a continuing relationship of mutual respect and commitment toward those she studies while maintaining a perspective that lends to her judgments a high degree of credibility. In reviewing *A Touch of Innocence,* Elizabeth Janeway noted: "The anthropological method has been absorbed and assimilated into a way of looking at the world with a kind of exact, tolerant, but not uncritical justice" (1959:54). The ability to perfectly suspend judgment while participating in and observing is a tightrope performance to which all anthropologists, with greater or less success, aspire. Katherine Dunham succeeded and proceeded to become a living exemplar of the ethical commitment to a broadly based humanism espoused by the pioneers of American anthropology. The Distinguished Service Award by the American Anthropological Association to Katherine Dunham was a belated recognition of her contributions to anthropology; a more substantive recognition, such as measures to rectify the neglect of the work of African-American anthropologists in whatever professional area they are working—thus expanding the boundaries of "accepted" anthropological practice—is long overdue. If such efforts were made, perhaps the lifework of those who, like Dunham, are marginal by current standards will be seen as essential to the spirit and scope of the anthropological endeavor.

References Cited

Aschenbrenner, Joyce. 1981. *Katherine Dunham: Reflections on the Social and Political Contexts of Afro-American Dance.* New York: Congress on Research in Dance.

———. 1991. "Katherine Dunham's Anthropology: Issues of Ethnographic Research and Presentation." Paper presented at the annual meeting of the American Anthropological Association. Chicago. Nov. 20.

Aschenbrenner, Joyce, and Carolyn Carr. 1989. "Katherine Dunham Technique as a Community Rite de Passage." *Western Journal of Black Studies* 13 (3): 139–43.

"Dance Magazine Award." 1969. *Dance Magazine* 43 (1): 66–67.

Dunham, Katherine. [1946] 1971. *Journey to Accompong.* Westport, Conn.: Negro Universities Press.

———. [1947] 1983. *Dances of Haiti.* Los Angeles: Center for Afro-American Studies, University of California at Los Angeles.

———. [1959a] 1969. *Island Possessed.* Chicago: University of Chicago Press.

———. [1959b] 1994. *A Touch of Innocence.* Chicago: University of Chicago Press.

———. 1968. *The Performing Arts of Africa.* First World Festival of Negro Arts Colloquium. Dakar: Editions Presence Africaine.

———. n.d. "Minefields." Ms. Author's possession.

———. Papers. 1919–68. Southern Illinois University at Carbondale.

Herskovits, Melville J. 1966. *The New World Negro: Selected Papers in Afro-American Studies.* Bloomington: Indiana University Press.

Janeway, Elizabeth. 1959. Review of *A Touch of Innocence* by Katherine Dunham. *New York Times Book Review,* Nov.: 54.

Lévi-Strauss, Claude. [1957] 1983. "Foreword to the French Edition." Translated by Jeanelle Stovall. In *Dances of Haiti* by Katherine Dunham. Los Angeles: Center for Afro-American Studies, University of California at Los Angeles. xv–xvii.

Linton, Ralph. 1946. Preface to *Journey to Accompong* by Katherine Dunham. New York: Henry Holt. viii.

Page, Ruth. 1978. *Page by Page.* New York: Dance Horizons.

Stocking, George W., Jr. 1983. *Observers Observed: Essays on Ethnographic Fieldwork.* Madison: University of Wisconsin Press.

Terry, Walter. 1969. Interview with Alvin Ailey. Phonotape. Dance Collection. New York Public Library.

7

Ellen Irene Diggs: Coming of Age in Atlanta, Havana, and Baltimore

A. Lynn Bolles

Ellen Irene Diggs was born in 1906 in Monmouth, Illinois, a small college town located in the state's agricultural belt near the Iowa border. She was raised in the supportive environment of an industrious but poor working-class black nuclear family. Her parents played together as children and were married fifty-five years when her father died. At a very young age Diggs became disturbed by conditions of poverty, social injustice, and inequitable wages. She recounted, "I just could not understand why and how people who did little or nothing had so much, while people who did the unpleasant, dirty work and worked so hard had so little" (Diggs 1978:7). Diggs's father was employed in and around the town of Monmouth, while her mother was a full-time homemaker. During her childhood the management of money was of primary concern for the family. Her father taught all of his children to calculate interest rates and to understand the importance of saving.

With her father's financial instructions Diggs learned other valuable life skills. Like many girls of her day, she learned handwork, such as needlepoint, crewel, and embroidery, under her mother's tutelage. Her mother also instilled in her an appreciation for and a knowledge of nature. Although Diggs was not allowed to cook because the family budget could not afford mistakes and wasted food, her mother would explain the various steps as she prepared meals.

Ellen Irene Diggs. (Courtesy of Irene Diggs)

During Diggs's youth the town of Monmouth had a population of about ten thousand, of which two to three hundred were black. Despite the college, the town was still isolated and rural. The lengthy winters provided an opportunity for the family to appreciate self-sufficiency. And, as in most black families of the era, education was perceived as the best way to become a "better person" because it enabled upward mobility. Books bought at the local bookstore, magazines read at the library, the local newspaper, and the Sunday Chicago newspaper, which her father brought home on Monday from another family in town, stimulated Diggs's interest in the outside world. From her voracious reading Diggs became determined to "visit and see these far distant places and people with my own eyes and for my own self" (1978:3). "As long as one read in our home," Diggs recalled, "one was excused from house chores" (1978:3). She added, "I was excused a great deal of time" (1978:4). And what she was not excused from, Diggs bartered with her siblings to have done. Because getting an education was of the utmost importance to her, young Irene Diggs resolved to learn as much as she could.

While she was in high school the Monmouth Chamber of Commerce awarded a tuition scholarship to the graduate with the highest academic achievement. The scholarship and accompanying gold medal went to Diggs, and she enrolled in Monmouth College. After one year, however, she transferred to the University of Minnesota, which had more extensive course offerings than the small liberal college in her hometown.

Enrolled in the College of Science, Literature, and Arts, Diggs majored in sociology, with a minor in psychology. At Minnesota she "was completely lost in a student body of ten—or twelve—maybe fourteen—thousand" (Diggs 1981). The university population was not only larger than that at Monmouth College but also larger than the population of her hometown. There, however, Diggs met a kind of racism she had never before encountered. So novel was this to her that she did not interpret racist incidents as such. For instance, a human behavior professor once warned her not to enroll in his class because it was "fast stepping." This comment was in keeping with the racial superiority theories then in vogue. Diggs responded, somewhat naively, "I am a fast stepper," and walked away.

Diggs viewed her years at Minnesota as valuable because she met both experiential and intellectual challenges. Due to racism—or neglect—Diggs did not have a single conversation with an academic counselor. She selected courses on her own, including those in economics and anthropology. She had never seen a magazine or newspaper written or edited by blacks. Her high school reading list had only two books authored by blacks, *Up from Slavery* by Booker T. Washington and *The Quest of the Silver Fleece* by W. E. B. Du Bois. Although Monmouth had two black churches, there were no outstanding black leaders from whom she could gain inspiration. She felt herself searching for a role model even as she received her bachelor of arts degree in 1928.

When her sister married a Baptist minister from Georgia, she accompanied them on their trip south by automobile. There a new vista opened. She toured colleges operated, governed, and designed by African Americans. A large black community included the intellectuals and leaders with whom Diggs longed to be associated. At that moment Diggs decided to go home, collect her belongings, and "return right back to Atlanta."

Atlanta

Diggs pursued a graduate degree in sociology and also read widely in the field of anthropology at Atlanta University. During her second semester W .E. B. Du Bois returned to the faculty as a professor of economics, history, and sociology. This was a momentous occasion for Diggs, as Du Bois was one of the black authors she had admired from her secondary school days in Monmouth. Diggs registered for two classes with Du Bois on blacks and the Reconstruction era, which reflected some of the historical and theoretical models that were hotly debated by many black intellectuals at that time. At the end of the semester Du Bois approached Diggs to offer a summer graduate assistantship to research a book. Feigning modesty, Diggs said that evidently "he appreciated my class work and reports" (Diggs 1981). That summer work began what would eventually be an eleven-year association.

Not only did Diggs research material for *Black Reconstruction in America, 1860–1880* (1935) but she also proofread and checked the footnotes. Du Bois's masterpiece would become cutting-edge scholarship on class, race, and politics in American life in the postbellum period. Du Bois argued that white Americans did not comprehend or seize the critical moment to advance black Americans newly freed from slavery. Economic, social, and political obstacles, in addition to the *Plessy vs. Ferguson* decision, impeded the recovery of the South for all—black and white, especially those of poor or working-class origins.

Under Du Bois's mentorship, Diggs received the university's first master's degree in sociology in 1933. She remained at Atlanta University as his research associate from 1932 to 1942, during which time she researched *Black Folk, Then and Now* (1939), which was an updated version of *The Negro* (1915), *Dusk of Dawn* (1940), and *The Encyclopedia of the Negro* (1945).

In 1940 Diggs and Du Bois cofounded *Phylon: A Review of Race and Culture,* in which they intended to feature literary and scientific articles from a black perspective. During Du Bois's and Diggs's editorship, *Phylon* became a leading black social science publication, ranking with Carter G. Woodson's *Journal of Negro History* and the *Journal of Negro Education. Phylon* was a remarkable achievement in the history of social analysis by, on, and for blacks. Pan-African in scope and design, it focused on class and race struggles within capitalism and highlighted the impact of class and race domination on black peoples.

Diggs's and Du Bois's most mammoth undertaking was *The Encyclopedia of the Negro,* which was finally published in 1945 as an extensive bibliography. With her usual understatement, Diggs confirmed that she "did a great deal of the work" (Diggs 1981). The original 125-page proposal called for four volumes of several thousand pages each. Entries were to be written by the best scholars working in the field of race relations, black history, society, and culture. From its inception, however, the project was plagued by internal fights among the black intelligentsia and lack of funding.

Diggs was reticent to discuss the nature of her working relationship with Du Bois because "it was so long ago," but clearly Du Bois demanded of her what he demanded of himself: high energy and excellence (Diggs 1981). Those expectations kept the young Irene Diggs working diligently for all those years in Atlanta. Both were also driven by the necessity of African historiography. Only this type of documentation would counter the flow of misinformation from white scholars. Both were also intent upon seriously studying peoples of African descent in the Americas from historical and cultural perspectives. Later this anthropological perspective became the mandate for Diggs's work on the African diaspora in Latin America.

Du Bois's imprint on Diggs's scholarship is recognizable in two main areas. The first is her numerous critical bibliographic essays that center on his writings. The second is *Black Chronology: From 4000 B.C. to the Abolition of the Slave Trade* (1983). In the early 1970s, Diggs wrote a number of essays for *A Current Bibliography on African Affairs* that focused on Du Bois's writings. Using Du Bois's articles from *Crisis* and other texts, Diggs organized her essays to convey the tremendous breadth of his scholarship and his grasp of current issues. Du Bois is the focus, but now and then Diggs makes her presence known. In the closing lines of the essay on Garvey, Diggs remarks: "There is awe for Du Bois; for Garvey there is adoration and sympathy. Both Du Bois and Garvey were strong, outspoken, aggressive. Both fought the battle, using different weapons and strategies, for the freedom of black people, but only Du Bois included all people in the search for identity, respite and equality" (1973:181). Similarly, Diggs inserts her opinions about Du Bois's work for suffrage: "Because Du Bois was aware of the way in which suffrage for women was interlocked with suffrage for blacks he was an early, consistent, constant advocate of women's suffrage. Every argument for Negro suffrage, he said, is an argument for woman's suffrage; every argument for woman suffrage is an argument for Negro suffrage. He predicted that the struggle for woman suffrage would lead to widespread discussion of Negro suffrage, North and South" (1974:279).

Du Bois's influence is obvious in *Black Chronology*, since its inception came during work on *The Encyclopedia of the Negro* although it was not published until 1983. In this reference book Diggs attempts to connect the histories of peoples of the African continent with the histories of peoples of the diaspora beginning with the rise of the first Egyptian empire in 4000 B.C. to 1888, when Brazil, the last slave-holding country in the Western Hemisphere, emancipated its slaves. This work was very much a part of the African-American intellectual vindication school because Diggs's purpose was to dispel the myth that Africans in the Americas had no histories—in science, technology, the arts, and culture—except what Europeans or European-Americans had constructed for them. Although the finished work did not live up to the enormous project outlined in the 1930s, it does tremendous justice to those early plans.

Havana

In 1941 Diggs took a well-deserved holiday to Cuba, her first trip out of the continental United States. Diggs immediately recognized the obvious African presence in the faces of the people and in the expressive Cuban culture. During this first trip Diggs visited the University of Havana, where she met scholars who encouraged her to return for an in-depth study. The next year Diggs returned and began taking intensive Spanish language courses at the University of Havana summer school. Her three-year stay was subsidized by a Roosevelt fellowship from the Institute of International Education at the University of Havana.

While at the university Diggs met with Fernando Ortiz, Cuba's "renaissance man" who at that time headed the department of ethnology. Ortiz's scholarly interests focused on Cuban culture, particularly African influence on society. Ortiz interpreted Cuba's transculturalism as a balancing act among the cultural components of European, African, and indigenous origins maintained by colonial and neocolonial formations firmly grounded in a historical framework. In his masterpiece, *Cuban Counterpoint,* he identified sugar and tobacco as symbols of a societal interplay between cultural forms and material conditions, suggesting a fluid creolization process (see Coronil 1995).

According to Diggs, "I was a guest in the palatial home of Ortiz at least once a week, and he saw to it that I witnessed many of the African survivals in Cuba" (Diggs 1981). As part of Ortiz's research team, Diggs examined pronounced Yoruba, Dahomey, or other African ethnic group characteristics in traditional black Cuban dance and music. The creative collaboration between the individual and the group in black Cuban music derives from African cultures with democratic qualities. On the basis of this ongoing research, however, Ortiz argues in *La Africania de la musica folklorica de Cuba:*

> The African traits, the Africanidad, of the Afrocuban are already diluted as a result of his acculturation to the Cuban melting pot. The vulgar demands of "turismo" have converted Havana into a crossroad of the world where the most repugnant aberrations are producing grotesque and vile deformations in Afrocuban dances. . . . Yet, in spite of turismo and the mechanization of life, the dance is the principal and the most enthusiastic diversion of Cuba, its genuinely indigenous production and its most universal exportation. (1950:248–49; author's trans.)

In Cuba Diggs focused her own studies on the impact and continuities of African cultural elements in Cuban society, particularly music and dance. She turned to areas where traditional black Cuban culture dominated. Although she did not specify locations, Diggs collected folklore, recorded music, photographed festivals, and observed rituals and dance in both rural and urban Cuba. In that Caribbean setting she became increasingly aware that certain elements of African cultures, such as dance, music, religious practices, and community relations, had survived into the twentieth century. Slaves had brought their culture with them to primarily the western part of the island, which was similar in climate, economy, and social stratification to their homes in West Africa. The slaves added to the social stratification rank by skin color and slave status. African influence on the culture was diminished, however, by the rich mix of indigenous peoples, Europeans, and Africans.

By Diggs's graduate student days Cuba had become a highly stratified neocolonial society heavily influenced by the United States and a long history of Spanish colonialism (1493–1897). As the only seat of higher education in the country, the University of Havana was reserved for elites, since only they could afford such a privilege. Most university students, as members of the upper classes, were white or light-skinned Cubans. Yet, because class counted more heavily than race, Diggs, as a student and an American, was perceived as upper class, despite her dark skin.

Cuba provided Diggs with opportunities for both fieldwork and international living, which laid the basis for future scholarship. As she conducted research for her dissertation on Afro-Cuban music and folklore and Ortiz's pursuit of African elements in Cuban society, Diggs formulated important questions concerning race and class. Working within the historical framework established by Du Bois and Ortiz, Diggs began to analyze the meanings of race: "Basically, the differences between the 'problem of race' in the United States and Latin America is their different definitions of who is white" (1971:107).

Like a number of other anthropologists working on race and race relations in the Americas at that time, such as Charles Wagley and Marvin Harris, Diggs argued that Latin American social systems developed largely through divisions on class and racial lines. As she discovered in her later work in Uruguay and Argentina, this fusion of white, black, and indigenous people

> produced new and alarming complications, difficult demographic problems, blendings and shades in color both surprising and pleasant. There is scarcely a single aspect of culture of this continent [South America] which does not reflect this reconstruction. It is evident in the intonation and pronunciation of the language, in the vocabulary, in the religious ceremonies and beliefs, in the folklore and superstitions, in the manner of living and thinking, in the cuisine, fiestas, dances, in the literature, music, painting and sculpture; it characterizes the individual and is the most typical expression of the ethos of these nations. (1971:108)

Unlike Wagley and Harris, however, Diggs concentrated on the black perspective. Instead of being crushed by slavery, Diggs found that transplanted Africans in South America were powerful: "The presence of such a large number of Negroes gave them a place of importance in the structure and life of the Rio de La Plata. In the colonial urban and rural centers the African not only performed the farm tasks and domestic services but side by side with the European immigrant he was the tailor, the cobbler, the blacksmith and the silversmith. Negroes, mulattos and mestizos were slaves, but also bull fighters, teachers of piano, actors, singers, coachmen, soldiers, barbers, venders, free men and freedmen" (1951:290).

With her work Diggs changed the focus of scholarship on slavery to the perspective of the slaves:

> Neither the tobacco, cotton, cane fields nor the mines decimated or consumed them [slaves] in the Rio de la Plata. Stories of the kindly relations between master and slave are always particularly touching manifestations of an unreserved feeling of kindness which can only exist when one's domestic servants are absolutely under one's domination. Each commentator assures his reader that slavery in his country was less cruel than in others. The background of physical loveliness is a familiar vignette of this make-believe. The owners and masters are beautiful in person, graceful in motion, generous, charming in conversation—careless geniuses in creating duties for others to perform. Contrasting with them are the childlike, primitive slaves, creatures of earth, singing, dancing, poor, malicious and vicious at times, contented always. There is nothing between—only spectacular extremes. But there is a void, a great aching silence about those things which must have existed but scarcely can be made to fit into this other wise perfect state. (1951:293–94)

Diggs discovered that the "castas" that appeared and disappeared indicated no harmonious "melting pot," but white supremacy leading to disenfranchisement, segregation, and social inequality:

> Colonization was an ethnic as well as a territorial conquest, and not only in the colonial epoch, for miscegenation in spite of legislation continued in the period of independence and continues today. Amalgamation became the leveler tending toward the dissolution of "castas" and resulted in the reconstruction, ethnic and cultural, of the continent. The arrival of the African in the Western Hemisphere complicated the ethnic categories and retarded the "whitening" of the Americas. The premium placed on the "tipo blanco," and the immigration of Europeans in the mid nineteenth century, speeded up the disappearance or dilution of the African. (1953:404)

All groups "suffered the oppression and tyranny of European hegemony. The attempt to make rigid and permanent the rights and duties of each not only served to unite them in the fight for liberation from a common oppressor but also resulted in a struggle, not yet complete, for emancipation from color and casta" (1953:427).

In contrast to the situation in Latin America, slavery in the United States fostered a two-tier color system that erased class differences. Although this stratification varied by region, the elevation of skin color was the legacy of slavery, the concept of "blood" purity, and white supremacy, as Du Bois argued in *Black Reconstruction in America, 1860–1880.* The massive social apparatus that maintained slavery was not dismantled or restructured even well into the twentieth century. If anything changed for blacks at all, it was through their own actions despite their oppressive social and economic conditions.

Although whites in the United States could move up the social hierarchy into a higher class, blacks could not, which was, according to Diggs, the "primary factor" in blacks' oppression: "Scarcely any public issue of importance can be considered without taking blacks into account. Racial attitudes and feelings penetrate and permeate every institutional structure of governance in the United States as well as the greater part of group and individual behavior. Wittingly or unwittingly, most of one's basic decisions are made in the context of black-white considerations" (1980: 157).

Also unlike Wagley and Harris, Diggs published primarily in black academic journals, such as the *Journal of Negro History* and *Phylon.* In the 1950s the black perspective was discounted in the predominantly Eurocentric academy and its associated presses. As a result, Diggs became a footnote, and not a primary resource, for most researchers.

Even her work on the fine arts was ignored by scholars. In her focus on black historical and contemporary artists Diggs could also put forth her anthropological theories. Acting as a patron as well as a researcher, she found an audience in *Americas* magazine, which published her articles in Spanish, Portuguese, English, and Italian. Antonio Francisco Lisboa, an eighteenth-century black Brazilian sculptor, offered a perfect subject. Born a slave, Lisboa "created examples of what the inquietude and sensitiveness of a 'new race,' a new culture, a new world might contribute despite Portuguese contempt and tradition" (Diggs 1950:25). At thirty-four Lisboa contracted an unknown disease that twisted his body and brought him the nickname "O Aleijadinho" (the Little Cripple). He continued his work for thirty-seven more years in chapels and cathedrals throughout Bahia and Minas Gerias. On the facade of the Church of Our Good Lord, Lisboa depicted St. Michael in a native cacique headdress, and he painted mestizo slave angels on the ceiling. He gave Christ slanted eyes; for Greek caryatids, the artist substituted Indian and mestizo figures. Diggs powerfully described the art, underscoring the emotions that the sculpture evoked and historicizing the body of work in its racial and national contexts.

Baltimore

In 1947 Diggs was invited to join the faculty of Morgan State College, a historically black college in Baltimore. Her teaching load was heavy by today's standards, though typical of that found in many black colleges and universities at that time. Diggs usually taught fifteen hours per week and prepared seven courses per year. Never did she teach fewer than twelve hours or five courses in the many years spent on the Morgan State campus. Her course offerings included introduction to sociology, introduction to anthropology, race relations in the Americas, and social stratification.

Because her classroom commitments were so extensive, she had little time to prepare book-length manuscripts. Still bitter about the experience, Diggs notes that presses were not interested in publishing her books, not even her dissertation. She did, however, publish many articles on blacks in Latin America and race relations in the United States, as well as over forty book reviews.

Today she is perhaps most well known in academic circles for her writings on W. E. B. Du Bois. Following his death at the age of ninety-five in self-imposed exile in Ghana, Diggs memorialized him:

> A non-payable debt we owe Du Bois for his thoughts and writings which laid the foundation for a revolutionary approach to the problem of color for much of what the nineteen-sixties have given wings to in the United States and in the world in the areas of freedom, equality and independence especially for non-whites.
>
> . . . He is not likely to be remembered as or made a saint—there will not be many myths about Du Bois but history will record him as an extraordinary productive writer, an unrelenting advocate of human dignity, a believer in the primacy of human conscience, a gentle jovial human being with a disarming air of simplicity, tough of purpose, with a biting but warm sense of satirical humor, persistent in his demands, shy but unafraid. (1965:19)

In addition Diggs wrote the introduction to the 1983 edition of Du Bois's *Dusk of Dawn* as a former student, research associate, secretary, and scholar in her own right. Diggs sets Du Bois's autobiographical essay in its proper sociohistorical setting and explains the changes of heart and intellectual direction Du Bois underwent while he wrote the piece. Despite her vital role in his work, most biographies of Du Bois do not acknowledge her existence, let alone her contribution to his scholarship (e.g., see Marable 1986). At most she is granted the status of "top aide."

Even though the academy ignored it, Diggs's work did appear in a wide range of popular media. Her tremendous contribution to the education of black America came in the popular press. Much of her scholarship on Latin America, material culture, and ethnography appeared in *Crisis,* the publication of the NAACP.

Diggs also appeared on television and radio programs in the Baltimore and Washington, D.C., area. The *Baltimore Sun* ran feature articles on Diggs, and she eventually contributed commentaries resulting from her extensive travels to eastern Europe, the former Soviet Union, the Far East, West Africa, and most of the islands in the Atlantic and Pacific.

Diggs as a Pioneer

Before her death in 1998 Irene Diggs was a fellow of the American Anthropological Association, the American Association for the Advancement of Science, the American Association of Physical Anthropologists, the Society for Applied Anthropologists, and the Evergreen House in Baltimore. Diggs also held memberships in other leading academic associations, such as the New York Academy of Science, the American Association of University Women, and the International African Institute. After retiring from Morgan State in 1976 she returned to Cuba as a special visitor to the United Nations International Seminar on the Eradication of Apartheid and in Support of the Struggle for Liberation in Southern Africa and provided accounts of the seminar as well as her impressions of how the country had changed since her fieldwork. She was also active in her community. She was a founding member of the Women's Committee of the Baltimore Art Museum and on the Women's Board of the Peabody Institute of Johns Hopkins University. Although she did not personally feel discriminated against—either at Morgan State or in the field of anthropology—she did become involved in women's issues through civic and statewide fact-finding commissions on mental health, corrections, and family welfare.

In 1978, the Association of Black Anthropologists honored Diggs for her five decades of valuable contributions to the study of peoples of African descent in the Western Hemisphere. In her speech she remarked on the history of blacks in the discipline as well as her own life experiences as a black intellectual: "I have found it difficult to get articles published in professional anthropological magazines, and when published elsewhere to have them mentioned in bibliographies and footnotes. I have not been invited to give papers at anthropological meetings which I have attended, with four or five exceptions, since 1947, to give papers, write reviews or appear on panels except on rare occasions" (Diggs 1978:7).

Diggs concluded her talk with a prescription for ending the intellectual isolation of blacks in the profession. She instructed young black anthropologists:

> it is your bounded duty, to continue with us and after us to create our own institutional structures wherein we study, work, write and educate students and have our work evaluated. . . . This means our institutional structure will be open to all who wish to join with us on a basis of equality. . . . This means we will have our own center and not be on the periphery of others, this does not mean that we will not work with and cooperate with others. . . . This means that we have no intention of isolating ourselves and in turn being isolated. (7)

The career of Irene Diggs offers a number of insights into the role that African Americans have played in anthropology and the academy. Diggs was most fortunate to be a student of two of the most distinguished scholars of the black world, W. E. B. Du Bois and Fernando Ortiz. Like many other African-American anthropologists, Diggs concentrated her work on the black experience and in the process combined common research techniques and theories to create new ones. Diggs transformed the work of her mentors to construct her own view of culture. For Diggs, culture consisted of learned patterns of adaptive behavior altered through time by processes of change. To understand the processes of change requires a historical, cultural, and economic analysis. Through her fieldwork Diggs was able to bring together the whole African experience both in and outside of Africa with emphasis on rebellions, ideologies, and the personalities and accomplishments of black people.

Like many black intellectuals, Diggs spent much of her time training young minds instead of publishing scholarship. In her nearly thirty years at Morgan State University Diggs was considered by students to be a formidable figure, even if she was not powerful within the discipline of anthropology. Diggs never did turn away from her field, however, believing emphatically "that anthropology can be, if properly taught, one of the most beneficial subjects black and whites can study" (Diggs 1978:7).

References Cited

Coronil, Fernando. 1995. "Transculturation and the Politics of Theory: Countering the Center, Cuban Counterpoint." In *Cuban Counterpoint: Tobacco and Sugar* by Fernando Ortiz. Trans. Harriet De Onis. Durham: Duke University Press. ix–lvi.

Diggs, Irene. 1950. "O Aleijadinho." *Americas* 3 (Oct.): 25–44.

———. 1951. "The Negro in the Viceroyalty of the Rio de la Plata." *Journal of Negro History* 36 (3): 281–301.

———. 1953. "Color in Colonial Spanish America." *Journal of Negro History* 38 (4): 403–27.

———. 1965. "Tribute to William Edward Burghardt Du Bois." *Freedomways* 5 (1): 18–19.

———. 1971. "Attitudes toward Color in South America." *Negro History Bulletin* 34 (5): 107–8.

———. 1973. "Du Bois and Marcus Garvey." *A Current Bibliography on African Affairs* 6 (2): 140–82.

———. 1974. "Du Bois and Women." *A Current Bibliography on African Affairs* 7 (3): 260–303.

———. 1978. "An Autobiography of the Discipline Anthropology." Speech delivered at the annual meeting of the Association of Black Anthropologists. Los Angeles. Nov. 17.

———. 1980. "The Biological and Cultural Impact of Blacks on the United States." *Phylon* 41 (1): 153–66.

———. 1981. Interview with the author. Notes. Baltimore, Md. Oct. 17.

———. 1983. *Black Chronology: From 4000 B.C. to the Abolition of the Slave Trade.* Westport: G. K. Hall.

———. 1991. Interview with the author. Notes. Baltimore, Md. Oct. 18.

Du Bois, W. E. B. 1915. *The Negro.* New York: Henry Holt.

——. 1935. *Black Reconstruction in America, 1860–1880.* New York: Harcourt, Brace.

——. 1939. *Black Folk Then and Now: An Essay in the History of Sociology of the Negro Race.* New York: Harcourt, Brace.

——. 1940. *Dusk of Dawn: An Essay toward an Autobiography of a Race Concept.* New York: Harcourt, Brace.

Du Bois, W. E. B., and Irene Diggs. 1945. *Encyclopedia of the Negro.* New York: H. W. Wilson.

Marable, Manning. 1986. *W. E. B. Du Bois, Black Radical Democrat.* Boston: Twayne.

Ortiz, Fernando. 1947. *Cuban Counterpoint: Tobacco and Sugar.* Trans. Harriet De Onis. New York: A. A. Knopf.

——. 1950. *La Africania de la musica folklorica de Cuba.* Havana: Ministerio de Educacion, Direccionde Cultura.

8

Across Class and Culture: Allison Davis and His Works

Dallas L. Browne

By focusing on the conjunctions of race, class, and culture, Allison Davis has contributed significantly to anthropology, sociology, and education. His descriptions of racial stratification and oppression in the South remain among the most provocative research in the United States. His examination of southern culture helped found environmentally based theories of racism and spurred such programs as Head Start. His critique of IQ tests demonstrated their cultural bias and led to less biased testing and evaluation of African-American students. Although his contributions to scholarship are significant, perhaps more important are his valuable insights into the structures and conflicts of American society and the individuals within it.

Early Influences

Allison Davis was born in Washington, D.C., on October 14, 1902, to John Davis, a clerk for the U.S. government, and Gabrielle Davis, a homemaker. Allison spent his first years on the family's farm in Nokesville near Manassas, Virginia, but the family, which included two other children, Dorothy and John Jr., moved to Washington, D.C., before Allison entered high school.

Allison Davis. (Courtesy of the Joseph Regenstein Memorial Library, University of Chicago)

John Davis Sr. had been valedictorian of his M Street High School class and was labeled one of the most promising young clerks in government employment by his co-workers. The years between 1901 and 1909 were exceptionally good for the Davis family because Theodore Roosevelt championed fairness in government hiring and staff promotion. Roosevelt's policies enabled John Davis Sr. to be promoted to clerk and head of a division in the Government Printing Office and earned Roosevelt admiration from him:

> Indeed he risked his very life in 1904 to vote for "Teddy" in rural Democratic Virginia. Already marked in a town of 236 citizens as the owner of one of the largest farms in Prince William County, he further angered the whites by registering and voting. A brave man himself, he admired beyond reason Roosevelt's stand against the great economic trusts of his day. He dressed like Teddy, trimmed his mustache like his, and wore pince-nez like his. He accepted Roosevelt unquestioningly and adopted his political ideas as his own. (Davis 1983:3)

The family's fortunes declined sharply after 1914 when Woodrow Wilson's administration reversed many of Roosevelt's policies. Wilson introduced segregation and racial exclusion, which cost many African Americans their government jobs. John Davis Sr. was demoted to a messenger in the Department of Defense War College. This demotion was a source of anger within the family, and Allison developed deep resentment against racial discrimination and blind prejudice.

The hostility Wilson generated with his policies culminated in the Washington race riots of 1921–22, which sowed seeds of fear and suspicion between blacks and whites and caused suffering and loss for many families. The riots convinced Davis that the primary motive for all racial discrimination was economic. To him the goal of the riots was to intimidate black workers into cowering at home and missing work for long periods of time. This would lead to their dismissal and the subsequent hiring of white workers to replace them.

By 1916 M Street High School had changed its name to Dunbar High School and had moved into a new building (Davis-Lucas 1993). Dunbar's faculty included an outstanding principal and renowned Latin and Greek scholars who could not find employment elsewhere, due to segregation. Most had earned degrees from the finest schools in the world, such as the University of Berlin, the Sorbonne, Harvard, Radcliffe, Amherst, Williams, and Wellesley. These administrators and teachers instilled in their students a desire to learn, a reverence for knowledge, and the belief that they were the best in the country and thereby produced a "model minority" (Sowell 1972). It is thus not surprising that Allison Davis's classmates included W. Montague Cobb, who would become a president of the NAACP. Allison Davis was at the forefront of this illustrious group. Like his father, he was valedictorian of his class. When reflecting on his early schooling Davis noted: "I went to an all-segregated high school in Washington, D.C. which was quite well known and had a good faculty. This is important because it shows that not all segregated schools are poor schools" (Turner 1972:22). Davis's achievements were not confined to academics, however. He played baseball for Dunbar and was captain of the tennis team, which was runner-up in the National Negro Tennis Tournament. He also served as captain of the junior cadet corps.

After graduation and World War I, a night job at the War Risk Insurance Corporation allowed Davis to earn money and acquire valuable experience. Allison was working there when the race riots erupted in 1921. Davis's mother feared that he would be harmed either going to or returning from work, yet his friends protected him. Davis himself, who had a fair complexion, feared traversing a black neighborhood because residents might assume he was white and then shoot him. Racial tensions caused problems within the Davis family as well. Davis's mother had an extremely fair complexion, straight hair, and blue eyes. Because she was often mistaken for white, she could move about the white sections of town without fear. Davis's father, however, was identifiably black, so feared for his life while traveling through white neighborhoods. The perceived unearned privileges accorded to Davis's mother, due solely to her fair complexion, created occasional tension between his parents (J. Davis 1992). Davis soon decided to fight the racial caste system because it threatened the happiness of his family and attempted to limit his opportunities (J. Davis 1992).

From Student to Practitioner

In 1924 Davis graduated as valedictorian and earned his bachelor of arts degree, summa cum laude, from Williams College in Williamstown, Massachusetts. Proceeding from there to Harvard, Davis earned his master of arts degree in English and comparative literature in 1925. From 1925 to 1931 he taught English at Hampton Institute, where he stimulated his students, including St. Clair Drake, to write and to think critically (Drake 1974:44). Davis said of the experience: "I taught English for a few years at a black missionary college in Virginia, but found that teaching in the standard manner made no sense for these poor and poorly schooled rural blacks. I decided that I didn't know anything really to teach them since our backgrounds were so different, yet, I wanted to do something to affect our students. I returned to Harvard to study social anthropology with W. Lloyd Warner" (Turner 1972:22).

Davis earned a second master's degree from Harvard in anthropology. A Rosenwald Fellowship for the 1932–33 school year allowed him to continue his anthropological studies at the London School of Economics. There he studied under Bronislaw Malinowski and Lancelot T. Hogben, a nondogmatic Marxist anthropologist. As Davis's tutor, Hogben influenced Davis's views on heredity and environment, just as Margaret Mead would later shape his perspective on comparative socialization. Davis was restless in England, however, and returned to the United States to continue his studies with W. Lloyd Warner at Harvard University. Warner had published *A Black Civilization: A Social Study of an Australian Tribe* and had decided to study an American town by using a similar thesis: social class was the main organizing principle in American life. Warner concluded that Americans were trying to get money and education and whatever else it took to climb the social ladder. As they climbed they crystallized into social classes. What resulted were the series of studies of fictional Yankee City, which Davis helped to research, and fame for Warner. When Warner left Harvard for a job at the University of Chicago, Davis transferred schools because Warner could help Davis grow intellectually: "While working under Warner, I had the opportunity to study the types of villages from which my past English students had come. I left Harvard as a team with Burleigh and Mary Gardner to study the two oldest cotton communities in Mississippi. This was the first time that social anthropology had been applied to a modern Southern community. . . . This study of Natchez represented a chance to break from my classical training to turn to the study of 'reality'" (Turner 1972:22).

Before conducting fieldwork in Mississippi, Davis was merely a student, but this experience enabled him to master the subtleties of American race relations better than anyone had before him. He emerged from Mississippi as a master anthropologist and an intellectual giant. After completing fieldwork for this study, he returned to the University of Chicago to finish his dissertation. While completing his dissertation he held many positions and received numerous grants. He was awarded a Rockefeller Fellowship from 1933 to 1935 and Rosenwald Fellowships from 1939 to 1940. He served as a professor of social anthropology at Dillard University from 1935 to 1939 and the director of research on black adolescent personality for the American Youth Commission of the American Council on Education from 1938 to 1939. From 1940 to 1942 he was on the staff of the Division of Child Development of the American Council of Education and was named head of the department of education at Atlanta University for 1941–42. Davis received his doctorate from the University of Chicago after finishing his doctoral dissertation, entitled "Caste, Economy, and Violence," under Warner's supervision in 1942.

Immediately after earning his Ph.D. Davis was recruited for the education department by the president of the University of Chicago, Robert Havighurst. Davis became the first African American with a Ph.D. to hold a tenure-track position at a predominantly white university in U.S. history. In 1947 the University of Chicago awarded Davis tenure, along with another black scholar named Abram Harris. By 1948 he had gained the rank of full professor, and in 1970 he earned the University of Chicago's coveted and fully endowed chair in education, the John Dewey Distinguished Professorship. His appointment to the University of Chicago profoundly affected his life: "it has made it possible for me to do things which I could not have done at a small black college" (Turner 1972:24).

In addition to fostering his own work, the position allowed him an opportunity to inspire others, such as St. Clair Drake, Charles P. Warren, and Leon Forrest, who earned advanced degrees in anthropology from the University of Chicago under Davis's tutelage. Three other students became heads of education departments at various colleges (letter from Dorothy Davis-Lucas, July 11, 1993, author's possession). In his teaching Davis was almost fatherly, which made him—and his profession—much more approachable. His strong family ties and successful relatives perhaps further encouraged others to follow in his path. His first wife, Elizabeth, was from an upper-middle-class Delaware family headed by her prominent physician father. She helped Davis conduct his research and organized the family's social life. Both sons, Allison Jr. and Gordon, became successful lawyers, and Gordon also served as commissioner of parks for New York City under Mayor John V. Lindsey. With these accomplishments, he was surely a source of inspiration for many African Americans and proof that blacks could be successful in institutions of higher education.

Lasting Legacy

Volume 27 of the January 1935 *Sociological Review* carried Davis's first publication, "The Distribution of the Blood Groups and Its Bearing on the Concept of Race." Although Davis had not studied with him for two years, Hogben obviously influenced his approach in this article. Hogben opposed the fashionable theory of biological determinism and maintained that the social environment was the decisive factor in individual development. Thus in this piece Davis focused on "iso-agglutination," or the clumping of red blood cells when brought into contact with the serum of another individual with a different blood type. He tried to correlate blood group with race, cephalic indexes, and stature, but discovered that "even using gradation of skin color and hair form distinguished by anthropologists, it is obvious that both these categories also cut across each of the traits dealt with. . . . Dark-brown skinned people, with curly hair, for example, can have every gradation of cephalic index, nasal index, and blood-group proportions, as can also white-skinned peoples with straight hair" (Davis 1935:28). Davis concluded: "while we can recognize certain restricted communities as natural races with well-defined limits, the bulk of mankind is not so classifiable," so blood type was not a reliable indicator of race (196). Hogben later reprinted this article in *Political Arithmetic* (Hogben 1938).

Davis's next publication would ignite a tremendous debate in the academic community. In "A Comparative Study of American Caste" Davis and W. Lloyd Warner equated race in America with the caste system in India (1939:229). Davis built on this work that same year with "The Socialization of the American Negro Child and Adolescent," in which he questioned the assumption that the "American Negro family . . . is relatively ineffective in training the Negro person to take on the normal sexual and familial behavior in American society" (1939:264). Davis found, conversely, that the race-caste system imposed social and economic limits upon many African-American families that were appropriate only to those in the lower classes and adversely affected those striving to join the middle class. According to Davis's findings, the larger society's low expectations for blacks generally led to inappropriate socialization by upwardly mobile blacks, which explained the atypical behavior of large numbers of African Americans.

In this article Davis also noted that because marriage between blacks and whites was prohibited in the South during the 1920s, it was impossible for many blacks to experience "normal" family life. Moreover, most lower-class blacks in the South were encouraged to foster common-law marriages, not legal commitments, and black illegitimacy was smiled upon. Training for professional, white-collar, managerial, and skilled occupations was offered only to white children. Illiteracy and the absence of traditional middle-class values among lower-class blacks reinforced this pattern of racial subordination.

This racial caste system prohibited mixed-race seating on buses and in theaters. Curfews did not allow blacks to remain in white areas after dark or own automobiles or wear expensive jewelry or even smoke cigarettes on "white" business streets. Blacks had to go to the back doors of restaurants to buy sandwiches and eat them in alleys, hidden from view. These caste barriers assured white superiority, privilege, and opportunity at the expense of blacks. Whites also gained a tremendous psychological boost from this system, not to mention shelter from black competition for resources. The racial caste system separated not only blacks from whites but also blacks from other blacks. African-American lower-class children were stigmatized at birth and forced to submit to a brutal system of control. They were taught that they were subservient to whites and could never become their social or economic equals in a segregated country. Although it was within their power to slow down work, come to work late, feign clumsiness, or even use flattery, humor, secrecy, or ignorance to outwit whites, violence against whites was taboo. Violence against other blacks, however, was encouraged through messages to fight if attacked.

By comparison, middle-class blacks were taught that they were separated from whites socially and must accept this, but in all other respects they were equal to whites. To such children, legal and social taboos did not imply subordination but merely difference. Middle-class African-American children were taught to minimize contact with whites or even to avoid them. They did not play with or talk to white children or adults unless it was absolutely necessary. They were trained to repress impulsive behavior and lead respectable lives.

However, upper-class African-American parents concealed their inferior caste status from their children. They hoped that one day these children could escape this stigma. As a result, upper-class children seldom thought of themselves as "Negroes" and did not act like lower-class blacks. At adolescence, they were taught to be critical of white society and told that they must use education and racial solidarity to destroy the race-caste system. In *Black Metropolis* St. Clair Drake and Horace R. Cayton noted that these children grew up thinking of themselves as "race men," or guardians and defenders of the black race, black pride, equal opportunity, and access to resources. They fought legally and intellectually, but did less than lower-class African Americans to resist white physical aggression.

This caste system forced most African-American women to work outside of the home while most white women remained within the home. The absence of parental supervision adversely affected black children's behavior, and Davis felt that it contributed to high truancy rates. In addition, in lower-class black families children routinely witnessed violent attacks by one parent upon the other, by siblings, and by neighbors. Since no one lost status or was punished for this aggression, children soon learned to carry knives, razors, or even guns and strike first to defend their lives. Violent adults were admired and respected within the culture as folk heroes and role models. Their prestige rose with each victory. Because the law offered lower-class African Americans little or no protection, a reputation for being tough accorded admiration, respect, and served as a survival technique in the lower-class world filled with gambling, drinking, cursing, and magic. Children were taught that personal strength, brute force, defiance, and aggression were essential. Their parents admired tyrants and bullies, yet middle-class school teachers punished aggressive behavior in school, where it was viewed as disruptive.

Violence frequently led to marital instability among lower-class African Americans. Most children experienced at least one parental separation within their first five years of life. Most families expected the early death of the father or his desertion. Many mothers subsequently either remarried or found another man to anchor their lives economically. For most children, according to Davis, "at least one of his brothers or sisters is likely to have an illegitimate child during adolescence, and his mother will almost certainly provide him with half-brothers and sisters, by men who fill the position of the sociological father to him for periods of relatively short duration. . . . In the lower-class . . . chances are very good that his father will disappear before he is born, and that neither he nor the other children in his family can identify their fathers" (1939:272).

Despite familial instability, religion filled an important role among the middle and upper classes.Among the lowest rungs of the lower class, however, church offered little. Preachers and deacons did not retrain children into new patterns of behavior at school, at home, or in society. Instead religious instruction focused on forbidding dancing, card playing, and playing baseball on Sundays, not altering fundamental values.

Davis found that although school was important and education was valued, playing hookey was socially acceptable, even chic, among the lower classes. These children frequently did not take their lessons or their teachers seriously. Since adults believed that upward mobility through education was virtually impossible, little emphasis was placed on learning. Neither teachers nor parents expected lower-class children to excel, so the children obliged by meeting their low expectations. The few professional jobs available to blacks required more deferred gratification and impulse renunciation than they had been trained to accept. Because the culture valued entertainers and athletes, lower-class black children were more likely to develop their talents in these areas than to acquire skilled jobs that would require more deferred gratification and impulse renunciation than they were accustomed to.

Davis made it clear that adolescence was much shorter for lower-class children than for others. By age fourteen or fifteen they were having regular sexual intercourse, holding jobs, and contributing to the family income. They had the privileges and obligations of adults and were often treated as such by the courts. Unlike middle- and upper-class adolescents, who could still lead the carefree lives of children, lower-class black adolescents were responding to specific environmental stimuli that encouraged illegitimacy, truancy, and poor school performance. Davis stressed the need for teachers and social workers to redirect the goals of these children and modify their environments if society wanted them to achieve upward mobility:

> Since the basic operational method of our class-system is that persons in any given class are subjected to systematic punishing by the classes above them, in order to keep them subordinated and at a defined social distance, it is not to be expected that lower-class children will be especially hopeful about social mobility, or be especially responsive to efforts of remedial workers along this line. The first step in the re-training of children, by teachers or social workers, therefore, is to stop punishing lower-class children by contempt or condescension along class lines. The second step is to make them understand that the social rewards of higher status are satisfying enough to justify hard work and renunciation on their part to change their behavior. (1939:274)

Davis went on to develop these ideas with John Dollard in *Children of Bondage,* a study of one hundred African-American high school students from the lower, middle, and upper classes of the black community in New Orleans and probably the first full-scale intensive study of the effects of socialization on the intelligence and behavior of middle- and lower-class African-American adolescents. Using Freudian psychology and life histories, they studied the development of the personality in black adolescents. They introduced traumatized lower-class youth, such as the "Frightened Amazon" Julia, who claims to "hate" whites because they "got all the money" (1940:42). Davis and Dollard argued that hatred and aggression are Julia's way of striking back at a system that has arbitrarily assigned her to an underprivileged life and a mother who had treated her harshly. Since the law rarely punished Southern lower-class blacks for acting out in their own community, Julia could curse, shoot, or cut people as much as she wanted, provided she did not harm a white person. Julia claimed she was rejected by her mother because "all of the other children are lighter than me" and she was glad when one boy stabbed another over her because this proved to her mother that "somebody does want me" (41). As Davis and Dollard point out, these statements and others merely rationalize Julia's behavior since her mother's favorite child, Earl, has darker skin than anyone in the family. Julia's hatred is rooted in deprivation and fear of white boys, who called her "nigger" and cut her simply because she was black. Compounding her fear and hatred is ambivalence because Julia knew "good white people" too (43). Davis and Dollard summarize her case:

> Essentially, Julia is a person with a grudge against life itself. It seems in the very beginning to have starved her and robbed her of gratifying and necessary habits, when she was incapable of protecting herself and unable to understand what was asked of her. Her deep animosity toward people stems from the hostile demands and the abrupt, traumatic training which she received from her mother and oldest sister. She has a just, but never to be requited, claim against the universe. Therefore, she can never expect anything good of most human beings, nor can she absolve them and her mother from having taken the good things of life away. Long ago, she learned not to expect support and guidance and love, and therefore not to move unless driven. Restitution is not to be made. She must take what she will not be given. She must abstract from people, by wile or force, what was taken from her. She will love, genuinely love, only herself. (43)

Davis and Dollard contrasted the deprived Julia with "Ellen Hill the winner," a middle-class black girl with numerous opportunities, not the least of which is a chance to attend college (181). They noted: "People like Ellen Hill, whose lives are largely organized around their efforts for upward mobility, must be constantly on the march. The sanctions of class position are continually pressing to keep them down in the class of their parents. In order to escape from the status to which they were born, such individuals must wage a powerful campaign for higher education, money, 'well-placed' friends, and an opportunity to learn the behavior of the social class above them" (185). According to Davis and Dollard, this process is most difficult for the lower classes and the upper middle class, who strive to break into the tiny upper class. Children who gain membership in the right cliques through athletics, academics, activities, or social contacts succeed, but few gain opportunities to learn the behavior acceptable to the class above their own.

The most mobile of all classes is the lower middle class. Children are under constant pressure to repress sexual impulses and aggression and avoid lower-class playmates so as not to fall further down the social scale. To "improve" themselves, they attend Sunday school regularly and avoid gambling, drinking, cursing, night clubs, and pool halls. Their goals include a high school education, a good skilled or white-collar job, and a strong marriage. Middle-class children are socialized to adhere to the norms and values of their own class. In this manner the middle class reproduces itself in each new generation. Physical pain and scolding or gratification and praise mold children's behavior. As they grow older they control their behavior by anticipating approval or disapproval from family and associates, which they learned by internalized expectations of peers, clique members, teachers, and others. Children quickly discover that the best way to avoid punishment is to imitate their parents. Thus, in the lower middle class "it pays" to be polite like their neighbors, to go to church like their fathers, to be quiet and refined like their teachers, and to keep sexual impulses hidden like their mothers.

By contrast, for children in the upper lower class it pays to be a hard worker like their mothers, to carry a knife and fight when necessary like their fathers, and to protect themselves from ridicule from their clique by beginning sexual relations early. Davis and Dollard observe:

> In their efforts to teach, lower-class Negro parents punish children with great energy and frequency and reward them seldom. They cannot offer the more effective status rewards to their children because both economic and educational privileges are class-bound and there are very few to which the child in the lower class has access. The chief reason for the relative lack of socialization of lower-class children seems to be that their incitement to learn, which means in part to renounce direct impulse gratification and to build up more complex habits and skills, is crippled by the scarcity of available rewards. (267)

The different methods of punishment affect more than children's behavior. Through delayed gratification, middle-class children learn to save money—and value—long-range goals, such as buying a book or a car. Because middle-class children learn to defer gratification at home, they then have little difficulty doing so in school. Lower-class children, in contrast, are less able to respond to traditional methods of teaching and to behave according to a middle-class teacher's expectations.

Davis later laid out the complete theoretical framework for his model of class and education in *Social Class Influences upon Learning:*

> In order to help the child learn, the teacher himself must discover the reference points from which the child starts. . . . Specifically, the teacher must learn a good deal about the pupil's cultural environment and his cultural motivation, if the teacher is to guide the child's new learning effectively. . . . The slum pupil . . . cannot learn the teacher's culture well until his teacher learns enough about the slum culture to understand what the pupil's words and learning acts mean. To encourage new learning, the teacher must discover the obstacles inherent in the pupil's old learning. She will need, therefore, to learn the pupil's cultural beliefs, his cultural definition of life-problems, the meaning of his words, and his culturally learned conceptions of the teacher herself and of the school.
>
> Then for the first time, the teaching situation becomes a reality-situation, in which the teacher can plan her own efforts with reference to some known points in the pupil's behavior. Only then does she begin to discover what her words mean to him, what he has to unlearn, and what learning experiences are pleasant or painful to him. (1948:1–2)

For Davis the close study of families and social cliques at each class level provided the master key to understanding how the system granted privileges to some and restricted access to others. Access to clique membership in a class above allowed for upward mobility, because that membership "provides the child or adult with the necessary models for imitation" (8). Without that access there is little possibility of advancement: "If a child associates intimately with no one but slum adults and children, he will learn only slum culture" (10). Davis concluded:

> Because the slum individual usually is responding to a different physical, economic, and cultural reality from that in which the middle-class individual is trained, the slum individual's habits and values also must be different if they are to be realistic. The behavior which we regard as "delinquent" or "shiftless" or "unmotivated" in slum groups is usually a perfectly realistic, adaptive and—in slum life—respectable response to reality.
>
> His social instigations and goals, his symbolic world and its evaluation are largely selected from the narrow culture of that class with which alone he can associate freely. (11)

Although he had focused on African-American children, Davis provided a model for studying the influences of class upon problems of learning generally. Davis attacked the notion that children from lower-class families were inferior in intelligence to their upper-class counterparts. He argued that as a direct result of defective intelligence testing, children in the lower two-thirds of American society were not getting adequate educations. Consequently, American society was being deprived of untapped human ability. With Kenneth Eells, a statistician who was Davis's graduate assistant, and Robert Havighurst, Davis would later identify, by item-analysis, the sources of cultural bias in standard IQ tests and challenge their use as reliable predictors of performance for members of minorities either in school or at work (Davis, Eells, and Havighurst 1953). Because this work focused on children of different races and social classes, the study led many cities, including New York, Chicago, Detroit, and San Francisco, to discontinue use of IQ tests in schools. Davis proclaimed, "This was one time I got what I wanted: a direct effect on society from social science research" (Turner 1972:24).

Later Davis critiqued the theory of cultural deprivation with Benjamin S. Bloom and Robert Hess in *Compensatory Education for Cultural Deprivation* (1965). They argued that disadvantaged children—those culturally deprived, regardless of race—did not receive experiences in their homes that prepared them for the types of learning needed to thrive either in school or in the larger society. Obviously this is a major hindrance in an economy that requires literacy as a precursor to success.

Deep South: A Social Anthropological Study of Caste and Class, the most comprehensive anthropological study of class and race available for a Southern town in the 1940s, was undertaken by Davis, Burleigh B. Gardner, and Mary R. Gardner. The Gardners, both psychologists, studied the white community while Davis, his wife Elizabeth, and St. Clair Drake studied the black community (Drake 1974). The researchers illustrated how damaged both blacks and whites were by the horrors of racial discrimination. For example, Southern whites believed that fighting, drinking, and gambling were not crimes if African Americans engaged in them but no white person witnessed the activity. If the same behavior came to the attention of whites, however, it was considered criminal and arrests were made. As one upper-class white woman remarked: "We have very little crime. Of course, Negroes knife each other occasionally, but there is little real crime. I mean Negroes against whites or whites against each other. Negroes will stab each other. There was quite a stir a while ago. A Negro man chased his wife out on the street and stabbed her to death in front of some white woman looking on. But there isn't much of that, even" (499). A white policeman added: "They don't often put them in jail or do anything to them for fighting among themselves unless they get too bad" (499).

Clearly, blacks' lives were devalued, even among other blacks. The black community referred to all hangings as *"legal lynchings,"* yet felt powerless to change the race-class system based on segregation and discrimination. Thus, most African Americans wore an emotional mask to disguise their resentment against this system. Power was the exclusive privilege of elite whites who used informal networks to control grants and jobs by securing bribes. Although poor whites had the illusion of power, they were almost as totally excluded and as exploited as blacks because of their inferior class. In 1936, when data for the book were collected, white supremacy's sacredness was widely accepted in the South. The authority of God ranked first, but the authority of white power—especially by elites—was a close second. The most virulently racist whites were upper lower-class whites, according to the study, because they were trying to win prestige and recognition from upper-class whites and defend their own interests. Lower lower-class whites and blacks, however, interacted freely.

This system provided trade-offs for many participants. A high status black woman with a white lover could funnel money into her church's fund-raising rallies. A white sheriff's black lover was also his informer. In return she could urge the sheriff to ignore offenses committed by her friends or relatives. If a black doctor needed money for his son who was in college, he could let his white landlord know. The landlord would line up his sharecropping tenants for "examinations." The landlord then deducted twenty dollars from each tenant's share of the crops. He kept ten dollars and the black doctor received ten dollars.

Despite its inherent prejudices, the system was held together by economics, according to Davis and his colleagues. In this system of trade-offs, both white and black elites preyed upon the black lower classes. The whole system existed for one purpose—to keep the labor supply intimidated so that landowners and employers secured the profits created by other people's labor, especially that of blacks. Davis, Gardner, and Gardner demonstrated that the racial caste and class systems merely reinforced a system of economic exploitation. If economic incentives were removed and people were taught new ways of relating to people from other economic and social classes, it was possible to change the caste system. Davis, Gardner, and Gardner thus definitively linked learned behavior and patterns of racial interaction, demonstrating that race prejudice was not inherited genetically, but culturally.

Davis turned again to intelligence when he teamed up with Robert J. Havighurst to produce *Father of the Man: How Your Child Gets His Personality* (1947), the first study by social scientists to compare the socialization and intelligence of middle-class and lower-class infants, children, and adolescents. Identical twin studies offered Davis and Havighurst impetus for studying the force of the environment in shaping personality. According to Minnesota and Soviet twin studies, when identical twins are given different educations and social environments, their IQs differ by as much as twenty-four points. Davis and Havighurst concluded: "When we consider such intricate patterns of behavior as intelligence, it becomes even clearer that environment, both pre-natal and post-natal, is able to modify, direct, and even to blot out the effect of hereditary similarities or differences between individuals" (63).

After demonstrating the primacy of environmental factors, the authors then reported the results of their study of fifty white middle-class mothers, fifty black middle-class mothers, fifty-one white lower-class mothers, and fifty-one black lower-class mothers. Birth order profoundly influenced their children's behavior. For example, "No matter what type of training he has received, no matter whether he was more indulgently or severely treated than the second child, the first child is still reported by mothers as being the more jealous and selfish" (127). They concluded that some degree of sibling rivalry was inevitable because no amount of training could overcome the first child's feeling that she or he had been replaced by the second child and therefore had lost the exclusive claim on parental love. Davis and Havighurst recommended reducing rivalry by creating a loving and caring family atmosphere and giving each child much affection and attention. Encouraging close relatives to interact with the children could also reduce rivalry.

Another way to create rivalry is through punishment and reward. Children learn to do what their parents want because they fear disapproval and desire love and acceptance. The strength of a behavioral habit, however, depends on the number of times it has been rewarded, the intensity of the reward, and the speed with which the reward is given. Children become rebellious when their parents' rewards and punishments are inconsistent or when the parents are violent and show little affection. Children learn by imitating models, but first they must learn to want social acceptance and understand the concept of authority. After this, socialization occurs rapidly, depending on the amount of love, fear, and admiration for parents.

Davis and Havighurst provided case studies of two sisters, Paulette and Mary, to illustrate these points. Mary, the older of the two girls, was born during the Great Depression amidst hard times for the family. Mary's mother resented her because she believed that the pregnancy and Mary's birth caused her poor health. As a result, Mary was not breast-fed for long. Paulette, by contrast, was a sickly baby, but this caused her mother to sympathize with her, give her added attention, and breast-feed her for eighteen months. In addition, Mary was sent to live with her grandmother throughout Paulette's nursing period. Mary resolved her conflict with her mother by resolving to be somebody else's little girl. Mary identified with her middle-class teachers and imitated them, while Paulette felt accepted by her lower-class mother so she imitated lower-class behavior. Although they had the same parents, a marked difference in their social environments resulted in markedly different personalities, aspirations, behaviors, and selections of adult models to imitate. Early rejection by her mother forced Mary to look outside of her family for a model and consequently she was more likely to become upwardly mobile. Davis and Havighurst suggested that the same motivation in a middle-class child may just as easily lead to downward mobility (166).

Morality according to Davis and Havighurst, then, develops when children receive complete love, in addition to appropriate prohibitions, from those who raise them. Punishment without love does not mold children's morality positively because it is only after children learn to love their parents that they want to be good. Children who lack love cannot develop a conscience.

Power also figures into moral development. Davis and Havighurst observed that birth order is a powerful motivator. Little children admire bigger children and strive to be like them, but ultimately imitate adults. Children view adults as free to come and go as they please with no restrictions or proscriptions on behavior. From the child's perspective, with age comes power.

Davis and Havighurst concluded by noting that the social environment of each child within a single family can vary, and this helps explain why brothers and sisters may behave differently. Many factors help shape whether a child will be more like the mother or the father: the mother's age and physical condition during pregnancy, the type of delivery, whether both parents desired the child, the level of the child's physiological drive, the nursing experience, the weaning experience, the response to toilet and cleanliness training, received attitudes toward genital exploration, training in exploration of the house, training in treating property, responses to age controls, level of identification with the parent of the same sex, and moral development.

One lesson to take from the study is that culture and environment shape and mold personality, even after adulthood:

> New situations and new stimuli will change not only a man's behavior—they will change his belief in himself. Men have been saved from despair, and vice, and from even the deep shadow of insanity by a change in their opportunities, by a chance to work, or to gain social distinction; by finding someone who loved them, and had faith in their ability and courage; by the birth of a son or daughter, and the new responsibility and hope that it brought.
>
> Old men learn to change their habits of living; selfish men learn to sacrifice. Even cowards, under a powerful surge of hope, or in new situations, or by gaining insight, learn to stand, and to hold their ground. The adult outgrows his childish fear of his father, or of God; even his fear of death as punishment. . . . Most of us "outgrow" or learn beyond the fears of childhood. Man, both as a helper in society, and as an individual survives by learning. (214)

The philosophy Davis and Havighurst espouse is evident in public policies and programs that offer children from the lower classes special training, tutoring, mentoring, and encouragement. Each program that enriches a child's environment helps reduce future crime and mold behavior along socially approved lines.

Davis's work profoundly affected other scholars. James Coleman's widely cited 1960s studies on the effect of socioeconomic status on performance in school built upon Davis's pioneering work on class, race, and intelligence. While working on *Children of Bondage* Davis wrote background papers for Gunnar Myrdal that influenced Myrdal's thinking about race, class, and caste in America, as demonstrated in his classic *An American Dilemma* (1944). In *The Negro Family in the United States* (1939) E. Franklin Frazier built on "The Socialization of the American Negro Child and Adolescent" by recording how illegitimacy, truancy, poor school performance, and desertion by mates decreased among African-American groups as their residential areas, incomes, occupations, and types of recreation improved. Leon Dash advanced a similar argument in *When Children Want Children: The Urban Crisis of Teenage Childbearing*

(1989). Davis's influence even extended to the law. Kenneth Clark used data from *Deep South* for the brief that won the landmark Supreme Court decision in *Brown vs. the Topeka Board of Education* in 1954.

For his final book, published one month before his death in 1983, Davis turned away from sociological and anthropological studies to look squarely at mutual hatred between ethnic, racial, and national groups. In *Leadership, Love, and Aggression* he posed several questions: "How can mankind learn to control and convert chronic anger and desire for revenge . . . violence and economic exploitation . . . conciliation and understanding?" (183). How can groups who fear and mistrust each other learn to love and understand each other? Davis believed that anger caused neighbors to kill one another. In an attempt to offer remedies to this anger, Davis examined the lives of Frederick Douglass, W. E. B. Du Bois, Richard Wright, and Martin Luther King Jr., and focused on how each directed his anger into reform.

He began *Leadership, Love, and Aggression* with a psychological and social analysis of Frederick Douglass, who once roared to a crowd, "'Those who profess to favor freedom and yet deprecate agitation . . . want crops without plowing . . . rain without . . . lightning . . . the ocean without the awful roar of its many waters. . . . This struggle may be a moral one, or it may be a physical one, but it must be a struggle. Power concedes nothing without a demand'" (17).

As a young slave Douglass had watched overseers break the spirits of other black men. He vowed that he would die before he would be spiritually defeated. Fighting the threat of oppression physically and mentally was cathartic for Douglass, who demanded power, not pity (40). According to Davis, Douglass developed personal excellence rather than excuses. Acting out his aggression through his work as an abolitionist freed him of hatred for whites, healed him, and helped him to be successful: he edited a newspaper, served as a federal marshal, was appointed the American ambassador to Haiti, became president of the Freedman's Bank, and served as an advisor to four American presidents. Although physical aggression was his last resort, it was the first step in a self-directed life of freedom. He advised other oppressed individuals in these words: "Heredity bondsmen, know ye not, who would be free themselves must strike the blow?" (40).

For Davis, W. E. B. Du Bois provided another model of healthy self-assertion. Du Bois began life uncertain of his identity. His father abandoned his mother soon after Du Bois's birth, and he often questioned his legitimacy. He and his mother lived in rented rooms in a poor Massachusetts neighborhood and depended upon white charity. In snobbish New England, his self-esteem came under constant attack. In *The Souls of Black Folk* (1903) he recounts his painful awareness of his color during a game at school when he was eleven years old: "'one girl, a tall newcomer, refused my card—refused it peremptorily. . . . Then it dawned upon me with a certain suddenness that I was different from the others . . . shut out from their world by a vast veil. . . . Why did God make me an outcast and a stranger in mine own house? . . . It is a peculiar sensation, this double consciousness, this sense of always looking at one's self through the eyes of others'" (qtd. in Davis 1983:110).

Like Douglass Du Bois believed that the best way to escape the bonds of color and discrimination was through excellence. His superior achievements in school bought his ticket out of poverty and shame. Ability and hard work were his formulas for success. At first Du Bois believed that racial prejudice could be changed by appeals to reason and objective evidence, but after completing his doctorate at Harvard, conducting research for thirteen years, and publishing over fifteen books, he concluded that he could not change Americans' attitudes unless he had power. Through his editorship of *Crisis,* the major publication of the NAACP, he attacked the injustice of America's race-caste system. He refused to behave subserviently and finally decided to leave the United States. He died in exile, viewed as a failure by his enemies but as a hero by many blacks and whites for his incorruptibility. Even though he never won acceptance as an equal from whites, their admiration for his accomplishments fostered greater mutual understanding and tolerance and dampened the fires of group hate.

Like Du Bois, Richard Wright articulated his anger through words, but he used fiction to make his point. Bigger Thomas of *Native Son* became the symbol of repressed anger building toward a rage-filled murderous explosion. Wright frightened and awakened America to the realization that it was producing Bigger Thomases across the country. Though Wright freed writers in America to express the existential rage of the oppressed, he was denied appropriate recognition for his work. According to Davis, his failure to reconcile his anger eventually destroyed him.

For Davis, Martin Luther King's philosophy exemplified the best way to constructively handle anger. King preached that we are no better than our neighbor, no worse, and no different. By example, this philosophy encourages us to rise above fear and hate and aggressively strive for change, reform, and the affiliation of all humanity. Davis felt that King's secret was never to direct his anger against an individual; rather he sought to destroy attitudes and behaviors that were harmful while transforming the person who hated into a whole, healed, and healthy individual whom he could treat with love, kindness, and concern. Davis argued that this remedy is needed throughout the world:

> King believed that men can save themselves from their own mutual hatreds, for they have the capacity to turn hatred into its opposite—mercy and love of mankind. He taught his followers to renounce hatred, to learn to deal with the enemy as fellow human beings, to give up the desire for personal revenge, and to forgive injuries once and for all. He was always willing to try again with people; he wholeheartedly asserted his faith in the human animal, who—however blinded, vindictive, and embittered—is capable of learning to love.
>
> It follows, that the cure for the world's repetitive hatred and revenge lies in seeking leaders who first can convert their own hatred into constructive initiative, and then can direct their full efforts toward saving mankind from its hatred, which otherwise will destroy it. Through this "sea-change" of hatred into compassion, a "brave new world" of love does indeed seem possible. (243)

After years of experiencing the anguish and pain of race and caste in America, perhaps it is fitting that Davis ended his career with *Leadership, Love, and Aggression*. Like his heroes, he hated the mistreatment of African Americans but directed his anger into a constructive analysis of race, caste, class, and intelligence in America. He described the terrible consequences of the caste system so vividly that it helped many see the necessity for change. His analysis of IQ tests led to a search for new methods of measuring the potential of every segment of American society. His contributions to anthropology are legendary, but above all, his life's work reminds us that good scholarship can help reshape the world we live in.

Note

I would like to gratefully acknowledge the support of the archives at the Regenstein Library, the University of Chicago, and the Department of Anthropology and the Graduate College at Southern Illinois University at Edwardsville.

References Cited

Davis, Allison. 1935. "The Distribution of the Blood Groups and Its Bearing on the Concept of Race." *Sociological Review* 27 (1): 19–34; 27 (2): 183–200. Reprinted in *Political Arithmetic: A Symposium of Population Studies.* Ed. Lancelot Hogben. London: G. Allen and Unwin, 1938. 503–31.

———. 1939. "The Socialization of the American Negro Child and Adolescent." *Journal of Negro Education* 8 (3): 264–74.

———. 1942. "Caste, Economy, and Violence." Ph.D. diss. University of Chicago.

———. 1948. *Social Class Influences upon Learning.* Cambridge, Mass.: Harvard University Press.

———. 1983. *Leadership, Love, and Aggression.* New York: Harcourt, Brace, Jovanovich.

Davis, Allison, Benjamin S. Bloom, and Robert Hess. 1965. *Compensatory Education for Cultural Deprivation.* Chicago: University of Chicago Press.

Davis, Allison, and John Dollard. 1940. *Children of Bondage: The Personality Development of Negro Youth in the Urban South.* Washington, D.C.: American Council on Education.

Davis, Allison, Kenneth Eells, and Robert Havighurst. 1953. *Intelligence and Cultural Differences: A Study of Cultural Learning and Problem-Solving.* Chicago: University of Chicago Press.

Davis, Allison, Burleigh B. Gardner, and Mary R. Gardner. 1941. *Deep South: A Social Anthropological Study of Caste and Class.* Chicago: University of Chicago Press.

Davis, Allison, and Robert Havighurst. 1943. "Child Socialization and the School." *Review of Educational Research* 13 (1): 29–38.

———. 1947. *Father of the Man: How Your Child Gets His Personality.* Cambridge, Mass.: Riverside Press.

Davis, Allison, and W. Lloyd Warner. 1939. "A Comparative Study of American Caste." In *Race Relations and Race Problems.* Ed. Edgar T. Thompson. Durham: Duke University Press. 219–45.

Davis, John. 1992. Telephone interview with the author. May 12.

Davis-Lucas, Dorothy. 1993. Telephone interview with the author. July 17.

Drake, St. Clair. 1974. "In the Mirror of Black Scholarship: W. Allison Davis and *Deep South.*" In *Education and Black Struggle: Notes from the Colonized World.* Ed. Institute of the Black World. Harvard Educational Review Monograph no. 2. Cambridge, Mass.: Harvard Educational Review. 42–54.

Drake, St. Clair, and Horace R. Cayton. 1945. *Black Metropolis: A Study of Negro Life in a Northern City.* 2 vols. New York: Harcourt, Brace.

Du Bois, W. E. B. 1903. *The Souls of Black Folk.* Chicago: A. C. McClurg.

Frazier, E. Franklin. 1939. *The Negro Family in the United States.* Chicago: University of Chicago Press.

Hogben, Lancelot, ed. 1938. *Political Arithmetic: A Symposium of Population Studies.* London: G. Allen and Unwin.

Myrdal, Gunnar. 1944. *An American Dilemma: The Negro Problem and Modern Democracy.* 2 vols. New York: Harper and Brothers.

Sowell, Thomas. 1972. *Black Education: Myths and Tragedies.* New York: McKay Books.

Turner, Barbara P. 1972. "Profile: Allison Davis, the Man and His Research." In *Education at Chicago.* Ed. Barbara P. Turner. Chicago: University of Chicago Graduate School of Education. 22–24.

9

St. Clair Drake: Scholar and Activist

Willie L. Baber

I was present at St. Clair Drake's memorial, held on the campus of Stanford University, and heard Ewart Thomas eulogize him as a "preacher man." Thomas's comments remind me of Drake's writing style, research interests, attire, use of description and narration in classroom lectures, and worldview. This preacher man image also reminds me of William Goldsborough's comments about St. Clair Drake. The men crossed paths at Hampton Institute in the 1930s, although Drake may not have known the younger Goldsborough, who became a highly distinguished educator in Greensboro, North Carolina. All Hampton students received instruction in theology, but Drake was referred to as "the preacher" by fellow Hampton students, and he could be so recognized by his black suits, pious behavior, and unusually serious attitude. Goldsborough also informed me that Drake's academic interests at that time were tied to liberation theology and "the race question."

Ewart Thomas's eulogy of Drake thus seemed to be consistent with Goldsborough's memory of him in the 1930s and with my knowledge of him at Stanford University in the 1970s. I was aware of Drake's secular use of the Bible, but I learned at his memorial that his favorite verse in the Bible is found in Ecclesiastes: "Whatsoever thy hand is able to do, do it earnestly: for neither work, nor reason, nor wisdom, nor knowledge

St. Clair Drake. (Courtesy of Willie L. Baber)

shall be in hell, whither thou art hastening" (9:10). Drake took up this charge by living and working the philosophy of vindicationism.

Vindication and Religion

Vindicationist scholars study racist ideas and behavior. They correct distorted interpretations of the African or African-American past or they develop counter ideologies for coping with the present. They may decide to take direct action, often giving up an otherwise comfortable existence in the interest of destroying racist beliefs and behaviors. As a scholar St. Clair Drake was interested in understanding patterns of racial domination and resistance in the black experience; however, through much of his life he refused to identify with a scholar's objectivist role. As an activist he was interested in destroying racial caste and in liberating peoples of African descent anywhere in the world. Drake's "black perspective" also refers to an association of Africa and the Americas and an exploration of societies, particularly the patterns of resistance, adaptation, and coping in the lives of peoples of African descent. He compared these survival strategies to strategies of subordination and control, such as co-optation, through which Africans and their descendants were subordinated as social groups.

Vindication means to defend in thought but it mattered to Drake that vindicationists "act in the streets." In later years he argued that normal standards of academic scholarship dissipates racist belief and action into some higher level of intellectual reflection in which counteraction is preempted. Indeed, nonaction had become an academic standard, a precondition of academic scholarship. This standard of detachment encouraged African-American scholars and intellectuals to set aside the most critical aspect of the black experience—how to combat racist behavior and discriminatory practice—or forfeit their claims to academic roles.

Drake's *Black Folks Here and There* (1987, 1990) is a two-volume work on white racism and the black experience written in the vindicationist tradition, an often difficult viewpoint to perceive or to accept given the objectivist nature of scholarship and nonaction as an academic standard. Is there any way to better understand a vindicationist tradition without violating objectivity or nonaction as academic standards?

One way to appreciate vindicationist writings is to place them alongside systems of philosophical relativism, such as Karl Mannheim's sociology of knowledge. In Mannheim's system all knowledge is partial. Knowledge is embedded in cultural difference that, in turn, functions according to the lived experiences of humans. Partial perspectives, including the subjectivity of white racism, are not an obstacle in the pursuit of truth (one may view the objectivity and nonaction of academic standards in the same way); rather, all partial perspectives become necessary to know the entire truth (Drake 1987:1). An approximation of total knowledge is impossible if data derived from the experiences of any known group are unavailable. Or, as Drake commented many times, "some things can be known only by those who have experienced them" (1987:1).

Fundamentally, racism is a process that excludes knowledge based in the experiences of others by those who have the power to do so. This we must note at the outset, and take seriously, if we are to understand St. Clair Drake "the preacher man." Theology, as a counterpoint to science, held an important place in Drake's life. During the prime years of his life science was used as a powerful instrument of racist oppression. W. E. B. Du Bois and other black leaders held in common the belief that "science" did not provide a means by which to discredit racist thought and behavior in American society, although they believed that it should. During the decades following the turn of the twentieth century, scientific racism actually contributed to racist oppression. This condition affected Drake's intellectual interests. In the 1930s black intellectuals were searching for practical strategies that would uplift the masses and discredit racist belief and behavior. These objectives were considered incompatible with beliefs in scientific standards, such as objectivity and nonaction. Du Bois, for example, acknowledges his failure to discredit racist theories using the techniques of science.

This situation is reversible if "scientific" knowledge is viewed as incomplete or partial, according to Mannheimian philosophy. Then the total "truth" would require concomitant knowledge of theology (and the axioms of subjectivity and action), to which Drake was exposed as a child. A synthesis of science and theology is possible. A synthesis of academic study, and the experiences that one lives, is also possible.

Even though Christian beliefs may function as in-group coping strategies and as rationalizations of racism, theology in general provides an important source of resistance to racist thought and behavior and to pseudo-scientific claims of inferiority based on race. The earliest vindicationists, a mature Drake notes, were black theologians such as Edward Wilmot Blyden (Drake 1971). Born in the Danish West Indies, Blyden held beliefs shaped by the Dutch Reformed church and the racist conditions he experienced during a visit to the United States. At twenty-five Blyden published *A Vindication of the African Race* (1857) in which he examined the original Hebrew verses of chapter 9 of the Book of Genesis; versus 25, 26, and 27 were in common usage as proof that blacks were under a curse and their enslavement was preordained. Blyden rejected the curse of enslavement, but retained the coping strategies associated with preordination and liberation. Recruited by the American Colonization Society, Blyden settled in Liberia with the intention of organizing an independent nation, which he believed to be the future of black liberation.

Drake's interest in Blyden and in liberation theology is reflexive. His early exposure to theology was combined with vindicationist scholarship in his paper "Destroy the Hamitic Myth" (1959). According to the myth Negroid peoples of Africa were predominantly agricultural and biologically inferior to the more Caucasoid pastoralists who wandered over the continent "conquering and spreading their superior culture and genes" (1). None of this made sense linguistically (Greenberg 1955), but the truth was "buried in the specialist literature or comes only to the attention of savants" (Drake 1959:14). Drake understood the power of ideology, and he called for an active effort to end this racist myth.

In the tradition of Blyden and liberation theology, Drake was an activist. He lived the tensions of theory and practice. Even today we are often reminded that the detached or objective goals of "scholarship" contradict those of activism. But this is only *one dilemma* in a host of contradictions and tensions that vindicationists face. As Drake notes in reference to Blyden: "What seems to be logical contradictions in Blyden's thought may seem less contradictory if they are related to time and place, and the degree of his power or powerlessness at specific periods in his life to attain goals he had set for himself" (1971:64). Seen as another axiom of Mannheimian philosophy, logical contradictions may recur as individuals need to integrate different perspectives over the course of their lives. But in this endeavor vindicationist scholars never lose sight of their fight against racism. Racism is central to the explanatory whole of behavior and belief, and from it all other contradictions flow; this is a condition that is known, deeply, only by those who have experienced it.

Drake issued challenges to all students, particularly those of African descent. We were encouraged to not only mark boundaries but also to cross them and to engage in a similar reflexive process: to read across academic disciplines and up and down class divisions to discover vindicationists wherever they might be. In this sense there were no boundaries of any kind in Drake's pedagogy other than those required to prove a point. He understood too well the need for each student to cultivate his or her own vindicationist perspective, admonishing us to "take from me whatever you can use and ignore the rest" (personal communication, June 13, 1980).

Background and Training

St. Clair Drake was born in Suffolk, Virginia, on January 2, 1911, to Bessie Lee Bowles Drake and the Reverend John Gibbs St. Clair Drake. Bessie Lee was an African American from Virginia, and John was an African West Indian from Barbados. Christian theology was the center of family activity. World War I movements into northern cities by African Americans included the Reverend Mr. Drake's move to Pittsburgh, where his son, St. Clair Drake, received an elementary education. At the age of eleven St. Clair Drake spent a year with paternal relatives in Barbados, where he attended an integrated school and lived in a middle-class neighborhood while hearing family members bemoan the ghettoes created by both blacks and whites (Jordan n.d.:3). During his adolescence Drake lived at his mother's family home in Staunton, Virginia, and experienced life among the lower classes after his parents divorced.

Drake's father was a formally educated preacher in Baptist and later Methodist traditions, and his mother was a devoted churchwoman, active in local women's organizations. Drake's father was a "race man," an activist who eventually served as an international organizer for Marcus Garvey's Universal Negro Improvement Association. During the 1926 convention of the association, Drake's father presented proposals to establish Liberty University near Jamestown, Virginia, and later became head of an attempt to train future generations of black leaders for the liberation of African peoples. It was shortly after this convention that Drake enrolled in Hampton Institute in 1927, graduating with a B.S. degree in biology in 1931.

Reflecting upon his years at Hampton, Drake states that the term *anthropology* was "only another word to me" (1978:90). He notes that the anthropometric data gathered by Franz Boas and his students, to disprove the idea of "pure" races, would not have gone over well at Hampton: "I suspect that many of us would have resented the idea of the white man at Howard using his post to measure the students' heads, to check under their arms with a color top, and to ask questions about the skin color of their parents and grandparents, and to inquire how 'white' or 'Indian' the family traditions claimed they were" (1978:90). Drake's intellectual heroes did not include anthropologists. He read the NAACP's

Crisis and the Urban League's *Opportunity* and he was schooled in the writings of the Joint Committee on Recovery at Howard University: Ralph Bunche in political science, E. Franklin Frazier in sociology, Charles Thompson in education, Abram Harris in economics, and Robert Weaver in economics.

Drake's activist disposition was expressed early in a month-long strike in 1927 protesting white intellectual and administrative domination of Hampton Institute. The race question, in Drake's opinion, was the problem of discrimination and domination, and not the concept of race per se.

Two lines of development began in Drake's years at Hampton, and they affected him the remainder of his years. He became a close friend of Mbiyu Koinange, who became minister of external affairs of Kenya and the author of *The People of Kenya Speak for Themselves* (1955). Koinange's friendship inspired Drake to devote himself to the African component of the diaspora. The African dimension to Drake's thought developed after World War II; the prevailing belief in the 1930s and 1940s was that Africans required the type of uplift argued for in Blyden's vindicationist perspective. An immediate influence during the Hampton years came through Drake's association with Allison Davis, who won the respect of students during the 1927 student-led strike.

In a book chapter entitled "In the Mirror of Black Scholarship: W. Allison Davis and *Deep South*," Drake recalls his disappointment that "there was not a black head of a department at Hampton, nor was there a black full professor. Emphasis was heavily on Booker T. Washington's philosophy" (1974:43). Drake attached himself to two faculty members at Hampton: Thomas W. Turner, a biologist who had come to Hampton from Howard University, and Davis, who held a master's degree in English from Harvard University. Davis's article "The Negro Deserts His People" (1929) challenged African-American intellectuals to attack the color line within the black community and to actively work for change in the heartland of the South, rather than to search out mythological "utopias" in the North.

Davis's teachings influenced Drake's opinion on scholarship in at least three ways: first, one should make some contribution to general theoretical work in one's discipline; second, one should become an expert at an empirical level; and third, one should select a problem that would make a contribution to the advancement of the race. These reflections are closely associated with Davis's turn from English literature to anthropology. After leaving Hampton, Drake prepared himself for study in social anthropology through his correspondence with Davis, who strongly suggested that Drake should take up this field of study because through it he could address the race question. Even as a very young man, however, Drake believed black intellectuals had additional obligations. First, they had an important role in "setting the historical record straight," best illustrated at the time by Carter G. Woodson's Association for the Study of Negro Life and History, Negro History Week, the *Journal of Negro History*, and *Negro History Bulletin*. Second, black intellectuals must challenge the biological and racial determinists at all levels of ideology. Third, black intellectuals must work on behalf of liberation of the masses. After reading the anthropological works of A. A. Goldenweisser, Franz Boas, and Lewis Henry Morgan, among others, it was not entirely clear to Drake how anthropology would address these additional activist concerns or goals.

Drake finished Hampton Institute in 1931 and then spent a year at Pendle Hill, a Quaker experimental graduate center near Swarthmore, Pennsylvania. The Quaker experiment in race relations, in which Drake himself was "sort of Exhibit A" (1978:89), did not compare with Drake's knowledge of what was being done by socialists and communists. Drake and others at the center organized the unemployed and sharecroppers, black and white, and considered ways to abolish the economic depression and racial discrimination. Through his correspondence with Davis, who had enrolled at Harvard University to study with W. Lloyd Warner, Drake managed to find interest in a few anthropological concepts. He found those of social anthropology interesting in their application to class, caste, and race relations: "It [social anthropology] did not offer any formula for social change . . . but, as applied to race relations in the United States, it did deal with some important aspects of that subject, which it seemed to me both Quakers and Marxists, as well as other anthropologists and sociologists, were, for one reason or another, ignoring" (1978:93). Drake's knowledge that Davis had sacrificed a promising career in English literature to retool as an anthropologist in response to Locke's "New Negro Movement" moved Drake closer to Warner's and Davis's anthropological studies. Davis became increasingly self-conscious about what obligations he should have to the masses. As Davis's student Drake easily shared these concerns "as members of that tiny college-trained group that had emerged in the sixty-odd years that had elapsed since slavery was abolished" (1978:2). Davis cooled Drake's activists needs, as Drake himself notes, by stating to him: "You can't really smash the system if you don't understand how it works. The problem is to learn the dynamics of the system" (1974:47). With some ambivalence, Drake accepted Davis's invitation to join Warner, a white anthropologist, to work on the research project that led to *Deep South.*

Race, Racism, and Deep South

Racist ideologies peaked during the 1930s. "Race" was applied to nation-states, ethnic groups, tribes, and skin colors along with judgments of inborn superiority or inferiority based on cultural expression or tradition. Theories of biological determinism were combined with white ethnocentric evaluations of black peoples, which led to hierarchies of superiority depending upon one's perceived relationship to a group or those within it. Evaluations of different groups were made as if behavioral and emotional traits were solely linked by genetics when such traits actually crossed a wide range of physical types (Drake 1987:31). In reference to black Americans, these ideological systems of race strengthened the color line within American society in both caste and class distinctions.

A confounding of biology and culture is found in Darwin's works and those of other early naturalists and extended into the work of nineteenth-century unilineal evolutionists, which created a climate of biological purity and determinism in human behavior. While most contemporary evolutionists are careful to point out Darwin's errors in evolutionary biology, similar errors today imply that those who do not survive are by definition weak and expendable and appear to support important cornerstones of laissez-faire capitalism, which, in turn, help to justify economic competition, profits, and capital accumulation. The newly emergent field of Mendelian genetics did little to clarify the situation because it was distorted by protagonists who claimed that black physical traits were an outward sign of an inner cognitive deficit and an inherited intellectual inferiority, thereby confirming, in circular reasoning, the social conditions of black people.

Drake believed in the political necessity of formulating philosophical perspectives that would challenge and change the racist ideologies of the status quo in ways that would strengthen group formation within and across racial or caste barriers. Drake credited Boas with shifting the scholarly burden of proof to the biological determinists in the debate about black intellect and abilities. But Drake also believed in social praxis. He could appreciate Davis's attraction to anthropology as an example of vindication through choice of problem. Drake's interest in the Warner school of race and caste, applied to Natchez, Mississippi, was motivated by a higher level of vindication—his desire to destroy a racist social system.

Davis completed his anthropological studies with Bronislaw Malinowski and Lancelot T. Hogben in 1933 and began Ph.D. work at Harvard. Warner had already gone to Harvard and had decided to study an American town to see if social class was the main organizing principle in American life. Later, Warner decided to try a comparative study in the South to test whether social class was linked to racial caste. This work led to *Deep South* (1941), in which Drake, Burleigh B. Gardner, and Mary R. Gardner participated.

The Gardners, a husband-and-wife team, worked among the whites in Natchez, Mississippi. Davis and his wife Elizabeth worked in the African-American section of town, but among the upper class. After working within this group the Davises had difficulty making contacts within the lower classes. Davis called upon his former student, Drake, to do participant-observation among the lowest classes. Drake responded: "I felt that what the Davis team was doing had historic import, so I went South" (1978:93).

The hypothesis guiding the analysis was that the social system of the South consisted of two racial castes within an overall class system divided by physical features, color, and descent. "What made the system interesting theoretically, was that within each racial caste there were social classes" (Drake 1974:47). This model of social structure raised the question of whether social interaction across class and caste lines occurred.

Drake decided to take on the work for *Deep South* because he was intrigued by the hypothesis, because he was satisfied with his role in it, and because at the time he could not totally commit himself to a communist or a socialist agenda. Although he was impressed by the communists' analysis of political economy and by their assertion that racism was organically linked to the development of capitalism, he found the class analysis made by communists and socialists too reductionist and was unsure about the long-term reliability of alliances between whites and blacks. In addition, Drake found that cooperation, conflict, accommodation, and assimilation as developmental concepts did not fit the realities of the North American black experience or fully explain lynching and Jim Crow.

The caste-class analysis of race relations promised to break down the habit of viewing black-white relations in terms of fixed categories of psychology or genetics. A caste and class analysis stressed the role of social structure, not values, as the independent variable. It asked new questions:

"How can a white person at point X in the caste-class structure be expected to act toward a person at point Y? How are individuals socialized to act toward cues of color and caste? If we changed the social structure of relations will attitudes begin to change 'on their own?' How can we change them?" (Drake 1980:22–23). Although *Deep South* was the best book on race relations in the South up to that time, *Caste and Class in a Southern Town* by John Dollard (1937) received much more attention.

After working two years on *Deep South*, Drake followed Warner and Davis from Harvard to the University of Chicago in 1937. Drake received a Rosenwald Fund Fellowship to continue his studies but was discouraged from anthropology by other graduate students:

> I chose the field, anyhow, partly out of stubborn defiance; partly because I liked it and the subfield of physical anthropology meant that my major in biology wouldn't be wasted; partly because it gave me a chance to specialize in African studies; but mainly because I was sure that Allison Davis was going to organize the first department of social anthropology in the country—at a black school, Dillard—and that an exciting Caribbean studies program he had already written was going to be part of it. (1978:95)

Here Drake considers practical issues: Where can any African American get a post teaching anthropology, and what else can you do with a degree in anthropology? Why choose to become a professional anthropologist? For Drake and Allison Davis the answer lay in their belief that anthropology could have practical value, explanatory value, and emancipatory potential in addressing the race question: "We believed the discipline had relevance to the liberation of black people from the devastating consequences of over four centuries of White racism" (Drake 1978:86).

The University of Chicago and Black Metropolis

Drake's years as a graduate student at the University of Chicago were interrupted by World War II, during which he served two years in the U.S. Maritime Service. Elizabeth Dewey Johns, a graduate student in sociology, introduced Drake to Mannheim's *Ideology and Utopia: An Introduction to the Sociology of Knowledge* (1936) because she had worked with Louis Wirth when he and Edward Shills edited it and translated it into English. Mannheim's model of cultural and behavioral relativism soon became central to Drake's thought and writings.

At Chicago Drake also met Horace Cayton, an African-American graduate student in sociology who shared his interests and held compatible political views. By the end of 1941 Drake and Cayton had compiled an impressive databank on the black community in Chicago. The work was initiated by the Works Project Administration but, under Cayton's direction, the pair added their own participant-observations and data from other graduate students, including research on the African-American lower classes overseen by Drake. These data were the basis for the now classic *Black Metropolis* (Drake and Cayton 1945). This two-volume work made use of all the prevailing sociological theories: Parkian sociology and the race relations cycle, British structural functionalism as developed by Radcliffe-Brown, the Warnerian caste-class model of race relations, Marxism, and black nationalist thought. The last of these orientations, often avoided by white scholars, was needed in a study of African-American life in Chicago in the late 1930s.

W. Lloyd Warner, a powerful name in anthropology, provided a methodological note at the end of the work. Although he compares it to *Deep South,* according to Glenn Jordan he "proceeds to seriously distort the empirical findings presented in *Black Metropolis*" (1982:8). Warner concluded that *Black Metropolis* illustrates great improvement in the status of black people, but a status system of caste best fit the data, not Cayton and Drake's argument for a more fluid casteless society. Jordan believes that Warner's distortion was deliberate, but accepted by Cayton and Drake as the cost of Warner's endorsement. Jordan, however, has set the record straight by enumerating the many significant contributions of *Black Metropolis:*

1. an analysis of the historical development of Black Chicago, and placed it within a larger social whole of American society;
2. a comparative analysis of the assimilation of white, non-Anglo ethnics into the mainstream of Chicago's economic and social life versus that of Afro-Americans;
3. a comparison of the form and content of the institutional life of Black Metropolis versus that of Chicago as a whole;
4. a comparative analysis of patterns of behavior and attributes among and within what Drake and Cayton refer to as the various socioeconomic classes of Black Chicago;
5. an implicit comparison of these classes with the "white middle-class";
6. a comparison of the ideology of freedom and democracy with the actual facts of Black life in Chicago (and elsewhere in the United States);

7. a comparison of Black-white race relations in the Deep South (i. e., as presented in Allison Davis, Burleigh Gardner and Mary Gardner, *Deep South: A Social Anthropological Study of Caste and Class*) with patterns of Black-white race relations in Chicago, a northern, industrial metropolis. (1982:7)

Faye V. Harrison (1988) was the first to bring critical appraisal of *Black Metropolis* as a classic work in the field of urban anthropology and notes its relative lack of visibility as a process of peripheralization of African-American scholars from the center of anthropological discourse and intellectual discourse in general. This pattern of peripheralization is obviously apparent in the careers of such preeminent intellectuals as W. E. B. Du Bois (Harrison and Nonini 1992), Allison Davis (Drake 1974), and Oliver C. Cox. Interestingly, each was well grounded in the philosophical positions expressed in Davis's "The Negro Deserts His People." And all three, in addition to Drake, found it necessary to associate patterns of exploitation in the lives of black people with racial stratification and capitalism as a world system. Why does this peripheralization process exist? Harrison responds: "it is important to understand that Du Bois, Davis, Drake and Cox struggled to produce conceptual and theoretical tools for building a free and just world. Unlike most of their counterparts in the [intellectual] center, they are part of an activist tradition" (1988:114). Then, one needs to assume a hegemonic center in which racism is protected and affirmed, for political reasons somewhat independent of racism.

For example, Davis demonstrated in *Deep South* that one ought to look at two systems of social relations, the economic (class) and the social (caste), and then ask, How do these interrelate? Drake has noted that data analysis linked to this question would move anyone theoretically closer to Marxist tenets: "Davis didn't consider himself a Marxist, but this was a Marxist approach" (1974:52). With its Marxist tenets, *Deep South* revealed the economic underpinnings of southern race relations in ways that no other work did at the time. This type of analysis is lacking in John Dollard's *Caste and Class in a Southern Town* (1937) and in Hortense Powdermaker's *After Freedom: A Cultural Study in the Deep South* (1939). Despite this lack, Harrison (1988:115) notes that Dollard's and Powdermaker's works not only received critical acclaim but also occupied the center of intellectual discourse at the time. The combination of race with economics may explain, post facto, Warner's lukewarm endorsement, and distortion, of *Black Metropolis*. How could Warner collaborate with African-American intellectuals using Marxism, in a racist social order, without discrediting himself? Drake defined this peripheralization process as institutional racism, which intensifies in response to a vindicationist perspective but functions normally in its absence.

The Africa Years

While completing his doctorate Drake in 1946 joined the faculty of Roosevelt University, an experimental institution founded with contributions from the Rosenwald Fund and the Marshall Field Foundation in opposition to anti-Semitism and white supremacy in education and explicitly dedicated to an active fight against racial discrimination and segregation. Post–World War II optimism about changing the attitudes and behavior of Americans found its way into the curriculum: "In one segment of our introductory sociology and anthropology courses at Roosevelt College between 1946 and 1953 we tried to deal with race thoroughly and frankly" (Drake 1978:87). With confidence, Drake believed that the battle against Arthur de Gobineau, Neville Chamberlain, Lothrop Stoddard, and cliques of reactionary biologists had been won. Black and white interactions in labor unions during the thirties and in the armed forces during the war reinforced optimism.

To complete his doctorate, Drake conducted fieldwork in Cardiff, Wales, in 1947–48. In "Value Systems, Social Structure, and Race Relations in the British Isles" Drake addresses the central problems of structural functionalism and combines insights from Mannheim's sociology of knowledge. This study of race relations in "Tiger Bay," where Asian and African colonials and their children resided permanently, integrates micro and macro levels of analysis and synchronic and diachronic data.

Drake's interest in Africa was renewed during his fieldwork in Britain, where he met Kwame Nkrumah, George Padmore, Mbiyu Koinange, and Somali nationalists who encouraged his participation in the pan-African cause: "With events moving so fast in Kenya and Ghana, and given my relations with Padmore, Bond, Koinange, and other Pan-Africanists, I felt a strong urge to be on the scene where the 'revolution' created at the Fifth Pan African Congress in 1945 was underway" (letter to Brokensha, Nov. 16, 1985, qtd. in Brokensha 1985:2).

Finally on the scene in 1954, first in Liberia and then in Ghana, Drake conducted several studies with his wife and colleague, Elizabeth Dewey Johns Drake. Drake's experience in Liberia led to "Who Will Liberate Liberia?" This, like so many of Drake's manuscripts, was considered too obviously personal to publish. While in Liberia, Drake was overjoyed to receive a letter indicating that he had received a Ford Foundation grant to study mass media in west Africa and Ghana (then known as the Gold Coast) for a year.

From 1958 to 1961 Drake served as head of the department of sociology at the University of Ghana. While in Ghana he analyzed the impact of resettlement plans for the village of Tema. This urban-based work was a major component of Nkrumah's development plans for the country. The building of a modern port at Tema was to supplement the existing facilities at Takoradi and to serve the Volta (Akosombo) Dam. In this work, according to David Brokensha, he combines the personal with the political: "Drake analyzes, in an understanding but critical manner, the government actions, which were generally sympathetic to the villagers (e.g., in respect of moving shrines) but which inevitably caused pain and suffering, especially to the older people who had to leave their homes" (1985:13).

Another example of Drake's research during this period is his study on nudity in northern Ghana. In the haste to build a modern nation, banning nudity became a political issue. Drake persuaded the government to postpone legislation enforcing the wearing of clothing until after the department of sociology had conducted a survey of the problem. The results of the research caused the government to abandon the proposed law and work out a planned program of adult education and a gradual achievement of goals (Brokensha 1985:12)

Drake's contacts in Ghana soon led him into increasingly important discussions. At the request of George Padmore, Nkrumah's advisor, Drake presented an important paper on racism at the All African People's Conference held at Accra in December 1958. Padmore also allowed Drake to participate in planning meetings for the conference and to record much of the proceedings. Padmore's friendship allowed Drake to acquire unrivaled knowledge of Ghana's political leaders. Drake, however, refused to place in print, or to analyze, any of this information out of his respect for Nkrumah and the pan-African cause, a clear indication that activism demands high standards of integrity: "I was having qualms about publishing participant-observation material gathered through Pan-African contacts, through interaction with friends and associates in Ghanaian internal politics. I've discarded a number of trial attempts at a book on 'The Nkrumah Years in Ghana,' and . . . this same kind of reluctance inhibited me from publishing my doctoral dissertation" (Drake 1978:99). The obligations of advancing the race far outweighed any desire for personal gain.

He further contributed by training a group of fifty American students who planned to work in Ghana for the Peace Corps. Drake participated in similar training programs, sometimes by visiting Ghana, in 1962 and 1964. Brokensha (1985:15) cites a letter from one of these students written twenty-four years after his Peace Corps experience:

> When I met Drake at Berkeley it was his anecdotal understanding of Ghana and his ineffable charm that impressed me[. . . .] He was a man of tremendous enthusiasm for the Ghanaian experiment; and he knew everyone of importance. He was a most inspirational teacher, enthusiastic about independence but not blinded, by euphoria, to political problems. I remember him most personally; a gentle man of considerable wisdom and much compassion, and he communicated this to a group of young Americans, most of whom were ignorant of the social and political forces which shaped his intellectual life. (letter from Thomas Livingston, October 16, 1985)

The Stanford Years

I crossed Drake's path a few years before his retirement from Stanford University, and I came to know a gentle, wise, and gracious man. But I also became aware of Drake's activist philosophy. In 1975 Stanford's commencement speaker described African-American family patterns based on work published in the 1960s. In protest, my father-in-law and Drake led a mass departure of families very different from those depicted in the speech.

Drake's involvement in direct action had begun as early as 1927, when he participated in the student-led Hampton strike. While conducting research for *Deep South* he organized sharecroppers in Natchez, Mississippi. Drake was slow in completing his dissertation because he was spending time with CORE, the NAACP, the National Negro Congress, and the Afro-World Fellowship, an organization based in Chicago helping to run an underground railroad for Kikuyu students trying to secure a college education (Drake 1978:98). In the 1950s Drake found himself in a fight with the University of Chicago over the means by which an orderly integrated neighborhood, with high community standards, was to be created, since those at the university wanted to "save the university upon which the ghetto seemed to be encroaching" (Bond 1988:777). When Drake returned from Ghana in 1961 he became involved with SNCC and in 1966 participated in the Meredith March, where Stokely Carmichael called for "black power." He was with Martin Luther King

Jr. during the assault of a mob in Gage Park in Chicago. To anthropology, then, Drake brought not just scholarship but action and the possibility of change.

When I met Drake I thought about the discipline of anthropology in the same way that Drake described it in his associations with Allison Davis: Racism has something to do with cultural differences and a good deal of anthropology depends upon both race and culture. But in my search for identity in the 1960s it did not occur to me that history, over millennia, shapes modern thinking as deeply as Drake's pedagogy often claimed. For example, it embarrasses me to admit that I initially understood Drake's interest in Egyptology as a product of "his time" rather than as part of an African diaspora discourse that borrows from Afrocentric and Eurocentric constructions and appropriations of ancient Egyptian culture, with racism and prejudice lurking at its core. I had learned, at a relatively young age, to appreciate ancient Egypt as an advanced African civilization and wondered why it was necessary to argue what was clearly known. I seriously believed then that everyone knew the facts, so racist beliefs involved a kind of mental game. It was, therefore, much easier to relate to Drake's activist disposition and his rich command of African-American intellectual thought.

Drake's appointment at Stanford University in 1969 included continuing to develop a program in African and Afro-American studies. This appointment entailed a balancing act better appreciated after I took a similar appointment at Purdue University as a young assistant professor. Drake faced several difficulties in his appointment at Stanford: polarization of black intellectual thought between extremes of black nationalism and pan-African Marxism; black students' demand for an autonomous department; and an unanticipated reversal of role expectations. According to Drake, a "*White* student had stalked out of the very first session of Comparative Urbanism stating that he was not going to waste his time on all that 'theory crap' while the cities were being polluted and rats were biting babies in the ghetto" (1978:101). Drake's reply was that nonutilitarian scholarly interests may make positive contributions in practical matters, and that such interests are not necessarily incompatible with activist goals.

My interests in anthropology moved me closer to Drake's knowledge of the Caribbean and Marxist theory. I studied Marxist theory under the direction of Bridget O'Laughlin, which undoubtedly pulled me along a narrower corridor of black intellectuals compared to the breadth of work contained in, and demanded by, Drake's vindicationist orientation.

Moreover, there was the constant pull of anthropological discourse at Stanford University that did not easily incorporate Drake's vindicationist views. Needless to say, my comprehension of Drake's intellectual breadth was limited at this time.

Drake's concept of Black Diaspora is one example of this breadth. Black Diaspora is global rather than regional and somewhat analogous to the modern world capitalist system but should not be confused with pan-Africanism. The Black Diaspora theory includes all of the socioeconomic forces that world economy theorists debate but adds the activist politics of liberation. This addition positions Drake's work as part of a trend to reinterpret history in view of subaltern experiences. The Black Diaspora involves the concept of "homeland" (a political statement) and the various situations outside of it into which individuals have migrated and where persisting "Diaspora communities" survive despite profound changes in the culture and physique of the people. Sub-Saharan Africa, the heart of the slave trade, is viewed as the homeland for many people of African descent today because our recent history marks the beginning of *racial slavery,* as compared to earlier forms of color prejudice. The Black Diaspora, however, is global when placed within a sufficient timeframe and would thus encompass Egypt and north Africa, the Middle East, India and China, Latin America, North America, the Caribbean, northern Europe, and Mediterranean Europe. Drake later referred to the Black Diaspora as a paradigm for research because it can counter hegemonic notions. The Black Diaspora paradigm is useful too in addressing institutional racism in a practical way because it can provide a vehicle for support of African-American scholars.

Drake elaborated on his concept of the Black Diaspora in the two-volume chronicle *Black Folk Here and There,* whose title is a variation on W. E. B. Du Bois's *Black Folk Then and Now: An Essay in the History and Sociology of the Negro Race,* published in 1939. In it Drake compares Africa prior to the slave raids with Africa after the introduction of European control that culminated in white racism. Although it was published long after he retired from Stanford, the work offers a rethinking of many issues Drake encountered at Stanford. One professor on the campus dismissed the claim that prejudice against those with dark skins did not exist in Greco-Roman antiquity: "This Colleague insisted with sincere conviction that it was 'natural' for all light-skinned peoples to be prejudiced against dark-skinned peoples" (Drake 1987:xx). A Nobel Prize winner in physics published articles in which he argued that the lower average IQ scores of blacks could be explained only by the greater causes of heredity. Such claims encouraged Drake to seriously address white racism, prejudice, and attitudes toward blackness through time.

In volume 1 Drake examines the interactions between ancient peoples of Egypt and Ethiopia as one historical case upon which to examine several prevailing theories about what happens when black people and white people interact. Drake concludes that over several millennia blackness was not evaluated negatively in the Nile Valley in any of the symbolic domains he identifies. Light skin color became salient only after Greeks and Romans settled in the area. From an examination of a Hebrew civilization in Palestine Drake concludes that anti-black prejudice and skin color consciousness did not develop in the Palestinian Judaic tradition, which also held a favorable attitude toward Ethiopians. After the defeats of Judah and Israel by the Assyrians and Babylonians a variation of Hebrew civilization that included negative attitudes toward black people developed among captives in the Mesopotamian diaspora. Pre-Christian Mediterranean civilizations in Greece accorded high status to Ethiopians and other people with dark skins, but with the establishment of Christianity as a powerful religion came a mixture of Greco-Roman and Judaic tradition. The early founders of Christianity had assimilated the Persian values of a Manichean cosmic struggle between light and darkness. This color symbolism may then have been transferred to social relations and to persons, suggesting that conversion of Ethiopians meant "washing them white." While color prejudice was clearly present during early Christianity, so was the insistence that black people could be "saved."

By the seventh century A.D. Islam had become the most important sociopolitical force throughout the Middle East, the African and European Mediterranean coasts, Spain, and Portugal. Drake concludes that prejudice against black people in the Middle East and Islamic world had its roots in slavery, not in color symbolism, since both positive and negative values were associated with people who had features considered Negroid. Furthermore, while there was certainly color prejudice in Muslim lands, it was "nowhere reinforced by a system of racial slavery such as the one that would emerge in the New World" (1990:184). The sixteenth century served as a turning point, and a defining moment, in black-white relations. As Drake argues, the transatlantic slave trade coincided with the restoration of old color prejudices, the assignment of them to an emerging stereotype of "Negro," and the systematic distortions of history, black and white, that vindicationists seek to correct.

Conclusion

St. Clair Drake's life can be seen as an expression of vindication that extends back to the 1930s and forward to scholars and students of the current generation. Drake's life work addressed the study of race and history, the integration of Mannheimian relativism, and the vindication of black peoples. Mannheim's philosophy is helpful in addressing the intellectual dilemma of conflict or confrontation, as an element of social change, compared to the "objectivity" of academic discourse. Both are parts of some greater truth, and Drake chose confrontation and conflict as a necessary aspect of his role in a larger system.

Despite this valuable work, despite his many teaching posts—including those at Dillard University, the University of Chicago, Boston University, Columbia University, the University of Liberia, the University of Ghana, and Stanford University—and despite his many honors, Drake was reluctant to situate himself as a significant figure in anthropology. When Glenn Jordan and Faye Harrison organized a session in his honor at the annual meeting of the American Anthropological Association in 1985, Drake was equally reluctant to agree to participate. Jordan and Harrison wanted some way to acknowledge his career and his numerous awards, among them the Du Bois–Johnson–Frazier Award from the American Sociological Association (1973); honorary doctorates from Roosevelt University (1976) and the University of Maryland at Baltimore (1985); Honorary Fellow of the Royal Anthropological Institute of Great Britain and Ireland (1986); senior scholar at the W. E. B. Du Bois Institute of Harvard University (1987); the Association of Black Anthropologists' Distinguished Achievement Award for Extraordinary Scholarship and Activism (1989); and the Society for Applied Anthropology's Bronislaw Malinowski Award (1990).

Drake's resistance to status within academic discourse is rooted in the life he lived, in his knowledge of academic politics, in the practical effects of institutional racism, and in the important need to force the black experience into its appropriate role in formulating the total truth. Drake died June 14, 1990. He managed to live one extraordinarily consistent life, as an activist and a scholar. His tribute to other black pioneers is more than fitting for St. Clair Drake: "Martin and Malcolm, W.E.B. Du Bois and Whitney Young are dead, as are Charles S. Johnson, Carter G. Woodson, and E. Franklin Frazier. For them, as well as for us who survive, I'd like to dedicate these lines.

IN US SOME SURGING ELEMENTAL POWER—
WE FOCUS FREEDOM'S RAYS INTO A BEAM
ILLUMINATE THE DESTINED HOUR
AND JUSTIFY THE DREAMER'S DREAM.
(1974:54)

References Cited

Blyden, Edward Wilmot. 1857. *A Vindication of the African Race.* Monrovia: G. Killian.

Bond, George C. 1988. "A Social Portrait of John Gibbs St. Clair Drake: An American Anthropologist." *American Ethnologist* 15 (4): 762–81.

Brokensha, David. 1985. "St. Clair Drake: The African Years, 1954–1966." Paper presented at the Association of Black Anthropologist's special session in honor of St. Clair Drake at the annual meeting of the American Anthropological Association. Washington, D.C. Dec. 6.

Davis, Allison. 1929. "The Negro Deserts His People." *Plain Talk* 5:49–54.

Davis, Allison, Burleigh B. Gardner, and Mary R. Gardner. 1941. *Deep South: A Social Anthropological Study of Caste and Class.* Chicago: University of Chicago Press.

Dollard, John. 1937. *Caste and Class in a Southern Town.* New Haven: Yale University Press.

Drake, St. Clair. 1954. "Value Systems, Social Structure, and Race Relations in the British Isles." Ph.D. diss., University of Chicago.

———. 1959. "Destroy the Hamitic Myth." *Presence Africaine.* Special issue entitled "The Unity of Negro African Cultures." 24–25:215–30.

———. 1971. *The Redemption of Africa and Black Religion.* Chicago: Third World Press.

———. 1974. "In the Mirror of Black Scholarship: W. Allison Davis and *Deep South.*" In *Education and Black Struggle: Notes from the Colonized World.* Ed. Institute of the Black World. Harvard Educational Review Monograph no. 2. Cambridge, Mass.: Harvard Educational Review. 42–54.

———. 1978. "Reflections on Anthropology and the Black Experience." *Anthropology and Education Quarterly* 9 (2): 85–109.

———. 1980. "Anthropology and the Black Experience." *Black Scholar* 11 (7): 2–31.

———. 1987. *Black Folk Here and There: An Essay in History and Anthropology.* Vol. 1. Los Angeles: Center for Afro-American Studies, University of California at Los Angeles.

———. 1990. *Black Folk Here and There: An Essay in History and Anthropology.* Vol. 2. Los Angeles: Center for Afro-American Studies, University of California at Los Angeles.

———. n.d. "Who Will Liberate Liberia?" Ms. Author's possession.

Drake, St. Clair, and Horace Cayton. 1945. *Black Metropolis: A Study of Negro Life in a Northern City.* 2 vols. New York: Harcourt, Brace.

Greenberg, Joseph. 1955. *Studies in African Linguistic Classification.* New Haven, Conn.: Compass.

Harrison, Faye V. 1988. "Introduction: An African Diaspora Perspective for Urban Anthropology." *Urban Anthropology and Studies of Cultural Systems and World Economic Development* 17 (2–3): 111–41.

Harrison, Faye V., and Donald Nonini. 1992. "Introduction: W. E. B. Du Bois and Anthropology." *Critique of Anthropology* 12 (3): 229–37.

Jordan, Glenn H. 1982. "Reading St. Clair Drake: A Methodological Essay with a Focus on *Black Metropolis.*" Urbana: Afro Scholar Working Papers, Afro-American Studies and Research Program, University of Illinois.

———. n.d. "St. Clair Drake: The Committed Intellectual." Ms. Author's possession.

Koinange, Mbiyu. 1955. *The People of Kenya Speak for Themselves.* Detroit: Kenya Publication Fund.

Mannheim, Karl. 1936. *Ideology and Utopia: An Introduction to the Sociology of Knowledge.* Ed. and trans. Louis Wirth and Edward Shils. New York: Harcourt, Brace.

Powdermaker, Hortense. 1939. *After Freedom: A Cultural Study in the Deep South.* New York: Viking Press.

10

Arthur Huff Fauset, Campaigner for Social Justice: A Symphony of Diversity

Carole H. Carpenter

Nature, nurture, history, and character combined forces to direct Arthur Huff Fauset along a difficult course. Born between two races in a time of segregation, he never accepted any of the racial identities imposed by society. Raised in an integrated home, Fauset imbibed a forceful humanism that served to impress upon him the manifold injustices and suffering in the world. He not only triumphed over them in his own life but also struggled against them on behalf of others. Due to his character and abilities, the primary tools in this struggle were intellectual, and his most comfortable arena, education. His was an ecumenical spirit as well as mind; his personal crusade was not fueled by a single ideology or centered around any religion despite strong religious connections within his family. Rather, he followed many paths opened by ideas, people, and circumstances and valued each for what it gave him at the time and what he could do along its course. He seemed, therefore, to be always on the edge (often the cutting edge) of groups, movements, and activities but central to none and wedded to no single one.

At one time or another, Fauset became an accomplished educator, political activist, community leader, anthropologist, folklorist, journalist, and creative writer. He rubbed shoulders and aligned himself with many who today are recognized as significant to various fields: Alain Locke, Adam Clayton Powell, A. Philip Randolph, Paul Robeson, Ralph

Arthur Huff Fauset. (Courtesy of Carole H. Carpenter)

J. Bunche, and others in the civil rights movement; Frank G. Speck and A. Irving Hallowell in anthropology; Elsie Clews Parsons and Zora Neale Hurston in folklore; and a great many published authors, including Hurston and his own half-sister, Jessie Fauset. Of all possible descriptions for himself, he chose "campaigner for social justice" (*Who's Who* 1950), but his campaign went beyond civil rights or any other movement. Rather, he fit the mold of a Renaissance humanist or a nineteenth-century reformer more than that of a social activist of this century.

Fauset can justly be celebrated within anthropology and folklore as a pioneer of black American cultural studies; he might just as readily be claimed by the civil rights movement, by the black community or by education in Philadelphia, or even by the world of letters. To appreciate fully Arthur Huff Fauset involves an understanding of his diversity, derived in no small measure from his marginality, conditioned by chance and by choice. He was to the end as he was born—a mélange, between worlds, uniquely himself. He struggled all his life to achieve unity and order among the diverse aspects of his existence, much as a composer of a symphony strives for a harmonious integration of distinct musical elements. As in music, so in life—the symphony of Arthur Fauset is greater than the sum of the parts, though an appreciation calls for close attention to exposition and development of themes and elements in those parts in progressing toward an ordered whole.[1]

Reconstructing the Composition

My first encounter with Fauset took place in Manhattan one bleak February day in 1970. The occasion remains sharply etched in my memory as the high point of my doctoral research, a study of Canadian folklore scholarship comparable to Richard Dorson's work *British Folklorists* (1969). I was attempting to interview all living persons who had done folklore research in Canada or on Canadian material, to uncover as many archival and collegial sources for deceased scholars as possible, and to produce a rationale for the scholarship and its influence as precursor to the current status of Canadian folklore work and its position in Canadian culture.

One name on my lengthy list was Arthur Huff Fauset, known to me then as the author of a book and an article on Nova Scotia folklore that dealt with traditions of the blacks and so-called half-breeds. Who was this person? What was his connection to Canada? Could he possibly still be alive? Standard searches produced only bibliographic references, so

I sought the assistance of a fellow graduate student at the University of Pennsylvania who was a black activist with good connections in the Philadelphia community from which Fauset came. Some time later, much to my surprise, a cryptic note arrived: "He's alive!" followed by an address in New York City (personal communication with Kathryn Morgan, fall 1969). I immediately wrote to Fauset and promptly received a cordial response expressing interest in our meeting. We agreed on a date for an interview that, with a subsequent one, I tape-recorded, providing the only extended commentary by Fauset on his life and work.

Fauset was a genteel, soft-spoken man of slight build and medium height. He welcomed me into his small apartment crammed with books, writing material, a typewriter table—the domain of a man of letters who, as I was quickly and forcefully informed, saw himself not as a scholar but as a person with a sociopolitical mission. Our meeting was most congenial—he was as delighted to be discovered by the academy as I was to find him, and he clearly wanted to influence the telling of his story. He spoke easily yet ardently and with straightforward clarity. His was a highly cultivated speech, indicative of his education and experience in expressing himself, and he was a most willing informant who took full advantage of this opportunity to explicate his life and work.

It was a strange encounter in some respects—between a young, Anglo-Saxon female from western Canada and an elderly (though he did not look it) man of color from the urban heartland of America. Yet it was deeply meaningful for both of us. Perhaps because as a foreigner I had no direct involvement with the civil rights movement, he could explain his own connection more easily; perhaps because I too came from a political family and had long been a student activist with a passion for causes, we developed a mutual appreciation. I was to meet with Fauset only once again, in June of the same year. At that time I sought to obtain some precise details missing from his life's story—especially about his wife and family—since I was contracted to write a biographical sketch for the reprinting of his *Black Gods of the Metropolis* by the University of Pennsylvania Press (127–28). But this immensely private individual was determined in his self-preservation, maintaining secrets through silence and by avoiding specifics, particularly dates, to camouflage his true years, for he was then considerably beyond retirement age, yet still teaching. The short biography, shaped according to his wishes, met with his approval prior to publication.

The real nature of this man is to be read as much from what was not told as from what he chose to tell. His life's narrative that follows is, with some additional facts and supplementary information, his own story as reconstructed by him in retrospect. The explanations and interpretations are essentially my own, though in keeping with my intention Fauset's voice resonates throughout.

First Movement: Exposition and Development of Themes

Arthur Huff Fauset was born in 1899 in Flemington, New Jersey, the second of three children from the union of Redmon Fauset and Bella Huff Fauset. It was the second marriage for both. Their resultant family included offspring of all three marriages, some of whom were adults by the time of Arthur's birth given that his father was much older than his mother.

Redmon Fauset (1837–1903) was a native Philadelphian, from one of the very old black families dating back some two hundred years in the city. He was a minister in the African Methodist Episcopal church and, as a radical within that radical movement, he did not get ahead in the church and never acquired a charge in a big city, but rather drew various small postings (such as near the Delaware Water Gap, where he met Bella, and Flemington, at the time Arthur was born). His son commented that Redmon Fauset was "noted for his forthright comment which frequently got him into difficulty,"[2] and he was widely recognized as being "very insistent in those things he believed; for years he was remembered for this insistence; on the other hand he paid a price for his strong beliefs—that is, he often made enemies in high places, both white and black; and for this he often had to be satisfied to occupy low places in the generally accepted hierarchy" (qtd. in Sylvander 1981:26).

The elder Fauset was nonetheless a cultural leader of black Philadelphia and therefore, owing to the prominence of the Philadelphia community, of black America during the late nineteenth century. He belonged to the established middle class, which valued education as a means of advancement and pursued the ideals of self-education then popular and being promoted in North America by Andrew Carnegie (of nearby Pittsburgh), among others. Redmon Fauset had no advanced education himself, but he was widely read and eagerly sought opportunities to discuss ideas as well as politics and religion. He believed in writing, for its own sake as discipline, as evidence of cultivation, and as a powerful means of expression and influence. So he wrote to improve himself and to shape others; his essays in particular contributed to his reputation for outspoken beliefs. Throughout his life, Redmon Fauset embraced the battle against the racial biases that fettered not just blacks but all his nation's people and strove for an integrated America without prejudice.

A powerful presence, Redmon Fauset strongly affected his children through his personality, ideas, and actions. Several of his offspring went to college (one, Jessie, to Cornell from where she graduated Phi Beta Kappa);[3] two became writers (the better known being Jessie); most were active in one way or another in the civil rights movement. Evidently part of the so-called talented tenth of Blacks, the family followed the philosophical orientation of W. E. B. Du Bois in accepting the social responsibility of becoming leaders amongst their people.

Redmon Fauset died during Arthur's fourth year, and the younger Fauset truly did not know his father in a conscious sense. Yet his influence persisted, for as Arthur was growing up people who knew his father frequently would liken the son to him and so encourage what Arthur came to see as "something within [his father's] own makeup that came to [him] also" (tape 2).

Redmon Fauset's ideals guided his family after his death because his widow shared a profound personal commitment to them. Bella Huff Fauset was white, born into a Jewish family, and raised primarily in Newark, New Jersey, where she met and married her first husband (Huff), also a black man. A Christian convert and an avowed integrationist, she "tolerated none of this business of slighting people because of color, or anything of that kind" (tape 2). It was her Jewish heritage that her son credited for her attitude toward education: "there was nothing that she prized more than education. . . . She spurred all of us children to go to school" (tape 2). Her brief five-year marriage to Redmon Fauset clearly brought her little financial security, for the family was quite poor, having to live mainly off meager church offerings. Yet, the union allowed her to bring into existence in the family's daily life the world she believed ought to be for all people—"complete harmony that can exist . . . between white and black" (tape 2). According to Fauset it was an interesting family life, as there were the decidedly black and older children from Redmon's first marriage; the half-black but very fair offspring from Bella Fauset's previous marriage; and Arthur and his two siblings, also half-black but somewhat darker children.

After his father's death, Arthur was raised mainly with his full brother and sister and his Huff half-siblings, a group with whom he had a "wonderful family relationship" (tape 2) for which he remained immensely grateful. This family unit lived in Philadelphia, where the Huff children were able to, and sometimes out of necessity did, pose as white people. Arthur experienced widespread tolerance within the black community but enough discrimination beyond it to fuel, early on, his determination to reshape the larger world in the image of his home. He did not feel full acceptance by any racially defined group, however. For one thing, he grew up a Presbyterian[4] and thereby felt somewhat alienated from the family's black connections through his father's church. He eventually disassociated himself from religion, declaring himself a "freethinker" (*Who's Who* 1950). His youthful experience of the broader world led Arthur Huff Fauset to develop a profound sense of marginality, which clearly fostered his discontent and generated his political awareness.

Fauset's family and childhood, then, had a lasting impact. A thirst for knowledge, the pursuit of education, a spiritual commitment, a passion for improving the human condition, an involvement with religion, a dedication to harmony amongst people of all colors—all prime attributes of the mature Arthur Huff Fauset—are traceable to his early experience and family connections that shaped his worldview which, in turn, guided his life's mission of social activism to eradicate racial injustice. He came to view himself as a legitimate radical, born to the condition through his father. Yet, once again, Arthur perceived himself as different:

> In my own family, I was more pronounced with regard to [radical politics] than any other member of the family, some of whom . . . even tended to be conservative. . . .
>
> I've often wondered what my father's attitude would have been toward me had he lived, because while he is acclaimed as a man of very outspoken views, I don't know what his views would have been with regard to radical politics. . . . I know that my two sisters, Helen and Jessie—that is to say, the ones by my father but not my mother—were much less outspoken than I. Inwardly they felt many of the things that I felt, but often thought that I was rash and foolish to express myself when I did. (tape 2)

Second Movement: In the Ivory Tower

Redmon Fauset would most certainly have approved of his son's bent for learning, evident early in Arthur's boyhood and pursued as a lifelong commitment to education through writing as well as classroom teaching. From his youth, Arthur Huff Fauset was a prodigious and diversified reader, so that in 1970, when asked to consider the influences on his life, he claimed "no person influenced me, with the exception of my mother perhaps, as much as books themselves" (tape 2).

An eager and accomplished student at Central High School, then a prestigious Philadelphia institution, Fauset went on to the Philadelphia School of Pedagogy for Men, qualified as a teacher, and got his first position in 1918 as an elementary teacher in the Philadelphia public system, earning sixty dollars per month. By this time Alain Locke had a considerable influence in his life. Well known to the entire Fauset family, Locke early assumed a role as Fauset's scholarly mentor and intellectual model. As years passed their connection also deepened into a mutual friendship. Locke recognized Fauset's potential and consequently "always kept before [him] the standard of scholarship" (tape 2) and gave some philosophical direction to his emerging activist inclinations. Later Locke quite naturally drew his young friend into the intellectual and artistic fervor of the Harlem Renaissance, engaging him with many other talented and promising people of color like himself.

With strong encouragement from his mother and supported by a small loan, Fauset managed to attend the University of Pennsylvania part-time while continuing to teach, and thus to earn his undergraduate degree (A.B.) in 1921. Locke then urged him to further his education at Harvard or in Europe so as to broaden his experience and better prepare for the racial situation Locke percipiently envisioned would develop. But Fauset was involved in formal academics primarily for intellectual exercise and self-improvement rather than to pursue some compelling scholarly or social quest. As he said, his study had "no particular aim other than study" (tape 2). Further, it was directed more by fortuitous circumstance than by premeditated design and from the outset was destined to be avocational. Distant institutions therefore had no great appeal; it was most comfortable to stay in Philadelphia where his job and other activities were.

Fauset never conceived of himself as primarily a scholar and had no intention of seeking an academic posting upon completion of his graduate work. He did not want a position such as Locke had at Howard University or one at any black institution in the South, but his racial ancestry barred him from an appointment at the University of Pennsylvania (or any similar northern school), so he gave little thought to university teaching. Rather, he sought advancement in the school system that treated him as black and, given the biases of the time, restricted him to teaching only at segregated schools for people of color. This meant he was limited to elementary school teaching as there was no all-black high school in Philadelphia. He took his principal's exams after four and half years of classroom work and in 1926 became principal of the Joseph

Singerly School, where he remained until 1946. Despite his advanced degrees, he was never promoted in public school work, as he said, "not because they didn't like me or because they had anything against me, but because they felt that I was not a conformist and they needed that in the public schools; they needed people who would take the instructions of the leaders" (tape 2).

Fauset was not inclined to follow an established order, to support any bureaucracy or institution to the extent of marching forward according to its demands; he was much more driven to challenge a system in an effort to transform it to accord with his social vision. Consequently, he frequently balked at the regime required in academe, but pursued scholarly work according to his convenience and his needs, though not beyond. Fortunately for anthropology, these needs included acquiring a doctorate, which seems to have been as much to fulfill his mother's dream (she died in 1923) as for himself.

While still an undergraduate, Fauset took a class with Frank Speck, who became his close personal friend as well as his primary academic influence: "I had gone into anthropology not necessarily to be in anthropology [though] the subject was something that did interest me, but especially because a Dr. Frank G. Speck (who was the head of the department of anthropology at the University of Pennsylvania at the time) was a very remarkable person, and once I got into a class of his I couldn't see much else at the University of Pennsylvania except work with him, or work in his department" (tape 1). Had it not been for Speck, who treated him as a "very favorite student" (tape 2), Fauset might just as easily have fed his catholic intellect by pursuing history, for later in his studies he encountered a historian, Roy Nicholls, who fired his enthusiasm for "studying the past" (tape 2). This interest was to persist so that Fauset could say in 1970 that he "gladly would have [gone into history] now, looking back" (tape 2). In many respects, history was more relevant to his sociopolitical interests, but in the early twenties, relevance in his studies was not really an issue for several reasons. First, Fauset did not become seriously involved in "things political," as he put it, until later in the decade. Second, applied scholarship was not a cultural goal of the period, which basically supported an ivory tower model for universities (definitely operative at Penn). In this one respect, at least, Fauset kept pace with his times. Third, and most important, Fauset himself never found scholarship to be an appropriate tool for his political activism; had he done so, it is just possible that he might have committed more fully to it. His experiences in academe led him to view scholarly work quite pragmatically as a means to personal development and thence to his making a greater contribution to the world he lived in.

While Fauset was still an undergraduate Speck recommended him to Elsie Clews Parsons as suitable for a summer fieldwork study she wished to pursue among the Negroes[5] in Nova Scotia. Fauset had no actual preparation in folklore, no special interest in the material, and no particular motivation connected with his heritage for undertaking the work:[6] "it was simply that Dr. Speck knew that I was interested in all things literary, and therefore interested in folk material . . . and for me it was a great opportunity" (tape 1). Fauset had not even known there were blacks in the Maritime provinces of Canada, but eagerly and promptly undertook a small research project—his first field study—to prove himself to Parsons. In part he used the students (primarily those in seventh grade) in his own school to gather the material that was later published under Parsons's aegis in the *Journal of American Folklore* as "Tales and Riddles Collected in Philadelphia" (1928).

Fauset spent approximately six weeks in Nova Scotia during the summer of 1923. Parsons not only took care of all expenses and remuneration but also accompanied her young protegé on some of the collecting forays. She impressed him as a "very remarkable person" (tape 1) who showed utter fearlessness in facing unknown people and places.[7] Despite her support, Fauset "had one devil of a time from the very beginning to the end" (tape 1) of the field trip, largely because of racial prejudice he encountered. While somewhat dissatisfied himself with the results of this first-ever collecting amongst blacks in Canada, Fauset found that Parsons was indeed pleased, enough to sponsor him on two later collecting expeditions: to the South (specifically Alabama, Mississippi, and Louisiana) in 1925 and to the West Indies (the British isles of the Lesser Antilles) in 1927. In fact, he was "the most successful of [Parsons's] recruits for collaborative research" (Zumwalt 1992:191). The anthropology department was sufficiently impressed to allow the text of his Nova Scotia collecting to serve as the thesis required for his master's degree. With little change other than comparative material supplied by Franz Boas and with financial support ($717) from Parsons, the thesis was eventually published as volume 24 of the Memoirs of the American Folklore Society, *Folklore from Nova Scotia* (1931).

To this point in his graduate work Fauset had never taken a single course on black culture. Even had he wanted to, none was offered at Penn, where the anthropology department emphasized studies of North American Indians. Nor had he actually studied folklore in any depth. The majority of his courses had been with A. Irving Hallowell, who had come to view him as not being seriously interested in anthropology, which in truth Fauset was not. Like most graduate students in Penn's department, Fauset belonged to the Philadelphia Anthropological Society. He also joined the American Anthropological Association, and for a time he was a member of the American Folklore Society, but never went to any academic meetings, which "tended only to bore [him] to death" (tape 1A). Unlike "virtually every important black intellectual in the nation" (Hemenway 1977:89), he was never active in the Association for the Study of Negro Life and History, a fact that further demonstrates his ambivalent identity and his limited involvement with scholarly cultural studies.

At the time Fauset believed there to be differences between himself and Hallowell stemming from disciplinary attitudes in anthropology. On reflection in 1970 he could not specify any of these differences, perhaps because for him the various scholarly stances and debates "didn't amount to much" (tape 2), seeming to be insignificant beyond the ivory tower. He did, however, identify Hallowell as directly responsible for his not pursuing work on folklore: "Hallowell did not think it was important enough to follow up" (tape 1). Consequently, Fauset claimed to have had no idea "the black thing was going to develop as it did," so he could "simply wash [his] hands of further folklore study" (tape 1) and turn his attention and energies to what was then his consuming interest: "the things that were happening out in the street" (tape 2).

While comfortable for Fauset in retrospect, this explanation totally ignores his significant personal connections to the Harlem Renaissance and its particular concerns with African-American folklore. But, rather than people or material, the cultural elitism inherent in the esthetics of the Harlem Renaissance seems to have resonated with Fauset's interests and intellectual background. In truth, he was more comfortable bridging the gap between western European high culture and African-American folk culture through literary means than he ever could be doing the precise, detailed observation and documentation demanded in scholarship on folk traditions. His involvement with the subject was productive for a time: it took him to interesting places, resulted in useful contacts and stimulating projects, and gave him material for his best creative works. It did not, however, captivate him for the long-term. Fauset's withdrawal from the area left it open to Zora Neale Hurston, who began collecting under Boas's guidance in 1927. Unlike Fauset, she soon embraced the material, the study, and the presentation of folklore. Hurston as a result quickly became the acknowledged authority on African-

American folklore, a position Fauset might have claimed, but emotionally and intellectually could not.

Urged by Speck and Hallowell, Fauset returned to academe some three or four years after his master's, but continued his studies "in a rather desultory manner" (tape 2). He took courses from time to time until late in the 1930s, primarily in anthropology from Hallowell, but also in history and English. There were no particular motivations for this study other than to nourish his intellectual curiosity and to stay in touch—with Speck and other academic friends at least as much as with scholarly trends. He was absolved of any deadlines and was thereby able to maintain gratifying academic connections with an institution that lent him prestige without formal responsibilities. His dissertation had to wait until he was inspired by a suitable and engaging topic.[8] This finally happened during a trip to California, where he conceived a project on urban black religious cults. It was to be a means of countering prevailing ideas concerning racial predisposition as the prime determinant of African-American culture. This study intrigued Fauset since it was scholarship for a social purpose, intended to foster greater understanding of the black experience and black culture in America.

In 1939 he began the research, involving considerable fieldwork (primarily in Philadelphia, but also in New York and Chicago) and, despite objections from some readers,[9] his degree was awarded in 1942. His personal and intellectual connection with E. Franklin Frazier was most useful in buttressing his arguments, which in some measure challenged claims in Melville Herskovits's *The Myth of the Negro Past,* which had appeared in 1941, just months before the completion of Fauset's dissertation. Again, not without contest,[10] *Black Gods of the Metropolis* was published in 1944 by the University of Pennsylvania as number 2 in the Brinton Memorial Series and volume 3 of the publications of the Philadelphia Anthropological Society, clearly marks of honor. In the foreword, the publication committee proclaimed the author's unique qualifications: "Himself partly of Negro origins, Dr. Fauset was endowed for this study with a background, point of view and an entrée to the field which could never have been possessed by one of exclusively European tradition and descent," as well as the work's special importance as an "important contribution to anthropological, psychological, and sociological research" (Mason, Brown, and Hallowell 1944). While quite well received at the time,[11] the volume only later became widely accepted, according to *Choice* on its republication in 1971, as the "most valuable study of Negro cults in the city."

Fauset was now one of America's first fully qualified anthropologists with black ancestry, yet apart from maintaining membership in the American Anthropological Association (of which he became a fellow), his formal academic connections ceased. He had wars to fight in other arenas. Nothing more should be made of this separation—Fauset was not bitter; nor did he feel misused, rejected, or even underappreciated. On the contrary, he felt that Penn had been very good to him and that he "happened to fall into nice things" there (tape 1). Quite simply, he had taken from academe what he could. It is fair to say that perhaps he had wanted more—some means to change the world. He said: "The thing that has been important to me in all my studies, far more than the studies themselves, is . . . how anything I gain from having gone through these disciplines, how any of that would help the general sociological situation in the United States, between the blacks and the whites" (tape 2). Whatever his disappointment, he certainly felt that any effort on his part had been well-rewarded.[12] To the benefit of later generations of scholars as well as the public he also produced some path-breaking work of lasting significance.

Recapitulation and Appreciation: Fruits of the Scholarly Campaign

It is likely that Elsie Clews Parsons, with political interests decidedly radical for her time and station in life, recognized a kindred spirit in the young Fauset and so concentrated some of her not inconsiderable energy on promoting him for himself, not merely because he could serve her interests. Certainly, she used her personality, intellect, money, and influence to encourage Fauset in his early research and to further its results. It was she, rather than Fauset's close friend and teacher Frank Speck, who shaped his collecting, influenced its publication, and promoted its recognition through her patronage.

Fauset's fieldwork in Nova Scotia unquestionably was groundbreaking. Never before had there been a study of black oral traditions anywhere in Canada; and the only persons of mixed blood to receive attention in Canadian anthropological literature until then had been the Métis in western Canada (primarily of French and aboriginal ancestry), not "half-breeds" such as Fauset studied, who included Negroid-Amerindians. It is important to note, though, that Fauset's publications based on his Canadian fieldwork did not directly stimulate further scholarship. Nor did they encourage any heightened cultural self-awareness within the Nova Scotian black community either at the time of their appearance or even much later in the 1960s. By then there was a strong local black movement that, though unconnected to Fauset, followed his preferred lines combining cultural concerns and activism.

The reasons for this lack of influence are several, but have little to do with the merit of the collecting or the resulting publications. More significant were the nature of the publications themselves, Fauset's relationship with Nova Scotia's blacks, and his position outside the mainstream of Canadian folklore activities. "Folklore from the Half-Breeds in Nova Scotia," published in the *Journal of American Folklore* (1925b), and *Folklore from Nova Scotia* (1931) were limited to a small audience of folklorists and anthropologists with folkloric interests. Few among that audience were Canadians, and those with Canadian interests were concerned primarily with the native people (as was Speck himself).[13] There never were any popular publications or significant media reports in Nova Scotia pertaining to Fauset, his field trip, or his publications.

Fauset had no personal contacts among Nova Scotian blacks, whom he found to be a people substantially different from his fellow Americans of color. For instance, he noted that "most things, including their stories, assume an air of 'Canadian' or 'British' in their lives rather than black or white which is unquestionably a feature of the mental frame of the Negro in the United States" (1931:ix). These black people and their culture were foreign to him, as was the blatant discriminatory treatment he received and regularly witnessed in Nova Scotia:

> When I arrived in Digby, the man behind the desk said, "We don't take your kind here, but I wouldn't turn a dog out in weather like this."... But it was raining so out there that I just had to stay in there because I couldn't go out in that weather.... I decided that I would get out of there as fast as I could, but the next morning it had cleared up and I came downstairs to go to breakfast and I was met with special decorum as I came into the dining hall, and felt, well, "I guess I'll have to change my opinion of this place," and I was taken to a far corner of the dining room and seated and while I was waiting for my breakfast to be brought to me I looked around and found that they had purposely seated me with my back to everybody in the dining room so that no one could see me. I didn't even eat my breakfast, just came out. Well, it was that kind of thing that occurred over and over. (tape 1)[14]

Fauset could not connect with the people, except as an interested observer; so he never explored the relationships between the material and the society beyond the titillating five-page introduction to *Folklore from*

Nova Scotia. Subsequent scholarship (by Helen Creighton and Frances Henry, among others)[15] has, however, supported his key observations, including the disappearance from tradition of particular folktales common amongst American blacks (such as animal stories) that were replaced by a British-oriented lore. But Fauset's explanations are somewhat superficial (e.g., African influences have faded due to the "pressure of western culture . . . because the Negroes of Nova Scotia are scattered about in comparatively small groups" [1931:viii]). It is noteworthy, given his involvement with Locke and the Harlem Renaissance, that his comments pay so little heed to the impact of the American experience in shaping a much more cohesive and enduring black culture in his homeland than he encountered in Nova Scotia. Nor does he take into account the prior experiences of Nova Scotia's black population in the West Indies, which made them twice-removed from their African heritage. He had done his West Indian collecting before the Nova Scotian material was published, yet surprisingly he did not alter his thinking or explore these cultural connections. But then, Fauset fully realized his limitations as a junior scholar and was keeping strictly to the established Boasian credo of cultural research, presenting his data with little interpretation or commentary.

Fauset found that "the reception of the people [his informants] generally was wonderful" (tape 1). Yet, despite recognizing "many personages who become dear as the distance increases" (1931:xi), he did not maintain any continuing contact with his Nova Scotian informants and never returned there, though he admitted to having "thought over and over what a glorious and beautiful part of the world Nova Scotia is" (tape 1).

Fauset did not know and was not known to any other collectors of folklore in Canada's Maritime region, such as W. Roy MacKenzie and Helen Creighton,[16] or anyone (most especially Marius Barbeau) at the National Museum in Ottawa, the focus of folklore activity in Canada at the time. Hence, his work, largely uninformed by prior study in the area, remained virtually unnoticed within Canadian folklore scholarship for decades.[17]

Although it has many of the shortcomings shared by works from that time, *Folklore from Nova Scotia* deserved better. Fauset collected without a recording device; nonetheless he tried to follow the current scholarly methodology, the virtually impossible task of reconstructing the material verbatim working from notes (see Zumwalt 1992:192): "frequently if you could feel that it would not impede the raconteur's momentum and so forth, you would take it down as he was giving it. In other cases where you couldn't be so sure you'd simply take a key word, keep on making these key words and then as quickly as possible get away from there and from your memory put everything down" (tape 1).

His entire field collection consisted of only a few very small notebooks since, as he maintained: "I can do a whole Memoir [a volume of the Memoirs of the American Folklore Society series] in a little notebook, I write so small . . . and then it was much more convenient to have a little notebook to put in your pocket, than to go around with a big book . . . so that all of the stuff that I've written for the Memoir [*Folklore from Nova Scotia*] and the *Journal* [*of American Folklore*] are embraced in a half-dozen little notebooks" (tape 2). These documents unfortunately do not appear to have survived beyond publication of the manuscript; Fauset himself claimed not to know "whatever became of them" (tape 2).

Fauset edited the collection, quite purposefully deleting from the original manuscript obscene material—"men's tales of the 'meanest' kind"—which were included in the finished book only upon Parsons's insistence. His fieldwork involved some of the single-minded pursuits common in folklore work then; for instance, he spent several days questing unsuccessfully after a Gaelic-speaking black person because Parsons was eager to find one. Still, the material he did collect is an invaluable record of a traditional voice that otherwise would have gone unheard for another generation.

Folklore of Nova Scotia is the work of a talented beginner. But this novice was clearly not so enamored of the field (and especially of such a participatory enterprise as folklore fieldwork) as to belabor what for him, reticent and marginal, was an unnatural enterprise. Folklore was not destined to keep him.

Fauset knew that "what reputation I have as a scholar, and I don't pretend to be a scholar, has been the result of *Black Gods*" (tape 2). The work is an important contribution to American studies broadly as well as to the disciplines of anthropology, folklore, sociology, religious studies, and history. Its significance derives, first, from Fauset's comprehensive cultural perspective, which led him to embrace the urban black cults as legitimate cultural expressions fully worthy of thorough study; and, second, from his sociopolitical orientation, which prompted him to recognize significance in these distinctive and popular contemporary cultural forms. Therefore, he endeavored to document in detail and from the perspective of the insider the actual beliefs and practices of the five cults he studied. He countered common opinion that these religious expressions involved bizarre, dangerous, or deviant behavior by providing ethnographic data to substantiate his claims that they were vigorous, coherent, and effective organizations with important psychological functions for individual members, social and economic functions for the community, and political functions for black Americans generally.

There is a certain temptation to suggest that Fauset's work was enabled by his contacts in the Philadelphia black community. He clearly did have access where others did not, for he knew some people in these churches, but not a great many. Such personal connections were often a liability for him, though, "especially in view of the fact that a great deal of [the collecting] had to be obtained rather furtively" (tape 2). Father Divine, the leader of the Father Divine Peace Mission Movement, was especially testy about outsiders peering into his group's activities. In Fauset's opinion, this was the most important and remarkable cult, and it had a special appeal for him[18] as an early interracial movement—"a forerunner of the contemporary love-not-hate world movement" (1971:xi). In his fieldwork, then, Fauset had to exercise great caution as he moved around in what he termed "Father Divine places" or in the Moorish Science Temple. Even though he had become very friendly with the latter's leader, he did not dare let on his real purpose.

Today questions may be raised about the ethics of conducting research virtually in defiance of the wishes of the cultural groups under study (see Clossen 1975). Fauset himself seems not to have been bothered by such concerns, the ends very much justifying the means for him. He commented at length about his difficulties in obtaining material on the Moorish Science Temple, which had much of the nature of a secret society: "If I had been white or looked white I would have had difficulty even getting into [their meetings]" (tape 1). The group had a Koran of its own that the members read from in the temple, and Fauset felt he had to "know what was in it and what they were saying . . . because it was the gist of my whole material" (tape 1). Since it was well known that he was not a member, he could never get a copy until he took a trip to the center of the Moors in Chicago. By some quirk he apparently met a Moor (or ex-member, he was not sure) who was interested in black history and wanted a copy of Fauset's book *For Freedom* (1927a). This individual was "lukewarm enough about his own group" to agree to Fauset's suggestion of an exchange for an old copy of the Koran (tape 1).

Fauset took on one of the great figures in North American anthropology when he challenged Melville Herskovits's idea that the proclivity of blacks for religion was a function of their African heritage. It was not unwillingness to submit to the establishment in this case (typically a reasonable expectation of Fauset), but vision and a capacity to express his insight in a lucid and compelling argument that set his study of black religion apart from others of this time. A dedicated academic in his position could have capitalized on the disagreement with a major scholar and likely built a substantial reputation in the process. It is indicative of Fauset's engagement with academe as an intellectual exercise for personal improvement rather than as his life's work that he did not follow such a course. Instead, he made his argument and left it to be pursued by others more committed to anthropology.

In contrast to Herskovits's rather dismissive treatment of the urban religious cults as contemporary manifestations of a historic religious tendency among blacks, Fauset maintained that these cults had particular importance in that "they provide for certain Negroes with imagination and other dynamic qualities, in an atmosphere free from embarrassment or apology, a place where they may experiment in activities such as business, politics, social reform, and social expression" (1944:107). Intervening years have more than supported this claim along with his conclusion that "the American Negro church is likely to witness a transformation from its purely religious function to functions which will accommodate the urgent social needs of the Negro masses under modern stresses of politics and economics" (1944:109). Fauset has earned the accolades of numerous later scholars, including John Szwed, who placed his work among "the writings of those who have best recognized the distinctiveness and power of Afro-American culture, and given it its proper place in the world" (1971:x).

A slim volume on religious fervor—scientific in its approach, clear in its analysis, inspired in its message—*Black Gods of the Metropolis* rests as the magnum opus of a fervent and intellectual observer. It is the apogee of his accomplishment in no small measure because it offered Fauset a means of integrating matters of consequence across the breadth of his interests, namely, an intellectual's quest for social significance in scholarship; an activist's concern for improving the social condition in America through his own work; a man's search to come to terms with his father (specifically here through an attachment to religion). One is left to speculate what might have been had this convergence of interests and energy occurred earlier in Fauset's career as did happen for Zora Neale Hurston.

Fauset's connections and contributions to African-American cultural studies can perhaps best be appreciated by comparing him with Hurston. The two shared much: each had a preacher father, a predilection for learning, a privileged education at an elite northern university, an involvement as a writer with the Harlem Renaissance, a prominent scholar/collector as mentor, a marked interest in black religious practices,[19] and a lifelong guardedness about private life. Both experienced frustration and limited success in their first collecting trips. They had various interests that were most thoroughly integrated in their writing, which stands for each as an enduring accomplishment.

Yet their differences were profound and ultimately telling in terms of their position and influence: he was of mixed heritage, whereas she was solidly southern black in her roots; he was naturally quiet and restrained while she was exuberant and gregarious, a natural communicator much more suited to oral traditional collecting. He came from the urban North while her connections were to small communities of the Deep South. Black folk traditions were essentially foreign to him owing to his thoroughly middle-class upbringing, experience, and identification, yet these folk traditions were experientially and emotionally central to her being. The impact of western European cultural elitism persisted throughout his intellectual life. She, on the other hand, moved beyond its initial influence to integrate a high art form with vital (not lesser) folk tradition. By so doing, she gave powerful voice to the African-American cultural identity that had become her chief concern. Her creative imagination and talent were decidedly richer than his and ultimately enabled her to weave the various elements of her life into a coherent whole leading to her prominence and success. His socialist and activist inclinations left him at odds with his conservative, elitist cultural philosophy, deflecting his attention away from black cultural politics to wide-ranging, integrationist concerns across all humankind. Far more than she, he remained the direct product of his parents—a thinker, writer, and rebel for social justice like his father; the perennial student and teacher of ecumenical living and humanitarianism nurtured by his mother; and, ultimately, a man between, bridging but not truly unifying ideas, peoples, and causes. His position as the marginal man may have detracted from his academic accomplishments and reputation. There can, however, be no doubt that it enhanced his perception of cultural movements on whose edges he hovered in pursuit of his social objectives.

Third Movement: Out in the Street

Like his father before him, Arthur Huff Fauset perceived his writing as a powerful means of expression and influence—a form of social activism for which he was especially suited. He had been dabbling in writing since rather early in his life. Following in the family tradition, he claimed: "I've always felt most at home when I could have a pen or a pencil in my hand" (tape 1). It was natural, then, that he become involved when his sister Jessie, a protégé of W. E. B. Du Bois, was appointed literary editor of the official NAACP publication, *Crisis*, in 1920. Du Bois intended to use this publication to foster the development of African-American literature—part of his effort to create independence through "a new society, built with black hands, segregated from white society, using black power" (Metcalf 1970:72). In 1922 Fauset published a short story based on folklore, "A Tale of the North Carolina Woods," in *Crisis* and thereby contributed to the upsurge of black creativity that was the Harlem Renaissance. At Locke's request, he prepared two items on folklore for *The New Negro* (1925), the volume that epitomizes the surge to black self-definition that characterized the movement. Locke asked him to write "American Negro Folk Literature" and to compile "Negro Folk Lore: A Bibliography" as a result of not only Fauset's research on black oral traditions but also their personal connection and basic philosophic accord, especially on American devaluation of this and other black culture.

While it was Locke to whom Fauset related most spiritually and philosophically, in personality he was more like Du Bois and could himself have said: "I never was, nor ever will be, personally popular. This was not simply because of my idiosyncrasies, but because I despise the essential demagoguery of personal leadership; of that hypnotic ascendancy over men which carries out objectives regardless of their value or validity simply by personal loyalty and admiration. In my case I withdrew sometimes ostentatiously from the personal nexus, but I sought all the more determinedly to force home essential ideas" (qtd. in Metcalf 1970:72). Fauset was evidently unprepared to commit passion, creative energy, and intellect to the Harlem Renaissance as Locke, Du Bois, and others he admired had done. His was not the mind-set of a true believer for this or any other ideology; hence, by design or default, he kept his inner being at the margins while outwardly and intellectually he was admitted to the inner circle.

The drive for civil rights and integration within American society as espoused by Du Bois and the NAACP appealed to Fauset far more than Marcus Garvey's coincident proposal that blacks reject America and return to Africa, there to unite internationally and oppose white domination. Like Du Bois and Locke, Fauset did have a pan-Africanist perspective but he was more activist than either in his determination to fight oppression. Consequently, he admired Garvey's willingness to act decisively.

Fauset's own activist tendencies were not exclusively racial in orientation, as he was philosophically against oppression of any sort. His most successful action occurred around 1932–33, involving reorganization of the teachers' union in Philadelphia; he became vice-president upon its establishment as AFT Local 192. Throughout this connection (as perhaps the only principal actively involved in the entire city), he remained highly respected by the senior administrators. They had already recognized his talents, in asking him to write *For Freedom* (1927a) specifically for the Philadelphia school system. As a result of this book, Benjamin Brawley (a literary associate of Du Bois who also knew Locke well) invited him to write one of an intended series of biographies of black people. Consequently, *Sojourner Truth: God's Faithful Pilgrim* appeared in 1938 though the series never materialized.

Fauset seems not to have possessed any particular urge to write for children, but he was a dedicated educator and ultimately produced three works specifically for youth. It is tempting to suggest that he identified with Du Bois and his favorite project of the midtwenties in the Harlem Renaissance, namely *Brownie's Book,* a short-lived magazine with cultural material and pointed commentary for African-American children. But, once again, Fauset seems simply to have eagerly grasped the opportunities presented to further his activist concerns—what he termed "people's activities" (tape 2)—and to have produced works of merit in the process. Driven substantially by his own sociocultural philosophy rather than simply by the cultural politics surrounding him, these "activities" were already focused on four themes that persisted throughout Fauset's life's work: promoting a black literature based on folklore; challenging racial stereotypes of any sort in America; developing black American self-definition and self-determination; and studying black history and culture (incorporating its African and pan-Africanist connections). Fauset's writing for children was, then, an early form of "engaged pedagogy" (in bell hook's terms [1994]), intended to promote the practice of cultural freedom in America.

Fauset's inclinations toward cultural forms were specifically literary, yet he harbored broad cultural interests that led him to cofound a Philadelphia-based arts movement, the Black Opals, and to coedit its literary review, *Black Opals.* He also continued his creative writing, the best of which directly incorporated folklore, such as his award-winning short story "Symphonesque" (1926), inspired by a baptism he witnessed while collecting near Mobile, Alabama.[20] Similar pieces include "Jumby" (1927b), concerning West Indian traditions,[21] and "Safe in the Arms of Jesus" (1929), about black worship. Through such stories he sought to heighten awareness of the black American soul which, in keeping with the romantic nationalist notions promoted by the Harlem Renaissance, he perceived as embodied in folklore: "the soul which underlies and permeates these songs of black folk is the same one which in latter years has burst forth into the luxuriant, mellifluous outpourings from the heart of such children as Dunbar, Du Bois and Countee Cullen" (1925d:348).

Over time Fauset's writing was also more pointedly directed toward sociocultural change as evident in various articles as well as his weekly column of critical commentary, "I Write as I See," in the *Philadelphia Tribune* during the late thirties. According to its author, the column was "highly esteemed for its forthrightness and candor" (tape 2). In the same period he produced similar pieces as signed editorials in the *Philadelphia Independent.*

Fauset had long been an active member of the Urban League, yet it failed to satisfy his drive to effect real changes in the world around him. With the establishment of the National Negro Congress (NNC), he believed he had finally found "the thing [he] had been looking for all [his] life" (tape 2). This organization particularly appealed to him because, while it advanced the same goals as the Urban League and the NAACP, it called for immediate militant action. Fauset joined enthusiastically and for several years was national vice-president as well as president of the Philadelphia council. Work with the NNC increasingly consumed his time and energy so that he sloughed off other activities, such as his dedicated involvement with the teachers' union. Eventually, however, he left the NNC because of conflict with its left wing. He objected to the NNC's involvement with (leftist) politics and to the dominance it was assuming over the organization's legitimate work—the battle for rights for black people. Though the NNC had fallen substantially under the control of the Communist party and the CIO, Fauset was not opposed so much to the ideology as to its application: for him, the group no longer represented and worked for black people. While he "never became disenchanted with Communists and their thought," he himself could not work within a communist organization (tape 2).

When America entered World War II and he had his Ph.D., Fauset volunteered for the army, though at forty-two years he was well past draft age. He felt compelled to become involved in this war, which he perceived as a direct means of bringing about "real freedom for the world's people" (tape 2). As might be expected, he also had a hidden agenda—to see what he personally could do about segregation in the military. He was admitted to Officers' Candidate School and also placed in Administrative School in Iowa before (just on the eve of his becoming a second lieutenant) "the Adjutant General's Office in Washington decided the Army would be better off without me," as he put it, because of his radical associations, especially with the NNC (tape 2).

Honorably discharged and armed with an excellent recommendation as well as extra money, Fauset returned in 1943 to Philadelphia, his school, and activism. He promptly joined the United Peoples' Action Committee, serving as its chairman until 1946. This group vigorously campaigned for black civil rights and was, Fauset claimed, "in many ways a spur to the NAACP . . . during the most trying times of the Philadelphia latter-day history" (tape 2). Never content with simply one project, he and some associates approached Adam Clayton Powell in New York and talked him into establishing a Philadelphia edition of the *People's Voice.* Fauset edited this newspaper until it became defunct shortly after Powell was elected to Congress.

In 1946, Fauset resigned from the Philadelphia school system, in very good graces though rather disillusioned with the educational bureaucracy. He also withdrew from the United Peoples' Action Committee and effectively separated from the civil rights movement, not so much because he encountered irresolvable philosophical differences or wished to terminate his involvement, but rather "because of the way things had developed in [his] own [personal] life" (tape 1). These developments involved the teachers' union he had been instrumental in reorganizing years before. After extended and dedicated service, he was (or at least he perceived himself as being) summarily thrown out in disgrace for his alleged affiliation with the communist movement. Fauset was simply humiliated and his apparent repudiation pervaded his relations across the Philadelphia community. Although he never said so in as many words, it seems that he felt betrayed, and by some of those people whose rights he had championed.

Changes were obviously in order, so Fauset the pragmatist made them, never again to commit himself outwardly to a cause though his thoughts remained "just as revolutionary as they ever were" (tape 2). He no longer felt he even knew what the answer to the social condition was let alone how to achieve it: "there are greater minds than my own, and probably some of those minds have the answer. I simply know that this [American society] is not the answer" (tape 2).

Fourth Movement: Recessional

For several years after 1946, Arthur Fauset "browsed about and went about" (tape 1). He traveled some—to Europe, Egypt (the only African country he ever visited), Mexico (where he lived for a year)—and he studied some, for instance, at Mexico City College in Berlitz language classes. But he "didn't do much of anything except note-taking" (tape 1). Like Du Bois in his later years, Fauset felt frustrated with the United States and uncomfortable within its boundaries, physical and social; but unlike Du Bois, he never left for good. In the fifties, he spent considerable time in New York City researching a historical novel (yet unpublished) on Shaka, a Zulu king from South Africa. Eventually he settled permanently in Manhattan, there to obtain yet another teaching position that saw him through until February 1960, at which time his background in activism again caught up with him, leading to his expulsion from the New York school system. It was now his country that had betrayed and marginalized him as tinged by communism because of his association with the United Peoples' Action Committee. While held in suspicion throughout the McCarthy era, this group never was officially blacklisted; nonetheless, Fauset suffered for his involvement.

Fortunately, an especially tolerant elderly couple befriended him and provided a job at the school they ran for recent immigrants. Upon their retirement in 1965, Fauset took his money out of the stocks in which he had fortuitously invested and used it to organize a school for Spanish-speaking people in which they could learn both English and business methods. The venture failed for lack of funds; Fauset liquidated the assets and paid his debts, whereupon he resolved to husband what remained by living modestly and just as he chose. Ever a survivor, he worked two nights a week as a receptionist at the Pratt Institute (for fine arts), but inflation eventually forced him to teach more.

In 1970, at the age of seventy-one, he was teaching English to foreign students at the Spanish American Institute—seven hours a day, five days a week—and considered himself fortunate to be doing something he enjoyed and undoubtedly (though he never claimed as much) doing it well. He lived in constant fear, however, that his real age would be discovered and he might end up "finding [himself] out on the bricks."[22] He had paid dearly "for being just as outspoken as ever [his] father was" (tape 2). Yet, he never completely gave up his crusade. In 1969 with the collaboration of another Philadelphia school principal, Nellie Rathbone Bright, he published a history of his country, *America: Red, White, Black,*

Yellow, from the point of view of prejudice and parallel racial development. This book for youngsters aimed at fighting racial stereotypes and promoting social justice for all.

Arthur Huff Fauset's life, while dense with incident and rich in productivity, was far from easy. His struggles to right the manifold wrongs he saw in society thwarted his attempts to advance. His marginal mindset was in some ways liberating, though it did preclude unqualified commitment to any one of his varied interests and the full development of his talents. For all that, he never failed to contribute significantly wherever his insatiable curiosity and profoundly human concerns carried him. Recognition of these contributions, however late, is justly deserved.

Upon his death in 1983, Fauset's obituary in the *Philadelphia Inquirer* recalled him as an "ex-principal," a "writer of several books on black history," a teacher, and "a servant of the community" ("Arthur Huff Fauset" 1983). None of these descriptives encapsulates his accomplishment better than "writer." Reflecting upon his career in 1970, Fauset commented that his writing projects "had never amounted to much" (tape 1) and that he had held "no major positions because [he] had never been associated with anything major" (tape 2). Such harsh self-judgment is unjustified, for the importance of his associations becomes ever more obvious and, if not an outstanding writer, he definitely had talent and purpose. It was in his writing that the various aspects of his life most fully merged, mutually influenced, and informed one another. His written works—some prize-winning, some influential, some deeply moving—stand as the greatest achievements of his lifelong social campaign.

Arthur Huff Fauset may never have been the visionary at the center of the action, but he was a most able officer soldiering for the causes he espoused. In his parting comments about his career Fauset wistfully remarked, "I always wished I might have been a fighting leader" (tape 2). Then, the rebellious campaigner had the last word as he proudly lifted his head and defiantly declared that, within the limits of Philadelphia and all the activities in which he had been engaged, he was just that—a fighting leader: "You ask any of the people who knew me in Philadelphia and know of my work and that is what they would say" (tape 2).

Notes

The Robarts Centre for Canadian Studies at York University facilitated this work on Fauset during my tenure as 1994–95 J. P. Robarts Professor of Canadian Studies. For this support, I am very grateful, as I am to Douglas Freake and Violetta

Maloney Halpert—cultural scholars, dear friends, and wordsmiths par excellence—for their invaluable comments on the penultimate draft, and to Ian Brookes, whose care and attention contributed immeasurably to the final version.

I dedicate this study to the memory of my dear friend, esteemed teacher, and cherished mentor, Kenneth S. Goldstein, another of Philadelphia's fighting leaders.

1. I am grateful to my friend the well-known trumpeter John Thiessen for the musical references. The symphonic analogy is here extended to frame Fauset's life as a special tribute to him given his marked preference among all his works for the 1926 short story "Symphonesque."

2. From the tape recording of my second interview with Fauset, June 29, 1970. This tape, the two tapes of the first interview on February 27, 1970, all the transcripts, and my notes are on deposit in the Memorial University of Newfoundland Folklore and Language Archive (St. John's) as well as in the Ontario Folklore-Folklife Archive of the Ontario Folklife Centre at York University (Toronto), which also holds additional documentation, photographs, and some publications of and concerning Arthur Huff Fauset. Hereafter, references to the interviews will be given in keeping with their archival designation as follows: (tape 1) refers to the first tape of the first interview; (tape 1A) refers to the second tape of the first interview; (tape 2) refers to the tape of the second interview.

3. Fauset noted that this "brilliant sister" attended Cornell because Bryn Mawr, her preferred choice located in the Philadelphia suburbs, "would not have her" (tape 1).

4. Seemingly his mother felt more comfortable in this denomination than in the highly politicized African Methodist Episcopal church associated with her deceased husband.

5. Following the general parlance of the time, both Parsons and Fauset used this term to identify the target informants. In *Folklore from Nova Scotia,* Fauset employed this same term along with "half-breeds." More interesting, however, is that he persisted in this usage during our 1970 interviews, a reflection perhaps of the profound differences he perceived between himself and his informants.

6. Fauset certainly did not think of or refer to himself as a "Negro" and, while technically a "half-breed," he felt no kinship with those he studied in Nova Scotia. His racial ancestry may, however, have contributed to Speck's recommending him for the work, though Speck's evident regard for this especially talented and mature student was likely more influential.

7. His expanded comments on Parsons's intrepidity are included in Zumwalt's discussion of their collaboration (1992:189).

8. As noted by Stuempfle (1985:21), around 1934 Fauset had been considering writing a thesis on the Maroons of Jamaica and had contacted Parsons by letter that year for information and suggestions of funding sources.

9. Fauset maintained that his dissertation was "almost thrown out" by the white social science reader, who objected to the number of slaves Fauset said were brought over. The reader claimed it was much lower, though Fauset's estimate

was closer to the "15–40 million quoted now [1970]." Said Fauset, "Black people weren't supposed to know as much about themselves as other people, notably white people" (tape 1A).

10. Madame Ida Robinson, the leader of Mt. Sinai Holy Church, one of the cults concerned, objected to having "the things that went on in their church publicized in that manner . . . and that [the book] was consequently an intrusion on the privacy of the institution" (tape 1). Fauset managed to dissuade those involved from filing suit against the University of Pennsylvania by convincing them that the work was not going to be extensively publicized.

11. Fauset himself referred to the positive reviews that appeared in the *American Anthropologist*, the *American Journal of Sociology*, the *American Sociological Review*, the *Annals of the American Academy*, the *Journal of American Folklore*, the *Journal of Negro History*, and the *New York Times* (tape 2). The few criticisms mainly concerned the limited descriptions and absence of comparative data on cults amongst people other than American blacks, though the reviewer for the *American Anthropologist*, Richard Waterman, was vehement in attacking Fauset's presentation of Herskovits's position on African-American culture as racist.

12. Fauset was never rewarded financially, however, for neither at the time nor later did he make anything from *Black Gods*, since the University of Pennsylvania Press "offered [him] the boon of paying for the dissertation publication if [he] would waive royalties . . . which [he] gladly did because . . . it was four or five hundred dollars to have the dissertation printed" (tape 1).

13. As I discussed in "Bridges and Boundaries" (1991), concern with the native people dominated American involvement with Canadian folklore well into the twentieth century through the influence and work of Franz Boas.

14. Such experiences were a major part of Fauset's difficulties during this fieldwork. They amazed (and no doubt disturbed) him all the more because he recalled Speck as having said prior to his field trip, "There's one thing that I'm very happy about in your case . . . that when you go up to Nova Scotia you won't have all this darn race situation that you have here in the United States. Therefore you're going to have a very pleasant time on your trip up there" (tape 1).

15. Creighton recorded some material from blacks in the course of her extensive collecting and included some (particularly narratives and beliefs) in a variety of her important works, such as *Bluenose Magic* (1968); with musicologist Kenneth Peacock, in 1969–70 Frances Henry undertook a study of black spirituals and gospel music in Nova Scotia sponsored by (and now housed at) the Canadian Centre for Folk Culture Studies at the National Museum, Ottawa. She also published the major socioanthropological overview of this group, *Forgotten Canadians: The Blacks of Nova Scotia* (1973).

16. Contact with them might possibly have encouraged Fauset's continued pursuit of folklore studies given their shared literary inclinations. MacKenzie's account of his collecting, *In Quest of the Ballad*, had appeared in 1919 and his

Ballads and Sea Songs of Nova Scotia came out in 1927, but Fauset only ever read the former and that near the end of his collecting (Zumwalt 1992:193). Meanwhile, Helen Creighton was actively collecting in the late twenties and the first of her many volumes appeared as *Folk Songs of Nova Scotia* in 1932. Neither worked specifically with blacks, to be sure, but more important is that neither was within the Parsons/Speck/Boas purview that directed Fauset's field experience. Creighton in particular might have influenced Fauset, for she was then engaged with folk traditions as a writer seeking interesting subject matter rather than as an academic scholar.

17. His work first came to the attention of many folklorists in Canada through its consideration in my book, *Many Voices* (1979).

18. An interesting connection emerged between Fauset and me early in the first interview when he discovered that I, like Father Divine's second wife, was from Vancouver. The tenor of our conversation changed, indicating a marked development of rapport as a result of this coincidence that obviously had significance for Fauset.

19. Some of Hurston's best strictly scholarly work concerned such practices, especially hoodoo. It came early in her career and profoundly affected the direction of her life's work, just as an earlier engagement with tradition of deeply personal meaning might have impacted on Fauset's vocation.

20. Originally published in *Opportunity* (June 1926), the journal of the National Urban League, this story won the *Opportunity* award for short stories and was reprinted numerous times, including in the 1926 edition of *The World's Best Short Stories of O'Henry* (tape 1A). The form of the story was modeled on a musical performance.

21. Fauset said he was inspired to write this piece by the British politician William Wilberforce (1759–1833) and his campaign for the abolition of slavery. The article was published in *Opportunity*, but Fauset also submitted it for a course in history at Penn (tape 2).

22. This explains his reticence with me regarding dates, as in his letter of 30 June 1970: "to give dates of my AB and MA degrees, or my teaching assignments in the Philadelphia system before about 1930, will come back to haunt me. . . . (This age factor is truly a bane!)."

References Cited

"Arthur H. Fauset, Ex-Principal in Philadelphia." 1983. *Philadelphia Inquirer*, 5 Sept.: B5.

Carpenter, Carole H., ed. 1979. *Many Voices: A Study of Folklore Activities in Canada and Their Role in Canadian Culture.* Diamond Jenness Memorial Volume, Canadian Centre for Folk Culture Studies Mercury Series no. 26. Ottawa: National Museum of Man.

———. 1991. "Bridges and Boundaries: Canada/U.S.A. Interactions." *Canadian Folklore Canadien* 13 (1): 3–6.

Clossen, David. 1975. "Diffusion in Process: Arthur Huff Fauset, Black Ethnography, and Esotericism." Ms. Department of Folklore-Folklife, University of Pennsylvania.

Creighton, Helen. 1932. *Folk Songs of Nova Scotia.* Toronto: Dent.

———. 1968. *Bluenose Magic: Popular Beliefs and Superstitions in Nova Scotia.* Toronto: McGraw-Hill Ryerson.

Dorson, Richard M. 1969. *British Folklorists: A History.* Chicago: University of Chicago Press.

Fauset, Arthur Huff. 1922. "A Tale of the North Carolina Woods." *Crisis* 23 (3): 111–13.

———. [1925a] 1969. "American Negro Folk Literature." In *The New Negro.* Ed. Alain Locke. New York: Atheneum. 238–44.

———. 1925b. "Folklore from the Half-Breeds in Nova Scotia." *Journal of American Folklore* 38 (148): 300–315.

———. [1925c] 1969. "Negro Folk Lore: A Bibliography." In *The New Negro.* Ed. Alain Locke. New York: Atheneum. 438–43.

———. 1925d. "The Negro's Cycle of Song—A Review." *Opportunity* 3 (Nov.): 333–35, 348.

———. 1926. "Symphonesque." *Opportunity* 4 (June): 178–80, 198–200.

———. 1927a. *For Freedom: A Biographical Story of the American Negro.* Philadelphia: Franklin Publishing and Supply.

———. 1927b. "Jumby." In *Ebony and Topaz.* Ed. Charles S. Johnson. New York: National Urban League. 15–20.

———. 1928. "Tales and Riddles Collected in Philadelphia." *Journal of American Folklore* 41 (162): 529–57.

———. 1929. "Safe in the Arms of Jesus." *Opportunity* 7 (Oct.): 124–28, 133.

———. 1931. *Folklore from Nova Scotia.* Memoirs of the American Folklore Society, vol. 24. New York: G. E. Stechert and Co.

———. [1938] 1971. *Sojourner Truth: God's Faithful Pilgrim.* Chapel Hill Series of Negro Biographies, vol. 1. New York: Russell and Russell.

———. 1944. *Black Gods of the Metropolis: Negro Religious Cults in the Urban North.* Publications of the Philadelphia Anthropological Society, vol. 3. Brinton Memorial Series of the Philadelphia Anthropological Society, no. 2. Philadelphia: University of Pennsylvania Press.

———. 1971. "Author's Note to the Paperback Edition." *Black Gods of the Metropolis.* Philadelphia: University of Pennsylvania Press. xi.

Fauset, Arthur Huff, and Nellie Rathbone Bright. 1969. *America: Red, White, Black, Yellow.* Philadelphia: Franklin Publishing and Supply.

Hemenway, Robert E. 1977. *Zora Neale Hurston: A Literary Biography.* Urbana: University of Illinois Press.

Henry, Frances. 1973. *Forgotten Canadians: The Blacks of Nova Scotia.* Don Mills, Ontario: Longman Canada.

Herskovits, Melville J. 1941. *The Myth of the Negro Past.* New York: Harper and Row.

hooks, bell. 1994. *Teaching to Transgress: Education as the Practice of Freedom.* New York: Routledge.

Locke, Alain, ed. 1925. *The New Negro: An Interpretation.* New York: Albert and Charles Boni.

MacKenzie, W. Roy. 1919. *In Quest of the Ballad.* Princeton: Princeton University Press.

———. [1927] 1963. *Ballads and Sea Songs of Nova Scotia.* Hatboro, Pa.: Folklore Associates.

Mason, J. Alden, W. Norman Brown, and A. Irving Hallowell. 1944. Foreword to *Black Gods of the Metropolis* by Arthur Huff Fauset. Publications of the Philadelphia Anthropological Society, vol. 3. Brinton Memorial Series of the Philadelphia Anthropological Society, no. 2. Philadelphia: University of Pennsylvania Press.

Metcalf, George R. 1970. *Black Profiles.* New York: McGraw-Hill.

Stuempfle, Steve. 1985. "The Folkloristic and Anthropological Scholarship of Arthur Huff Fauset." Ms. Department of Folklore-Folklife, University of Pennsylvania.

Sylvander, Carolyn W. 1981. *Jessie Redmon Fauset, Black American Writer.* Troy: Witston.

Szwed, John. 1971. Introduction to *Black Gods of the Metropolis: Negro Religious Cults in the Urban North* by Arthur Huff Fauset. Philadelphia: University of Pennsylvania Press. v–x.

Who's Who in Colored America. 1950. 7th ed. Yonkers-on-Hudson, N.Y.: C. E. Burckel.

Zumwalt, Rosemary Lévy. 1992. *Wealth and Rebellion: Elsie Clews Parsons, Anthropologist and Folklorist.* Publications of the American Folklore Society, New Series. Urbana: University of Illinois Press.

11

Skeletons in the Anthropological Closet: The Life and Work of William S. Willis Jr.

Peggy Reeves Sanday

> We must . . . view anthropology from the perspectives of colored peoples, from Richard Wright's "frog perspectives" of looking upward from below. When we do this, the importance of color erupts, and the world of E.B. Tylor, Franz Boas, and A.R. Radcliffe-Brown becomes articulated with the world of W.E.B. Du Bois, Richard Wright, and Frantz Fanon. The "frog perspectives" reveal surprising insights about anthropology, and these insights are the skeletons in the anthropological closet.
>
> —William S. Willis Jr. 1972

William S. Willis Jr. was passionately committed to anthropology as the academic discipline that could help bring "the end of poverty and powerlessness among colored peoples" through studying the exploitation of these peoples for "the prosperity of white societies" (1972:149, 125). Much of his scholarship served as a model for the anthropology he envisioned. Willis provided particularistic descriptions of the historical trends and sociopolitical processes that kept the dominated peoples of the part of the world he chose to study, the American southern colonial frontier, from achieving freedom and equality. In the process he contributed significantly to our understanding of the dynamics of intercultural contact, exchange, domination, and subjugation in multicultural contexts.

In this chapter I look at the life experiences and research interests that led Willis to conclude that anthropology was not what it claimed to be. It was not "the science of culture," he suggested, but the social science that studied "dominated colored peoples—and their ancestors—living outside the boundaries of modern white societies" (1972:123). Willis exposed and analyzed what he saw as the two faces of anthropology: rac-

William S. Willis Jr. (Courtesy of Gene Willis)

ism and antiracism. As a person and a professional he was caught in the struggle between the two. He recognized that although the racist part was never openly expressed, it was always there, hidden behind the "apolitical masks" of nearly a century of anthropological scholarship that ignored colonial domination abroad and racism at home—the "skeletons in the anthropological closet." Willis experienced the racist part of anthropology more personally in the difficulty he had getting an academic job and in his treatment during his short tenure at Southern Methodist University in Dallas. Despite the insensitivity and sometimes demeaning attitudes he encountered in his professional life, however, Willis did not give up on anthropology.

This summary of Willis's critique of anthropology would not be complete without examining Willis's views of the "scientific antiracism" of Franz Boas and the Boasian school. Willis expressed considerable ambivalence on this topic because he believed that antiracism was not conceived primarily to defend African Americans but "to attack racial discrimination among white groups, especially Nordicism and anti-Semitism" (1972:138). According to Willis, that "scientific antiracism was concerned only secondarily with colored peoples" explained the detachment of Boasian anthropologists from the civil rights movement (139). While this angered Willis it did not keep him from recognizing the significant contributions made by Boas in extending the concept of cultural conditioning to blacks as well as to whites.

At the end of his life Willis was engaged in an extensive examination of Boas's life work, which might have helped him resolve the paradox of Boasian anthropology. It is clear from Willis's unpublished work and letters on file at the American Philosophical Society that he felt a close kinship with Boas because of the difficulties Boas encountered in attempting to deal with the race issue in America and his research efforts to collect and preserve black folklore. Willis saw parallels between Boas's experience with anti-Semitism and his own experience with racism. Writing to his friend and colleague Morton Fried in 1973, Willis concluded that anti-Semitism was as "inherent and pervasive in Christian society" as "color prejudice" was in white society. The stereotype of the "cowardice of Jews" was as strong as the stereotype of "the shiftless black," he suggested. Willis expressed admiration for the younger Boas at the turn of the twentieth century because he was the "*only* Jew in anthropology in this country and he was making daring innovations in the world of white Protestant anthropology" (Willis to Fried, March 17, 1973, American Philosophical Society; hereafter APS). I suggest that Willis's research on Boas became the means by which he vented his frustration with racism and expressed his hope in anthropology as the intellectual discipline that could offer a way out despite the failure of the Boasians to participate in the American civil rights struggle.

Throughout his life, Willis maintained an active correspondence with anthropological colleagues and students. I was among his first students, and we stayed in contact until his death. I met him in the spring of 1958 at Columbia University. The course was Anthropology 6: Indians of North America. He was the instructor, I was one of twenty-five undergraduate students. It was a first for both of us. It was his first time teaching at Columbia as a new Ph.D. It was my first semester as an undergraduate major in anthropology. That semester I also took courses from Margaret Mead and Morton Fried. As teachers Mead was famous, Fried was charismatic, Willis was thorough. To a lowly undergraduate female who had just arrived from Catholic University in Washington, D.C., Willis was the least daunting and the most personable of the three. All students were important to him, regardless of who they were, especially if they shared his commitment to the field. He was a skilled, hard-working teacher who came to class with piles of notes on lecture cards, which he often read. His perfectionism would have been tedious were it not accompanied by a fascination with anthropological theory and the great respect and interest he showed for students. I was grateful for his concern and encouragement. Willis was the first professor at Columbia who made me feel that there might be a future for me in anthropology. Although we lost touch for many years, we reestablished contact in Philadelphia in the 1970s: He arrived in the years after resigning from Southern Methodist University; I arrived to start my tenure as an associate professor at the department of anthropology of the University of Pennsylvania. We discovered that once again we had in common the experience of being first, he as the first black hired at SMU, I as the first tenured woman hired by Penn's anthropology department, one of the oldest in the country. Although we never explicitly discussed the indignities he suffered at SMU or those I encountered at Penn, I realized through researching his life work that we had this in common also. But that is another story.

Early Life and School Experiences

Willis was born into an affluent family in Waco, Texas, on July 11, 1921, the only son of college-educated parents. William S. Willis Sr. was principal of a black high school. In protest against the subservience expected of him by the Waco school board, he resigned and organized a construction company that built houses for poor blacks. Such sense of community responsibility ran in the family. William Jr.'s uncle cofounded the Negro Progressive Voters League of Dallas and used his own money, earned through his profitable business, to help register and transport African-American voters to the polls. William Sr. later became grand chancellor of the Colored Knights of Pythians of Texas, a black fraternal organization. Partly in response to an ultimatum from the Waco Ku Klux Klan, William Sr. moved his family to Dallas in 1923 into a stately Federal-style home he had built in the early 1920s (Gene Willis 1983).

The Willis family entertained their friends in the black community, traveled, and spent every summer in Chicago, where they owned another home. Willis Sr.'s business brought him into frequent, friendly contact with the white business community of Dallas, a relationship few African Americans could establish given the restrictions imposed by segregation. William Sr. died suddenly when William Jr. was eight years old.

After attending a segregated elementary school and graduating from the segregated Booker T. Washington High School, Willis attended Howard University. As a history major Willis became very close to the historian Rayford Logan. Willis also studied under Sterling Brown, Ralph Bunche, E. Franklin Frazier, Alain Locke, and Charles Wesley. Through studying history Willis was able to intensify his long-standing fascination with black history and culture, which had been nurtured by the many books in his family's home library.

Shortly after graduating cum laude in 1942 he volunteered for service in the U.S. Coast Guard. After shore patrol duty in Boston and combat duty in the North Atlantic, he was honorably discharged in 1944. It was a confusing time, and Willis was torn between a number of options for pursuing further study. His Howard mentor, Rayford Logan, suggested that he try Harvard Law School. Willis, however, was more interested in social science and black history and culture.

Graduate Work in Anthropology

In 1945 Willis began graduate study at Columbia University, first in political science and then in anthropology. In two applications submitted to the Guggenheim Foundation in the 1970s, Willis explained what led him into anthropology. In the first account, he wrote that he "was led into anthropology by the appeal of the scientific antiracism of the Boasian tradition" (undated, but circa 1971, APS). In the second account he expanded this explanation: "In 1945, I began graduate study at Columbia University, first in political science and then in anthropology. I shifted to anthropology because I assumed that this discipline was the vanguard in the attack against racist thought. I tried to reconcile the concentration on North American Indians that then prevailed in anthropology with my strong interests in history and in the study of Black people by selecting Black-Indian relations in Southeastern North America as the problem for my dissertation" (undated, but circa 1976, APS).

Despite the enormous influence of Boas and the Boasian tradition of cultural as opposed to biological determinism in American anthropology, Willis encountered discrimination immediately upon entering the field as a graduate student. When he went to register in the department of anthropology, which for many years had been Boas's academic home, a well-known professor advised him not to pursue graduate work because there would be no place for him in the field (Gene Willis 1983). Nevertheless, he persisted and received a Ph.D. at Columbia in 1955. His classmates comprised a distinguished list: Eric Wolf, Sidney Mintz, Morton Fried, Robert Murphy, Elliot Skinner, and Marvin Harris.

Willis was not able to develop his interest in scientific antiracism and black culture and history during his graduate years at Columbia. The Boasian tradition was no longer prevalent in the department and the study of North American Indians dominated American anthropology, despite Boas's efforts to turn attention to North American blacks. The closest Willis could get to studying dominated people of color in America was to examine Indian-black relations in southeastern North America. He selected this problem for his dissertation but soon discovered that it could not be handled adequately without first gaining satisfactory knowledge of sociocultural change among eighteenth-century Native Americans in this region. Willis soon focused on the economic, military, and political patterns among the Cherokee. Research for the dissertation was partly financed by a John Hay Whitney Opportunity Fellowship awarded him in 1949. In the same year he married Georgine E. Upshur of Philadelphia, who was studying for an M.S. degree at the New York School of Social Work. Willis finally completed "Colonial Conflict and the Cherokee Indians, 1710–1760" in 1955. His research on the impact of the Anglo-Spanish-French trade and political rivalry on Cherokee society and culture and his documentation of the sociocultural change, assimilation, and adaptation of an Indian people in a colonial setting made him into an ethnohistorian and convinced him of the importance of the historical approach in anthropology.

Early Work

Willis applied immediately to the Ford Foundation for a training fellowship in West African culture and history. At Columbia he had been able to take only one survey course on Africa offered by Gene Weltfish. His plan was to spend an academic year beginning in September 1956 studying Africa at some university before going to West Africa for fieldwork. He wrote to Melville Herskovits in November 1955 asking for sponsorship at Northwestern. Herskovits responded by return mail welcoming him to Northwestern and promising to do whatever was necessary to help Willis receive training.

In his proposal to the Ford Foundation Willis stressed his ethnohistorical background and his desire to focus his project on the "study of the processes of cultural change through time," noting that concern with historical depth had been ignored by the structural-functional approach of British anthropology. He wrote that he would be "especially concerned with the ethnohistory of the emergent African political systems, particularly with those in British West Africa," specifically the Gold Coast and Nigeria. He emphasized that his maturation as a scholar would be facilitated by an intense concentration upon an area so different in its history and ethnography as the U.S. Southeast. Another reason he gave for his interest was the recent political developments in West Africa, which he said were "especially important and immensely fascinating" (Ford Foundation proposal for Foreign Area Training Fellowship in Africa, APS). Such a concern with nationalist politics and change over time was quite unusual in African studies in the 1950s.

Also unusual at the time was his emphasis on the importance of studying African women. In the application he wrote that his wife would accompany him throughout the program of study. He explained that she would "be able to form contacts with African women" that would not be available to him. Accordingly he included her qualifications in the application: "an A.B. degree from the University of Pennsylvania where she was a major in Sociology and a M.S. degree from the New York School of Social Work." "Moreover," he concluded, "she has had six years' experience as a social worker." Perhaps his proposal was perceived as too political and naive given the academic and global politics of the time, because the Ford Foundation turned him down.

Denied the chance to engage in black ethnography abroad and at home, Willis turned back to the ethnohistory of southeastern Native American relations. On February 13, 1957, he wrote to William N. Fenton, then the premier ethnohistorian of northeastern Indians, for advice on possibilities for employment or grants but was careful not to mention his interest in Indian-black relations: "my belief is very strong that one of the most important needs in American anthropology is for more historical research in the documentary materials pertaining to the American Indians." Fenton's response must have been devastating to the young scholar. Agreeing that anthropology needed more historical research, Fenton stated that he knew of "no way" in which a young man of Willis's talents and training could "find gainful employment at it" (Fenton to Willis, Mar. 5, 1957, APS). Several months later, after reading Willis's first published article, "The Nation of Bread" (1957), Fenton wrote Willis a congratulatory letter, calling it "a sharp piece of writing" (Fenton to Willis, July 24, 1957, APS).

From 1955 to 1964 Willis was able to get only part-time teaching positions at Columbia and City College of New York, probably because employment opportunities for black scholars in white schools were minimal, as were opportunities for anthropologists in black schools. During this time he pursued his research interest in early colonial southeastern North America, publishing two articles on Native American culture patterns and black-Indian-white relations.

In both articles Willis established his significant abilities as an ethnohistorian by correcting the record regarding certain issues Willis felt had been misreported. His approach was innovative. In addition to examining the standard historical treatises, he looked for "ethnographic facts found now and then in routine documents written by busy officials and semi-literate traders" and compared these facts with extended descriptions by more sophisticated authors (1957:125). The scholarship was enlivened by the personal interest Willis took in the five groups he studied: Cherokee, Choctaw, Chickasaw, Creeks, and Seminoles. He often wrote informally about these groups, mentioning the names of leaders and warriors and discussing the relationships between slaves, former slaves, and Native Americans as if he lived among them. The result was a fascinating look at the cultural complexity and diversity of early southeastern colonial life, which often belied the neat anthropological analyses fitting Native American cultures into preconceived theoretical categories devised by anthropologists for comparative analyses of social organization.

In "Patrilineal Institutions in Southeastern North America" (1963b) Willis documented numerous examples of patrilineal practices in this supposedly matrilineal area, using eighteenth-century sources that had been largely ignored. He suggested the interesting hypothesis that the matrilineal institutions, which existed alongside the patrilineal, may have seemed prominent to later observers "because native patrilineal institutions were swamped and obscured by newer patrilineal institutions that developed as a result of White contact" (1963b:260–61). He suggested that because patrilineal institutions may have been less formalized than the matrilineal clan system, they would have been more difficult to see.

In these two articles Willis combined the historical method with Boasian particularism. Explaining his research approach in a letter to Charles H. Fairbanks, who was then head of the department of anthropology at the University of Florida, Willis characterized the complexity of eighteenth-century southeastern Indian culture, emphasizing the "great deal of cultural variation" that often included "outright contradictions." The well-known confederacies of the Creeks, Cherokee, and Choctaw, which some anthropologists treated as homogeneous cultural units, he saw as "confederacies of different cultural units." Each of the tribal towns, he suggested, had a different culture, which meant that the unit of significance was not the large Creek nation, but the tribal town (Dec. 18, 1963, APS).

During this time Willis did not turn away from his interest in African-American culture and history. In 1957 he wrote to his trusted Howard mentor, Rayford Logan, saying that he wanted to shift his research toward "problems dealing with the Negro" (Feb. 24, 1957, APS). In his first article on this subject Willis examined the relationship among blacks, Native Americans, and white European groups on the southeastern colonial frontier. Entitled "Divide and Rule: Red, White, and Black in the Southeast," the paper was published in the *Journal of Negro History* in 1963 and reprinted four times thereafter.

This was a masterpiece of particularistic analysis of eighteenth-century multiculturalism in the midst of intense political struggle. As he stated, "the Colonial southeast was an arena of an unremitting struggle for empire among Whites: English, French, Spanish, and later Americans" (1963a:159). Whites competed for the allegiance of Indian groups and sought to drive a wedge between Native Americans and African Americans, as well as between various Indian tribes, so as to control them all.

This article demonstrated that Willis had come of age as a scholar. In a letter of recommendation written the following year, Morton Fried recognized Willis as "one of the country's authorities on the Colonial period in the Southeastern United States" (Fried to Whom It May Concern, Oct. 7, 1964, APS). Fried expressed the belief that Willis had "an unusually acute grasp of the historical problems (of this area) in terms of the triangle constituted by Indians, Negroes and the European settlers." "Any thorough study of the race problem in any culture," he concluded, "requires some use of Willis' contribution."

Academic Tenure at Southern Methodist University

In 1964, still without a job and despairing of ever getting one in the Northeast, Willis and his wife moved into his family home in Dallas. His mother had lived in the big house alone until her death of a heart attack at the age of seventy-six in June 1963. Willis wrote in a letter to Dorothy Libby that it was a "very sudden and unexpected tragedy" (July 17, 1963, APS). He had remained close to his mother, visiting three or four times a year to check on her. She died a few days after he had arrived for one of these visits.

The year after he moved to Dallas, Willis became the first black faculty member at Southern Methodist University in Dallas. Looking to head off trouble rising from civil rights struggles all over the country, the Department of Sociology and Anthropology at Southern Methodist made Willis a special offer. The suggested appointment required him to spend two-thirds of his time at SMU, a white upper middle-class school located at one end of the city of Dallas, and the other third of his time at Bishop College, a black Baptist school with a lower-income student body, located at the other end, miles apart. The job was exhausting, involving a great deal of travel time between the schools to adhere to often conflicting class schedules, attend faculty meetings, and meet with students.

Willis spent only one year in the joint appointment. Fearing that the arrangement would become stabilized, thus precluding a full-time appointment at SMU, he gave up the Bishop position and taught part-time as an assistant professor at SMU in 1966–67, sustaining a temporary loss of income. He became a full-time assistant professor in the fall of 1967 and was promoted to associate professor in May 1968 with tenure.

The years at SMU were bittersweet but filled with close friendships. Edward B. Jelks, for example, was an archaeologist who came to SMU with his wife the same year that Willis joined the SMU faculty. The two couples struck up a friendship that Gene Willis continued in the years after her husband died. In 1988 Jelks dedicated his book, *The Historical*

Dictionary of North American Archaeology, on which his wife worked as assistant editor, "to the memory of William S. Willis, Jr." In the preface he offered special thanks to Willis, "whose encouragement led to my undertaking this project in the first place." Jelks left SMU in 1968 to go to Illinois State University.

After his first year at SMU Willis seemed exhausted when he wrote to Fried that he and his wife had "made it." However, he hastened to add that he and his wife could not have asked for a more "cordial and warm reception." They were readily accepted by the SMU social community and Willis was elected to several boards in Dallas (May 17, 1966, APS). The following year Willis interpreted their social acceptance as evidence that he and his wife's "efforts to integrate had been successful to a large extent" (Willis to Fried, Mar. 26, 1967, APS).

The exhilaration he felt in surmounting the many challenges continued. In the fall of 1967 he summed up his feelings in a letter to Fried: "this experience has probably been the most exciting, most significant, and most revealing one in our lives. There are so many aspects about us, about Negroes, and Whites that we did not dream of until we went through this ordeal. We feel we are the richer for it. We only wish that it had come much earlier in our lives, but then America was not ready and we were probably not ready" (Oct. 9, 1967, APS).

The first signs of trouble came that fall when Willis found that, due to his popularity as a teacher, he was carrying almost half of the students in a nine-member department and was the only faculty member faced with three separate preparations. He felt he was the "workhorse of the department" but received the least pay (Willis to Elliot Skinner, Sept. 23, 1967, APS). It seemed that although he had managed to achieve his primary goal of full-time status and integration at SMU, the costs to his peace of mind were severe.

Thereafter, his letters express growing frustration and desperation. Willis soon began to feel isolated and helpless. At SMU the problem was "white lethargy" and in Dallas it was "black hostility." To the black community, he wrote in a letter to Elliot Skinner, "I am a criticism, a threat, a challenge, and an overt desertion." SMU, on the other hand, had in him "its integration too easily and too cheaply." He felt that he would have to apply new pressure to be treated equally. He thought he would have to "de-emphasize teaching and general behavioral acceptability" to "reduce anxiety and exhaustion." Other solutions were to publish, invite outside offers, "become more difficult," and "be prepared to resign" (Willis to Skinner, May 31, 1967, APS).

Skinner responded by commenting on the interpersonal dynamics facing one who crosses the line separating the races. The African-American community Willis left behind would prevent him from "playing the role of precursor," Skinner suggested. On the other hand, the "danger at SMU" was that Willis would be made welcome "but like a virus intruder judged ultimately as subversive of the system" and, thus, he would be "surrounded and consumed by *leucocyte.*" Commenting on the solutions Willis had proposed, Skinner, who knew Willis well as a close friend, doubted very much that he could deemphasize his teaching because he was always eager to do his best. "I cannot see you behaving badly," Skinner said. "You are too much of a gentleman for that." Publishing and inviting outside offers were better solutions, Skinner advised, along with playing politics. According to Skinner, the political was the key to most things in American society if one had the cynicism necessary to play the game (July 27, 1967, APS).

Willis followed Skinner's advice by asking for more equal treatment and an office. For unknown reasons, Willis was not given an office in the anthropology department. The first office assigned to him was one vacated by someone on leave in January 1968. Before that he had to make do with an office in the now separate sociology department. Willis continued to be the lowest paid faculty member and still carried the most new courses. The situation changed somewhat when he was promoted to associate professor with tenure in the spring of 1968 and was granted a leave of absence for the fall semester.

His growing militancy was evident when he was invited during this leave to give a lecture at the University of Texas at Austin in a major series devoted to the blacks in American history. He delivered a paper entitled "Anthropology and Negroes on the Southern Colonial Frontier" to an enthusiastic audience of five hundred. He felt that the paper established good rapport with the black students without antagonizing the white students and eventually published it.

In the lecture Willis departed from mainstream anthropology by stressing the importance of studying African Americans in the United States and by opposing the almost exclusive emphasis on Native Americans. He suggested that the reason for the neglect of blacks was directly related to the evolution of modern Western anthropology as the study of colonized peoples and others outside the boundaries of Western civilization. Native Americans fit this conventional approach better than blacks because the reservation was the functional equivalent of the colony of imperialism. Furthermore, he pointed out, it was impossible to find funding from the federal government or northern philanthropy because neither was willing "to risk Southern white anger for the sake of a mere exercise in scholarship" (1970:37).

In addition to challenging anthropology's neglect of black culture and history, Willis also attacked the "lily-white composition of anthropology," pointing out that there were no more than ten African Americans in the country holding Ph.D. degrees in anthropology (38). He attributed the scarcity to few employment opportunities for blacks in white institutions and little enthusiasm for anthropology in black institutions. In his opinion, black colleges were operated "by and for middle-class mulattos," who were concerned with assimilating white middle-class culture (39). Studying exotic peoples in other countries or on reservations at home was irrelevant for people struggling with prejudice and discrimination on a daily basis, he suggested.

This talk demonstrated the direction in which Willis was moving in anthropology. His four years in Texas had radicalized him, he wrote to Skinner at the time he gave the talk (Nov. 23, 1968, APS). About this time he proposed a new course entitled the Anthropology of New World Negroes. Upon his return to SMU in the spring of 1969, he began to take an increasingly vocal position both in and out of the classroom. He soon presented a stronger version of his Austin talk to the SMU Anthropology Club and entitled it "Why U.S. Anthropology Has Neglected U.S. Negroes" (Willis to Skinner, Apr. 12, 1969, APS).

During the spring semester black students at SMU occupied the president's office for a few hours to protest their treatment. There was no violence and some constructive agreements were reached, including the establishment of the Institute of Afro-American Studies. Although Willis was involved in some of these proceedings he did not take a militant position. When approached to serve as a sponsor for a separatist black organization on campus, he expressed the wish to remain neutral. He saw himself as occupying a middle ground in the increasingly polarized discourse of the time. He did not want to be identified as a "black anthropologist" because of his commitment to integration and his opposition to any form of racism. Above all, he cherished his identity as an anthropologist (Willis to Skinner, Apr. 12, 1969; Willis to George Foster, May 20, 1969; Willis to Sidney Mintz, May 20, 1969, all in APS).

As time progressed, the demands at SMU and the problems of negotiating the various black factions in the Dallas community together with a longing to be closer to his anthropological colleagues and their professional stimulus in New York led Willis and his wife to begin thinking seriously of leaving Dallas. His salary was extraordinarily low for an associate professor with tenure ($13,500 in 1970). He was continually frustrated and discouraged by the petty annoyances and outright insults he suffered in the department. In the fall of 1970 he resigned from the graduate faculty in protest when he learned that in his absence and without his consultation his colleagues had reduced his one graduate course to an undergraduate one and gave it a new name. He withdrew his resignation only after receiving a letter of apology from the department chair and the dean.

There were other more serious incidents. One in particular demonstrated the extraordinary insensitivity of the chairman of the department, Fred Wendorf. In April 1971, Wendorf distributed copies of a peculiar document to the faculty at a departmental meeting. The year-end "Report of Activities for the Calendar Year 1971" contained racist and sexist slurs directed at black students, women, and the Afro-American Studies Program signed by a fictitious professor named P. O. Stamp (APS). Under the heading "Teaching" was an account of a course called "Black Stamps." According to its author, this course "was well received by majors in the program of Afro-American Studies, who were much impressed by my slides of the British one-penny black. Unfortunately, some of my students were misled by these exhibits to conclude that Queen Victoria was a black woman, a misconception which was corrected only after intensive studies of subsequent issues featuring Edward VII and George V." Under "Awards and Honors" the author listed an "Honorary D. Ph. (Doctor of Philately) from Balls State University." Under "Community Service" he listed himself as "an advisor to the League of Women Bloaters (a society for the promotion of pregnancy)."

Willis was not present when the document was distributed and was told later that at the meeting Wendorf claimed that the document had come from the provost. Willis wrote immediately to the provost, protesting the existence of this document with its "unfortunate racial slurs and off-color vulgarisms" and indicated that he did not believe that it originated in the provost's office (Willis to H. Neil McFarland, Apr. 29, 1971, APS). The provost replied that the document had not originated in his office and apologized for the "affront." However, the provost belittled the seriousness of the affair by concluding that it was no more than "one person's effort at humor" and should be treated as nothing more than "poor taste" (McFarland to Willis, May 3, 1971, APS).

However, this was not the end of the matter. Soon after, Wendorf placed a large placard on the departmental bulletin board announcing a party at his home with P. O. Stamp as the guest of honor. Willis did not attend the party but learned that the honored guest was the dean of the graduate school, who had just been promoted to vice provost (Willis to Charles V. Willie, June 27, 1971, APS).

About this time Willis learned that his request for a leave without pay for the year 1971–72 had been officially approved by the board of trustees as a terminal leave of absence. When he protested to the provost, he was informed that this was done because Wendorf and the dean, the newly revealed P. O. Stamp, had understood that when Willis made the request for the leave he had indicated his intention not to return to the university. The provost took all of this to be "a misunderstanding," but did not provide much comfort when he assured Willis of his "willingness" to discuss with him his relationship to the university at any time during the period of the leave. Willis finally received clarification of the issue in a letter from the president, who apologized for the whole incident and removed the word *terminal* from the record (Willis to James E. Brooks, May 20, 1971; James E. Brooks and H. Neil McFarland to Willis, May 22, 1971; Willis M. Tate to Willis, June 4, 1971, all in APS).

On April 27, 1972, Willis sent a letter of resignation to Willis M. Tate, the chancellor (APS):

> Dear Dr. Tate:
>
> When I was invited in 1965 to become the first black faculty member at Southern Methodist University, I had some hope that a step toward racial justice was being taken and that such a step might lead to more important changes and greater racial understanding.
>
> In practice, however, quite the contrary has happened. The treatment which I received from Dr. Fred Wendorf, Chairman of the Department of Anthropology, at first surprised and then infuriated me. I have brought specific instances to the attention of the central administration on numerous occasions. It has eventually become sadly obvious to me that the administration is unwilling to demonstrate the courage and vision necessary to deal effectively with the problem and permit me to function with dignity. As a result, my position in the Department of Anthropology under Dr. Wendorf is intolerable.
>
> I resign herewith my tenured appointment as an associate professor, effective immediately. This is a sad ending for what I began so hopefully in 1965, and I fear that it is another victory for what in my opinion is a deplorable attitude. Nevertheless, I can no longer function effectively in my work while having to cope with the treatment accorded me.

In a draft of this letter Willis had added that although he could not prove "that this treatment by Professor Wendorf is due to racial bigotry, the impact on me is the same" (APS).

The resignation came after Willis had suffered further indignities by Wendorf, who, in his absence, had removed all of Willis's personal effects from his office and sent them to an office in another building. Writing about this and other incidents to Sidney Mintz, Willis expressed his incredulity over the way he had been treated, especially since the department had received a National Science Foundation Developmental Grant of $600,000, "the only one given an anthropology department, with the special provision that the new focus of [the] Department would be in urban ethnography, especially minority problems" (Nov. 8, 1971, APS). Willis felt that his color and intellect had been exploited by Wendorf to get the grant but then his contributions to the department could be overlooked. Willis was not even mentioned as a member of the department when news of the grant was published in the newsletter of the American Anthropological Association.

Later Work

The same year that Willis resigned, his article "Skeletons in the Anthropological Closet" (1972) appeared in *Reinventing Anthropology,* the controversial book edited by Dell Hymes. Hymes had invited Willis to contribute an article because of his Austin lecture, which had been published in *The Black Experience* (1970). *Reinventing Anthropology* was part of a series of books intended to address important problems not covered in standard textbooks. Hymes wanted the book to cover a range of questions. For example, what would anthropology be like if reinvented now? What would it be like if reinvented in an age of film? How much of anthropology is the way it is because of the goals of anthropology and how much because it has become an American academic profession? Hymes also included critiques of the limitations of anthropological study of culture change in the context of colonialism (Hymes to Willis, Oct. 16, 1970, APS).

Originally Willis thought of entitling his contribution "The Anthropologist as Vulture" or "The Anthropologist as Exploiter." He finished the final draft in June 1971, just after the P. O. Stamp incident and the attempt to ease him out of SMU. He admitted that the essay was written "in bitterness and under considerable strain" and that the perspective he developed was due to his six years in Dallas (Willis to Hymes,

June 17, 1971, APS). With his usual honesty, he wondered whether the bitterness and the isolation he had endured at SMU might have introduced in the argument an "element of distortion" (Willis to Morton Fried, June 17, 1971, APS).

In his essay Willis argues that anthropology's virtual silence on the domination of people of color at home and abroad was inconsistent with its tradition of scientific antiracism. He points out that although scientific antiracism had been developed as a theory to establish the irrelevancy of race as an explanation of differing sociocultural patterns, it was "*not* conceived primarily to defend colored peoples" (1972:138). Instead, it was used to establish "the irrelevancy of racial explanations in regard to white groups" (139). As Boas himself admitted, Willis continued, most scientific antiracism was an "effort to combat the anti-Semitic drift" in the white world (139). Willis was incensed at the detachment of many Boasians from the civil rights movement. He pointed out that Herskovits, for example, used black populations to confirm antiracist conclusions in the physical anthropology of Boas, yet excluded ending "discrimination against New World blacks as a goal of Afro-American studies" (139).

Willis concluded that most anthropologists are "at best committed only to gradual socio-cultural change," thereby postponing the end of imperialism to a distant future (144). Moreover, the equilibrium model of functionalism so prevalent in British social anthropology could be seen as a defense of the status quo. Such models "locate the causes of change inside artificial boundaries of small communities and not in the world-wide system of capitalist imperialism" (145). By misplacing causation, he claimed, anthropology provided both an inadequate guide to change and insufficient theories of change. Thus, anthropology was unable to either properly describe or provide "any scientific basis for a program of socio-cultural change" (145).

This strong essay was virtually ignored when it was published and some of its points still have not been addressed. Although many concerns, including the effects of national political and economic processes on local sociocultural forms, are currently accepted, anthropological practices toward peoples of color have yet to be fully confronted or even recognized.

After moving to Philadelphia, his wife's home, Willis continued his intensive examination of the Boas papers on file at the American Philosophical Society, which include over sixty thousand letters. Because he did not complete this work before his death, we do not know what Willis might have finally concluded from this research. However, there are a few clues. His first piece on Boas was completed in 1973, not long after his resignation. Entitled "Franz Boas and the Study of Black Folklore" (1975), the article includes a description of Boas's efforts to encourage the collection of black folklore and to train black professionals in the fields of anthropology and folklore. Willis details how together with Elsie Clews Parsons, a wealthy sociologist-turned-anthropologist, Boas sought out black students who then received financial backing from Parsons to collect black folklore. Frank Speck introduced them to Arthur Huff Fauset in the twenties, who was eventually awarded a Ph.D. from Pennsylvania in 1942. Gladys Reichard introduced them to Zora Neale Hurston, who studied briefly at Columbia. Both Fauset and Hurston became competent folklorists under the guidance of Boas and Parsons (1975:320–21).

In this piece Willis suggests that "the main key to Boas as a person and as a scientist" was the conflict he felt between his personal politics and his desire to professionalize anthropology as a discipline. According to Willis, Boas's interest in black folklore "arose from political commitments that shaped his vision of anthropology." These commitments, Willis suggests, "were more fundamental than the professionalization of anthropology, although professionalism was sometimes strong enough to clash successfully with Boas's politics." Even though professionalism might have "acted as a break on Boas's political activism" until his later years, Willis concludes that this "professionalism was often an apolitical mask for deeper political convictions" (309).

In an interview taped for a PBS special on Boas in 1979, Willis went even further to propose that race was Boas's fundamental concern in anthropology. According to Willis, Boas's contribution to the study of race was unique for four reasons: he introduced a new way of looking at race by minimizing the importance of race as a determinant of human behavior; he tried to shift the main focus of anthropological research from Native Americans to others, especially to black people in the United States; he tried to establish a "black presence" in anthropology by drawing black students into Ph.D. programs; and he tried to establish close cooperation between anthropology as a discipline and black scholars and political leaders interested in studying black people in the United States and elsewhere in the world (Transcript of Odyssey Production Tape, 1979, APS).

Boas's interest in African Americans is evident in "Boas in Atlanta," a paper Willis was working on at the time of his death. In it Willis describes his surprise at Boas's trip to Atlanta in 1906 to deliver the commencement address at Atlanta University, one of the major black colleges in the United States. Although by 1906 Boas had attained a certain eminence in anthropology, he had powerful enemies in the field who as late as the 1920s came close to expelling him from the American Anthropological Association: "That Boas would make this visit when there existed this limitation on his predominance in anthropology tells something significant about Boas and what this trip meant to him. . . . He was risking giving his opponents ammunition against him when we take into consideration the state of race relations at that time" (n.d.:1–2).

According to Willis, racial politics at the time pitted Booker T. Washington against W. E. B. Du Bois, who invited Boas to Atlanta. Since Washington controlled white philanthropy Willis thought that if Boas wanted funds to study blacks he made "a strategic blunder in accepting the invitation to speak at Atlanta" (15). However, even if Washington was offended at Boas's acceptance of the invitation there was nothing in the speech delivered by Boas that was inconsistent with Washington's position. Willis characterized Boas's speech as follows:

> He used euphemisms. He did not advocate political agitation. He did not condemn the white man. He urged the student to self help, to work hard, to be patient, to be smiling and cheerful. This was all straight BTW. No it was not what Boas said at Atlanta, but the very fact that he went to Atlanta at the invitation of Dubois. Boas unknowingly was in the enemy camp. Boas soon recognized his blunder. Then began his attempts to mend fences with BTW. [He had a] secret meeting with BTW. This might be one reason for the strange coolness that persisted between DuBois and Boas. Boas might have resented that DuBois got him involved in the racial politics [without warning him]. (15–16)

Although Willis was clearly ambivalent about the talk Boas delivered in Atlanta, he appreciated Boas's emphasis on culture in explaining the position of American blacks in the United States:

> He did not think that American Negroes had achieved very much so far in the United States. He did not believe that this lack of achievement should be taken to mean that Negroes were biologically incapable of making a contribution. He used the relatively high level of African cultural development to show what the Negro was capable of achieving when not hindered by whites. Africa was used to indicate Negro capability and to counteract the idea that the Negro was incapable. . . . In addition to praise for Africa, he used this to give the Negroes hope. He urged them to self-help, to have hope, to be patient, to be cheerful. (4)

Willis was not happy with Boas's stress on the Protestant work ethic, "gradualism," and especially with all that he did not say in this speech:

> In the first place, he soft-pedalled what the white man had done. He did not explicitly refer to the slave trade, slavery, segregation, imperialism, discrimination, exploitation, lynching. Instead, he resorted to euphemism: innocuous gloss of these events. Moreover, Boas did not advocate protest and agitation. He did not advocate immediatism. He did not advocate that Negroes should immediately agitate and protest for their rights. He did not condemn what whites had and were doing to Negroes. (4–5)

At the time of his death, Willis may have been trying to resolve his ambivalence about Boas's contribution to "antiracism." The day before he died he requested photocopies of two letters on file at the American Philosophical Society. One was a letter written on May 6, 1935, by William K. Gregory resigning as chairman of the Galton Society in protest against anti-Semitism and the society's alignment with Germany. The second letter was written by Raymond Pearl in response to Gregory's letter. Dated May 8, Pearl's response poses the central dilemma that Willis undoubtedly felt confronted Boas, namely how to resolve the clash between professionalism and politics.

Pearl's resolution of this dilemma was not one with which Willis would have agreed. Although sharing, "in considerable part," Gregory's views "about the current political philosophy of Germany," Pearl questioned the wisdom of Gregory's resigning. "I have a deep conviction," he wrote, "that political considerations should never be allowed to play a part in science." Pearl went on to express the hope that since Gregory's action was "motivated by political rather than scientific considerations," he would reconsider his resignation (Pearl to Gregory, May 8, 1935, APS).

Conclusion

Willis understood the professional minefield of racism yet despite his race, which ensured his marginality in the field, and emboldened by the civil rights movement, Willis was always direct and outspoken. In his letters, teaching, activism, and publications, he did not hide behind the apolitical masks of scientific professionalism. He was the gentleman scholar who remained true to his beliefs in science, anthropology, and human betterment. Despite the discrimination he experienced, he did not prevaricate or dissemble. He resented all stereotypes and suffered when thoughtless colleagues applied them to him. Although he identified with his race, he was intellectually aligned with the many anthropologists with whom he corresponded on a regular basis. His correspondence with students and colleagues of like mind—George Foster, Morton Fried, Elliot Skinner, Sidney Mintz, Marvin Harris, Dell Hymes, Charles Fairbanks, Rayford Logan, and Arthur Huff Fauset—demonstrated a man of a fertile, inquiring mind with deep feelings, always loyal, and unwaveringly committed to anthropology, as some are committed to family.

Although Willis did not receive his just reward from the field to which he devoted his life, his many friends in the field will never forget him. I feel confident in saying that all who knew William S. Willis Jr. would be glad to add their voices to the letter Stephen Catlett wrote to Gene Willis on August 9, 1983, a few days after his death:

> It just will not yet sink into my mind that I will not be seeing your husband's kind, loving face again. . . . His, and your, generosity and concern over the years, to me and others . . . has always seemed . . . to be an almost unique quality that is to be treasured. . . . I will never be able to think of Franz Boas again and not be lovingly reminded of Dr. Willis. It only saddens me more to think that he was not able to publish more from the wealth of information he had amassed in his head and on paper over these many years of research. (Gene Willis's possession)

Note

This essay is dedicated to the memory of William S. Willis Jr., who was my first mentor in anthropology. I am grateful to his wife, Gene Willis, for her generous cooperation in the research for this essay and for her willingness to critique drafts.

References Cited

Hymes, Dell. 1972. *Reinventing Anthropology.* New York: Pantheon Books.
Jelks, Edward B. 1988. Preface to *The Historical Dictionary of North American Archaeology.* New York: Greenwood Press.
Willis, Gene. 1983. Interview with the author. Philadelphia. Aug. 9.
Willis, William S., Jr. 1955. "Colonial Conflict and the Cherokee Indians, 1710–1760." Ph.D. diss. Columbia University.
———. 1957. "The Nation of Bread." *Ethnohistory* 4 (2): 125–49.
———. 1963a. "Divide and Rule: Red, White, and Black in the Southeast." *Journal of Negro History* 48 (3): 157–76.
———. 1963b. "Patrilineal Institutions in Southeastern North America." *Ethnohistory* 10 (3): 250–69.

———. 1970. "Anthropology and Negroes on the Southern Colonial Frontier." In *The Black Experience in America: Selected Essays.* Ed. James C. Curtis and Lewis L. Gould. Austin: University of Texas Press. 33–50.

———. 1972. "Skeletons in the Anthropological Closet." In *Reinventing Anthropology.* Ed. Dell Hymes. New York: Pantheon Books. 121–52.

———. 1975. "Franz Boas and the Study of Black Folklore." In *The New Ethnicity: Perspectives from Ethnology.* Ed. John W. Bennett. St. Paul: West Publishing. 307–34.

———. n.d. "Boas Goes to Atlanta." Ms. American Philosophical Society.

12

Hubert B. Ross, the Anthropologist Who Was

Ira E. Harrison

I first met Hubert B. Ross on December 5, 1981, at the annual meeting of the American Anthropological Association in Los Angeles. I had just finished chairing a symposium and presenting a paper on pioneer African-American anthropologists. He told me that he was a graduate of Columbia, but had never heard of fellow graduate Louis Eugene King, and was quite pleased with my presentation. We soon discovered that we were interested in the same area. He had been researching African Americans earning doctorates in the social sciences, while I was trying to learn about pioneering African Americans in the field of anthropology. We had just begun a warm collegial relationship that would continue up to Ross's death in 1995. I eventually discovered how unusual Hubert Ross was. Since anthropology is still not an established discipline in black colleges and universities, Ross's employment as a black anthropologist at a historically black institution was rare indeed (Harrison 1994, 1979).

Background and Training

Hubert Barnes Ross was born in Boston on April 2, 1918, to Carolyn Barnes and Hubert Heaton Washington Ross. His father had dropped out of Yale due to financial problems, but later graduated from Harvard

Hubert B. Ross. (Courtesy of the Ross family)

dental school and practiced dentistry in Boston, where he married Carolyn Barnes from Indianapolis in 1916. She was a graduate of Teachers College in Columbia and had taught geography at Tuskegee Institute before moving to Boston in 1916. Ross was born two years later on April 2, but his mother died on April 26. Ross was sent to New Haven, Connecticut, to be raised by his father's sister and grew up in a neighborhood full of Irish, Italian, Russian, and Slavic families.

Ross applied to Williams College, but after the college wrote him that he would not be happy there he attended Wesleyan University instead. When the president of Wesleyan was asked how he felt about having Ross at the university he is reported to have replied, "I think that it is nice to have *one* here." Despite this lukewarm reception, Ross's undergraduate experience was pleasant. Although interested in the social sciences, he had to major in ethics and religion because neither sociology nor anthropology was offered. Failing to receive an Urban League Fellowship, Ross enrolled in the graduate sociology program at Yale University in 1939. Ross reflects that had he known that he was interested in anthropology, he could have studied with Allison Davis and St. Clair Drake at Dillard University or with W. E. B. Du Bois and Ira De A. Reid at Atlanta University, especially since his cousin was teaching at Spelman and wanted him to come to Atlanta.

At Yale Ross could live at home and walk to school, both important for saving money but not completely necessary since his college education had been partially paid for by the philanthropist and family friend Madame C. J. Walker, who had established a trust for Ross upon the death of his mother. He took seminars with Geoffrey Gorer, Hortense Powdermaker, John Dollard, Leo Simmons, Maurice Davies, Raymond Kennedy, and George Peter Murdock, as relations between sociologists and anthropologists were quite cordial. Yale sociologists called themselves cultural sociologists, descendants of the William Graham Sumner tradition. Murdock in particular impressed Ross with the idea that culture rather than just biology was the basis of behavior and emphasized that anthropology is more historical, holistic, and cross-cultural than the other social sciences. Ross decided that anthropology appeared less racist than the other social sciences and thus majored in it, but he soon was inducted into the Army Corps of Engineers and served from 1941 to 1945.

Although he had his moorings in white academia at Wesleyan and Yale, was a charter member of Alpha Phi Alpha fraternity at Yale—the oldest black college fraternity—and was a promising anthropologist under Hortense Powdermaker and George Peter Murdock, he felt that the world had changed. Feeling this way, and having saved his money while in the army, Ross took a year off to read in the New Haven Public Library and the Yale University Library. He returned to Yale to finish his master's degree in sociology, but afterward left for New York City, not quite sure of what to do next.

Ross at Columbia University

In the summer of 1948 Ross took a course in anthropology at Columbia University under the linguist Joseph Greenberg, who had just postulated his theory on African language classification. Greenberg's theory turned Ross's attention again to anthropology. Charles Wagley, a specialist in Brazil, further focused Ross's interest. When Ross showed Wagley a paper he had written at Yale on Portuguese Angola, which had been inspired by the missionary activities in Angola of his home Congregational church, Wagley suggested that Ross enroll immediately in his cultural anthropology course in the winter session. Ross furthered his studies by taking a physical anthropology course with Harry Shapiro, one on linguistics with Joseph Greenberg, cultural anthropology under Charles Wagley, one on southwest archaeology with Julian Steward, and an introductory course in African studies with Gene Weltfish.

As a graduate student, however, Ross did not have complete autonomy over choosing his classes. He was not interested in archaeology, but when Julian Steward called him into his office to inquire why he was not taking his course, he immediately enrolled in it. Ross had not enrolled for Gene Weltfish's course either, but she called him into her office saying, "Although I am a woman and although I do not have professorial rank, I still have some status around here." So graduate student Ross took her course, and she, subsequently, became chair of his doctoral committee. William Willis was a year behind Ross, and Elliot Skinner was already in the field. Although they knew of each other, Ross did not have a course with them or become acquainted with them as students.

In 1950 Wagley received a grant for three graduate students to conduct fieldwork in Brazil. Wagley had in mind Harry Hutchinson, Ben Zimmerman, and Ross, but Ross would soon marry Edith Mae Lively, a social worker. As a result, graduate student Marvin Harris replaced Ross but Ross married the woman that he loved and remained with her until her death in 1984.

Ross completed his coursework by 1952 and returned to New Haven to support his wife and baby daughter by working in a factory while writing his dissertation. Ross had wanted to try fieldwork in Angola, but the Portuguese government failed to grant approval. He was also relying on Melville Herskovits to speak in his behalf, but had not received a response. Herskovits appeared unsupportive of African Americans at this time, believing them to be too emotional and to lack objectivity in studying themselves or people of color.[1] Thus, Ross chose a completely different topic that Wagley had lectured on.

Ross's dissertation, "The Diffusion of the Manioc Plant from South America to Africa: An Essay in Ethnobotanical Culture History" (1954), is a pioneering work in that he employs comparative, historiographic, botanical, archaeological, and linguistic data to reconstruct the diffusion of the *manihot esculenta* plant—known also as manioc, cassava, or tapioca—from South America to Africa. Whereas Herskovits demonstrated the importance of African culture to those who had traveled to the Americas, Ross did the reverse by describing the cultural influences of diet and food cultivation of the Tupinamba on Africans in the sixteenth century. During colonization the Portuguese learned that manioc was the staple diet of aboriginal Brazilians, so they adopted it instead of transplanting wheat. Manioc was soon used to make flour and biscuits on ships traveling to and from Brazil, Europe, and Africa. Previously unknown in Africa, manioc cultivation spread from Santiago Island, in the Cape Verde group, to Senegal, Gambia, Guinea, Guinea-Bissau, Sierra Leone, and Liberia. It was also introduced into the area from the Ivory Coast west to Cameroon, north to the Congo River, and later on the east coast. Because it is easy to cultivate, requires little care, can exist on the ground in a state of self-storage, and is a locust-free crop, manioc has become a staple crop in Africa. Ross concluded that even "in the absence of personal contacts, the manioc cultivating and eating peoples of South America exerted a cultural influence upon the peoples of West and Central Africa" (1954:121).

Ross's Career in Anthropology

After earning his doctorate in 1954, with the help of a John Hayes Whitney Fellowship in 1952, Ross became a fellow in the Johns Hopkins School for Advanced International Studies Summer Seminar on Africa. At a cocktail party he met Horace Mann Bond, president of Lincoln University, who sounded him out about a job. The president submitted Ross's application to a committee headed by Laurence Foster, who was head of the social science department. Ross was hired as an instructor in sociology and history in 1954 and was an assistant professor of sociology from 1955 to 1960. During these few years he taught each of the following courses:

Art 204	Art of Negro Africa
History 203	The Negro and the Old World
History 203	Peoples and Cultures of Africa
History 204	The Negro and the New World
Seminar 407	Seminar in Sociology
Seminar 408	Seminar in Social Theory
Sociology 201	Introduction to Sociology
Sociology 202	Race Relations
Sociology 203	Anthropology
Sociology 208	Community
Sociology 301	Marriage and the Family
Sociology 303	Social Anthropology
Sociology 304	Prehistory
Sociology 307	Criminology
Sociology 308	Urban Sociology
Sociology 403	Social Thought (Contemporary Social Theory)

This teaching load is the norm in historically black colleges but must be shocking to those familiar with the requirements of publishing-intensive white academia.

Ross spent the summer of 1955 as a visiting associate professor of sociology at Texas Southern University, another historically black institution. In 1960, while attending a meeting of the American Society for the Study of Africa, Ross met Sam Westerfield, dean of the Atlanta University School of Business Administration. Westerfield told Ross that Atlanta University needed an anthropologist. Since Ross was interested, Westerfield called the president and Ross and family were promptly invited to Atlanta University. It was a great move for not just Ross but also his wife because Atlanta University had one of the nation's best schools of social work. Ross was promoted to associate professor and had an opportunity to teach more courses in anthropology:

Anthropology 571	General Anthropology
Anthropology 572	Peoples of the World
Anthropology 573	Social and Cultural Anthropology
Anthropology 573	Biology, Technology, and Culture

Anthropology 573	Cultural Ecology
Anthropology 574	Personality, Society, and Culture
Anthropology 575	Introduction to African Studies
Anthropology 575	Africa: People and Problems
Anthropology 575	Anthropological Linguistics
Anthropology 577	Introduction to Afro-American Studies
Anthropology 578	Social Organization
Anthropology 579	Racial and Cultural Anthropology
Anthropology 579	Ethnic Relations
Anthropology 580	Introduction to Afro-American Studies
Anthropology 583	Psychological Anthropological
Anthropology 585	Anthropological Linguistics
Sociology 400	The Study of Society
Sociology 400	Contemporary Sociological Theory
Sociology 502	Contemporary Sociological Theory

Ross continued to teach in the Atlanta University system, which includes Morehouse and Spelman colleges, finally becoming a full professor of anthropology in 1969. During his thirty-five years he did more than teach numerous courses. He served several times as chair of the department of sociology and anthropology; he wrote articles on W. E. B. Du Bois, Oliver C. Cox, Caroline Bond Day, and numerous book reviews; he edited *Phylon: The Atlanta University Review of Race and Culture*; and he participated in various symposiums at American Anthropological Association meetings. He also was director of the Atlanta Project Association for the Study of Afro-American Life and History; principal investigator for an ethnographic study of Hancock County, Georgia; editor of the African correspondence of Claude A. Barnett; a research consultant to the History Group, an Atlanta-based organization studying black neighborhoods; and an avid compiler of information on the academic careers and contributions of African-American pioneer anthropologists.

Still active, Ross died of a heart attack at the age of seventy-five on March 9, 1995, in Atlanta. Ross's influence is evident in this reflection on his career:

> I concentrated on teaching because when I came here, the president said that's what he wanted. And I think he was right because there were . . . at least fifty people who have gotten Ph.D.'s in sociology or anthropology or education from AU who have come out of the department. I think that we have a function particularly in preparing people to the extent that

> when they go to Chicago or Berkeley or wherever, they can stand the competition, which is tight. . . . I have had a modest career here at AU. . . . The students that I have been associated with, if they think about going on to study at the Ph.D. level, then in a sense you might say that the program has served as a prep school in the best sense.

The Significance of Hubert B. Ross

It is difficult to speculate on how the history of American anthropology was affected when Marvin Harris replaced Hubert Ross on Wagley's study of Brazil, but certainly Ross's students benefited. Lucky for them Ross arrived in Atlanta at the beginning of the 1960s, when African studies had emerged as a viable area of concentration, the civil rights movement was at its height, and white academia was beginning to consider allowing more blacks to enter higher education. Ross's position at Atlanta University, the center of historically black institutions in the South's major metropolitan area, his teaching methods, and his consultative skills enabled him to introduce many students to the discipline of anthropology and to encourage them to pursue doctoral studies in anthropology, sociology, social work, and education.

Ross was able to continue the legacy of eminent social scientists who had taught in the Atlanta University system and researched the history, life, and culture of African and African-American peoples: W. E. B. Du Bois, Ira De A. Reid, Albert N. Whiting, Mozell C. Hill, William Hale, Hylan Garnet Lewis, Walter R. Chivers, John Reid, James Conyers, Caroline Bond Day, Morris Siegel, and Robert G. Armstrong.

Notes

Most of this chapter was read and approved by Ross prior to his death. It is based upon many discussions that we have had over the years, but mostly on a videotaping of Ross on April 21, 1993, at his home.

1. Louis Eugene King told me that he got no help from Herskovits while he was at Columbia or afterward. William J. Willis Jr. was extremely reserved with me when I mentioned Herskovits to him in 1983. I had invited him to be a discussant for my symposium on African-American anthropology at the meeting of the American Anthropological Association, which was held in Chicago. He told me that he had to give it a lot of thought because he had given up on the American Anthropological Association years ago and had no desire to go to Chicago, the site of Herskovits's empire. Willis died of a heart attack prior to the meeting, so I do not know if he would have attended. Elliot Skinner did not get to conduct fieldwork

in Africa until after he had completed his doctoral studies, not while he was a student under Herskovits. Another pioneer anthropologist told me that she stopped going to Anthropological Association meetings when Herskovits said in a meeting that "Negroes were too emotional to study each other."

References Cited

Harrison, Ira E. 1979. "Black Anthropologists in the Southern Region." *Anthropology and Education Quarterly* 10 (4): 269–75.

———. 1994. "A History of the Committee on Anthropology in Predominantly Minority Institutions." Paper presented at the annual meeting of the American Anthropological Association. Atlanta. Nov. 30.

Ross, Hubert B. 1954. "The Diffusion of the Manioc Plant from South America to Africa: An Essay in Ethnobotanical Culture History." Ph.D. diss., Columbia University.

13

The Continuing Dialogue: The Life and Work of Elliot Skinner as Exemplar of the African-American/African Dialectic

Cheryl Mwaria

Elliot Percival Skinner, statesman and scholar, is arguably one of the most prolific anthropologists of our time. In a period spanning four decades he has written twelve books and over seventy-five articles. He focused much of his work on the dialectical tensions between African Americans and Africans and exemplified those same tensions in his life as an African-American Africanist scholar and ambassador to Africa.

Elliot Skinner, the son of Joseph McDonald and Ettice Francis, was born in Trinidad and Tobago, West Indies, on June 20, 1924, and grew up in the household of his Barbadian maternal aunt. This experience shaped his early intellectual interests by heightening his awareness of the nuances of cultural difference. He was, in his own words, "always open to other cultures" (Skinner 1994a). Nurtured in a climate of intellectual competition, Skinner was exposed to white power and privilege but had no sense of limitations that could be imposed on him. When he finally realized that there were few job opportunities for him in Trinidad, he grew eager to join his father in the United States. He arrived in Harlem, land of his cultural heroes W. E. B. Du Bois, Duke Ellington, and Cab Calloway, at the age of seventeen and was soon drafted into the army. The U.S. armed forces were segregated at that time and it was believed that blacks were unsuited for more than the more menial jobs in support areas. Skinner was assigned to a stevedore unit despite his desire to serve in the infantry and soon

Elliot Skinner. (Courtesy of Elliot Skinner)

learned that even German prisoners of war were allowed privileges denied to him and his fellow black servicemen. He was an avid reader and had studied French in high school. When his company was sent to France during the war, he took every opportunity to improve his knowledge of the language and became an interpreter for the company. This in turn put him in a position to take advantage of the army's educational program at the University of Neufchatel. While there, he studied Swiss culture, anthropology, parasitology, and comparative anatomy. He left after three months, determined to go to college and earn his bachelor's degree and perhaps enter dental school despite warnings from friends that racial discrimination would prevent him from doing so.

After discharge from the army in 1946, Skinner returned to his father's house in a West Indian neighborhood in Harlem. It was here that he first began to notice the "stranger syndrome" initially articulated by Georg Simmel and about which he was later to write. At that time there was a tension between West Indians and African Americans exhibited through mutual distrust and distaste. According to Skinner, "West Indians discovered economic niches that African Americans overlooked or didn't want and subsequently felt that African Americans didn't take full advantage of the opportunities in front of them. African Americans for their part felt that this was their country and they shouldn't have to accept the lowest jobs that immigrants were willing to take" (Skinner 1994a). Skinner, who was then engaged to his first wife, Thelma Givens, an African American, recognized these attitudes from his childhood in his aunt's home. His maternal relatives were Barbadian immigrants to Trinidad and the two communities disliked each other for similar reasons. Skinner asserts that he refused to "buy into it" either time. It was remarkable, he felt, how immigrant communities could so easily forget their admiration for their host communities, which had led in part to their migration in the first place, and how quickly resident communities could become resentful of immigrants they initially welcomed (Skinner 1994a).

Skinner's interest in the complex relationship between people marginalized by culture, social roles, spatial distance, and social status from their host communities led him to be the first to systematically apply Simmel's concept to African societies. In his pioneering article "Strangers in West African Societies" (1963) Skinner noted the presence of permanent stranger communities as early as the eighteenth century in Ghana, Malle, Gao, Djenne, and Timbuktu and described how changes in status and role of these communities, in relation to their hosts, affected their political and legal positions. Skinner opined that unlike the situation that was to emerge with the advent of colonialism, these African strangers were to remain "under the control of the local African political authorities, and stayed only at the sufferance of their hosts" (308). Colonialism brought about new conditions resulting in local polities being involuntary hosts to uninvited migrants who often enjoyed considerable autonomy and answered not to local authorities but to European administrators, themselves uninvited strangers. Tensions arising out of economic aggression on the part of the strangers sometimes resulted in overt clashes. At other times it resulted in the expulsion of locals from their traditional economic pursuits, such as in the Ivory Coast when Togolese and other outsiders took over the fishing industry. Skinner argued that what had come to be called "tribalism" in the context of modern African states is better understood through an examination of the factors, such as changes in political autonomy and independence, that have altered economic positions and have made for conflict between locals and "strangers." In other words, these conflicts were reflections of the ancient and universal problem of the "stranger." His work in this area pointed the way for new avenues of research both within and outside of the African context.

Mentorship and the Making of an Anthropologist: The NYU and Columbia Years

Skinner entered University College at New York University under the G.I. Bill following his discharge from the service. There he met John Landgraf, a relatively new faculty member teaching in the sociology department. According to Landgraf the two made an immediate, though unexpected, connection, and Landgraf was to become Skinner's lifelong friend and mentor. In those days University College was an all-male institution with a somewhat misogynist orientation. The students were mature, many of them returning veterans like Skinner. The major difference was that most of them were white and Jewish. This did not bother Skinner, who felt he could hold his own anywhere and was willing to work hard to overcome any obstacles he might face. Landgraf, an anthropologist, had studied at Harvard under Clyde Kluckholm, who had sent him to Columbia for a brief stint to study with Ralph Linton. Landgraf's career was interrupted by the war when he was sent overseas to serve in the navy. In 1945 he returned to Harvard and from there was sent to NYU, where he began teaching in 1946. By his second year he had established a reputation for being a flamboyant teacher and faculty advisor for Phi Beta Kappa. Both Landgraf and Skinner were married and had young children by that time. Skinner enrolled in Landgraf's course, but was still uncertain about what he wanted to do with his life. He considered dentistry but soon was captured by cultural anthropology. On reflection he stated, "My discovery of anthropology while pursuing what I considered to be the unwelcome intrusion of a 'social science' requirement in an exacting pre-dental undergraduate curriculum, changed my career plans and profoundly affected my life" (1994a). In those days anthropology had not yet been widely established as an independent discipline, but it was growing and mentorship played a crucial role in the establishment of careers. It was common for mentors to guide their students with respect not only to what they should study but where and with whom. Nor did the guidance end there, for the old boys' club of mentors was critical in gaining future appointments. In Landgraf, Skinner fortunately had found an able and willing mentor. Landgraf was impressed by Skinner's ambition, perseverance, and discipline. "Skinner," he said, "was aggressive and intensely concentrated on his work" (1996). Nor was Skinner afforded the luxury of spending all of his time on his studies. With a wife and young children to support, he was forced to find work wherever he could. Consequently, with few opportunities open to him, he took whatever menial jobs he could find as long as they paid the bills. Although work, study, and family left little free time, Skinner found opportunities to develop a friendship with Landgraf. After his application to study at Northwestern under Herskovits had been turned down, Skinner decided (with Landgraf's approval) to attend Columbia for graduate training. Landgraf, who had been a student with Charles Wagley, called his old friend and paved the way for Skinner's graduate career (Skinner 1996).

When Skinner entered Columbia in 1951, there were still relatively few blacks in white institutions of higher learning, particularly in anthropology. Columbia had hosted Zora Neale Hurston, Hubert B. Ross, and William S. Willis Jr., himself a contemporary of Skinner. True integration was yet to come. This did not deter Skinner, who was determined to pursue his doctorate at what was arguably the premier anthropology department of that time.

Skinner studied under Julian Steward, Alfred Louis Kroeber, Elman Service, Harry Shapiro, William B. Schwab, Charles Wagley, Gene Weltfish, Joseph Greenberg, and young Marvin Harris. The mentorship he was to receive at Columbia, like that at NYU, proved invaluable, and coupled with his own high standards and competitive nature was to set him firmly on the road to establishment success, which remained closed to many of his African-American peers. After completing his master's thesis on African monarchies within a year, Skinner began to investigate, under the direction of Julian Steward, the adaptation of the Bush Negroes of Guyana to the South American tropical rain forest. This work was designed to accomplish three goals: work with Steward; deepen his understanding of an African population; and satisfy his curiosity about acculturation (1994b). Skinner's initial library work on this topic brought him to the attention of Morton Fried, who had begun to work on Chinese communities overseas and invited him to join his project in Guyana. With Fried's backing Skinner obtained money to conduct fieldwork in Guyana on ethnic relations and acculturation, which became the basis of his doctoral dissertation. Fried served as his guide: teaching him how to conduct an interview, hiring him as his research assistant, and serving as his sponsor on his dissertation committee. Landgraf, too, played a role by teaching him how to drive a car and keeping note of his progress.

With his doctoral degree in hand, Skinner was able to turn his attention once again to Africa. Joseph Greenberg had pointed out that Skinner had omitted reference to sahelian monarchies in his master's thesis and drew his attention to the Mossi. It was then that his life-long involvement with the Mossi began:

> Well, the point is that I was really interested in the political organization of the Mossi because they were the one population in the entire Sudan which had preserved their political organization since the fourteenth century. They had been in contact with the Malian Empire, and the Malian Empire had bitten the dust. The Songhai who had come after them had bitten the dust. The barbarous states had bitten the dust, and here were these people that I considered fossils, and I wanted to take a look at their political organization to see exactly what it was all about and, I suspect, to answer the old accusation that black kings, black ambassadors, black men of affairs could not be found simply because certain people didn't know they existed. I wanted to go check that out. (Skinner 1994b)

Armed with a Ford Foundation Foreign Area Fellowship, Skinner set off to conduct fieldwork in Africa, the first trained African-American anthropologist to do so. Knowing that although French ethnologists had published works on the Mossi no such work had been published in English, Skinner was determined to become the first anthropologist to do that as well.

It should be remembered that in the midfifties fieldwork in Africa was still dominated by the British and the French, each holding a considerable amount of Africa as colonies. Though the movement for independence was underway in a number of African countries, colonialism had not yet begun to fade significantly. Skinner, recognizing the power white European ethnologists had over who would be allowed to work where and ever mindful of the need to make connections, wrote Madame Schaftner (Denise Paulme) at the Musee de l'Homme in Paris, Robert Mauny at the Institute Français in Dakar, and E. E. Evans-Pritchard at Oxford: "In those days you couldn't go to Africa unless you went through those Europeans, so I showed up at Oxford and met Herskovits for the first time, serendipitously. We were all waiting for the great E.-P., and of course as director of African studies, he knew I was Greenberg's student, and we talked, and then, of course we finally saw E.-P., who began to raise hell with us for going to Africa without permission. I was scandalized, but Herskovits wasn't, he just winked at me and that was that" (Skinner 1994b). Skinner's entree to Africa as a research scholar was relatively smooth, despite being seated at a segregated table with several Africans on the ship transporting him there, because he had establishment help. Other African-American scholars had to find their own way to Africa.

This vignette is all the more remarkable because at that time research in Africa was firmly in the hands of whites, whether European or American. The Americans were upstarts in the eyes of European scholars in part because, with the exception of Liberia, the United States came late to the battle for hegemonic control in Africa. As a result there had been little effort or emphasis on anthropological research there by Americans. This, of course, would change as the cold war heated up and African states gained independence. As for anthropologists, Herskovits himself was the man largely in control of who got financed to study where. The word was that even his own students, who were African American, were not able to conduct research in Africa under the pretext that fieldwork must first be conducted among a population quite different from one's own.

Meanwhile, the curious and often unacknowledged triad between Africans, African Americans, and whites was about to undergo substantial changes. The civil rights movement was beginning in the South, sparked in part by the brutal torture, lynching, and mutilation of Emmet Till, an African-American teenager, and his mother's courageous decision to have an open casket funeral to let the world know what had happened to her son. The news spread even to Africa, where Skinner was approached by countless Africans who wanted to discuss the case with him. As Skinner wrote in "African, Afro-American, White American: A Case of Pride and Prejudice":

> The early attitude of Africans to American whites, however appears to be [more] complicated, influenced as they were by the various skeins of relationship between white and Negro Americans. There were the intricate relationships between the missionaries, and their converts, compounded of gratitude for education and Christianity, yet soured by the whites' attitudes of racial superiority, their paternalism, and their disdain for African culture. There was the respect and admiration for an America, once a colony, which had thrown off the colonial yoke and become great. Yet matching this was the feeling of disappointment when Africans heard reports that Americans treated their black citizens much worse than the Europeans treated their black subjects. These disillusioned views of America were further circulated when, beginning in the 1930's, African students returned home from study in America and reported that while white Americans lauded the effort of Africans to get an education, they usually banished them to Negro colleges and humiliated them because of their blackness. (1965:384–85)

Skinner was the receiver of this African reception, for the Mossi were both welcoming and curious about the stranger in their midst. Skinner's initial fifteen-month sojourn among the Mossi proved to be fruitful. When he returned to the States in 1957, unbeknownst to Skinner at the time, the old boys' club once again played a role in his future. When Skinner failed to get a job at the University of Minnesota after an interview with E. Adamson Hoebel, Landgraf and Wagley decided he would be "better off" at Columbia (Landgraf 1996). Skinner then joined the faculty at Columbia as a visiting assistant professor and began work on a series of articles on Mossi migration, kinship, politics, and economic life.

A closer look at the articles he published at this time reveal Skinner to be a first-rate anthropologist with not only keen observational and analytical skills but also a critical awareness of the role anthropology and anthropologists, particularly those of color, could play during the emergence of independent African states by voicing the plight of the commoner and bucking the trend of earlier myopic analyses. Skinner frequently focused on the impact of rapid social change on indigenous customs and institutions. In "Labour Migration and Its Relationship to Socio-Cultural Change in Mossi Society" he wrote:

> Socio-cultural change is fairly rapid in present-day Africa, and because of this, many anthropologists have a tendency to regard African societies as in various states of "disequilibrium." The Wilsons, among others, believe that this is due mainly to the "failure to adjust novelty with tradition—a change in one respect without changes in other respects." (G. and M. Wilson, "The Analysis of Social Change Based on Observations in Central Africa", Cambridge, 1945: 132). The belief is that only gradual changes can prevent disequilibrium. The major shortcoming of this concept as an analytical tool for studying socio-cultural change is that it cannot deal with situations of constant and accelerated changes. The belief that social systems return to equilibrium tends to obscure the analysis of the new emergent institutions and practices which are of vital concern to those interested in studying and understanding the processes of transformation in modern Africa. Given the context of change today, where the institutions of African societies are still changing with no end in sight, the most profitable concern is not with equilibrium or disequilibrium, with all the problems of valuation or value or value positions that such concern implies, but with the direction and process of change. (1960a:376)

Skinner thereby shifted from the more arcane theoretical perspectives dominant at the time and focused attention on the consequences of social processes initiated by European activities and the resilience and creativity of African societies, particularly the Mossi, in responding to them. His analysis in this article was nothing short of a tour de force, providing not only careful historical documentation of the changes in labor patterns forced upon the Mossi but also a detailed ethnographic description and analysis of newly emerging Mossi patterns of adaptation and change. He was among the first to note the changing position of women in Mossi society as reflected in marriage patterns initiated by the women themselves, in open defiance of both the neglect of their husbands as a result of labor migration patterns and of the traditional pattern of arranged marriages among the Mossi known as the *pogsioure.* The newly independent position of many Mossi women came through opportunities opened up by increased mobility and economic autonomy coinciding with labor migration patterns of Mossi men.

Not all of Skinner's articles on the Mossi were concerned with social change. That same year, 1960, he published "The Mossi Pogsioure" in the journal *Man.* Building on the analysis of cultural systems in terms of obligations between individuals and groups pioneered by Marcel Mauss and Claude Lévi-Strauss, Skinner described the Mossi institution of the *pogsioure* in which women (also called *pogsioure*) were used "1) to channel goods and services to the chiefs; 2) to establish or strengthen political bonds and benefactor dependent relationships between chiefs and their subjects; and 3) to incorporate strangers into the political and social structure of the districts" (1960b:20). This article, though brief, demonstrated Skinner's grasp of the concerns of an earlier, more classic anthropological approach to ethnographic description of "traditional" societies. It also delineated the ways in which Mossi elders and district chiefs solidified political patronage through the exchange of women, whose agricultural labor and fecundity were highly valued.

Skinner's fieldwork among the Mossi laid the foundation for his monograph, *The Mossi of Upper Volta* (1964), which received rather mixed reviews. In his review for the *American Anthropologist* Peter Hammond characterized the book as one that provides the reader with "a detailed descriptive account, skillfully synthesized from earlier documents, Mossi oral tradition (perhaps relied on too uncritically), contemporary reports, and Skinner's own field research" that provided a "clearer picture of how the system is set up than of how it *works*" (1965:133). The reviewer in *Current History* was less critical, though quite brief, referring to the book as a "lucid account of the impact of enforced modernization on a fascinating African setting" (Apr. 1965:234). The important thing to be remembered here is that Skinner's work was being published and reviewed in first-rank anthropological journals, an arena previously almost exclusively reserved for white scholars, and that he was one of the first African Americans to do so. The publication of *The Mossi of Upper Volta* coincided with a growing demand for information about the peoples of Africa, whose quest for independence was imminent. Once again Skinner was ready to take advantage of opportunity. In 1959, again with Landgraf's support, Skinner joined the faculty of New York University. While there, he gave a series of lectures on WCBS-TV's Sunrise Semester Courses on Africa, from 1960 to 1962. After his brief stint at NYU Skinner joined the faculty of Columbia once again in 1963, this time as the first African-American anthropologist with tenure at an Ivy League university.

The Ambassador Years

In 1966 Skinner was appointed U.S. ambassador to Upper Volta (Burkina Faso) by Lyndon Johnson and served there for the next three years. He was with Ambassador Edwin O. Reischauer, a former envoy to Japan, "the only Head of Mission to speak what were considered exotic languages" (Skinner n.d. "Anthropology":6) at that time. In many ways this appointment amounted to a homecoming. His ambassadorship represented the growing role for African Americans in the U.S. foreign service. Prior to the growing independence movements in Africa, white men were rarely sent as ambassadors to Africa. Indeed, the first American representatives to African states were African Americans, dating back to the nineteenth century when James Milton Turner and later Henry Highland Garnet were appointed ministers resident, and for Turner consul general as well, to Liberia. The independence of Ghana in 1957 posed a problem for the American government because for the first time, as Skinner notes, "America found itself compelled by world events to deal with black men on the basis of full equality":

> The first problem was a racial one. Was the prospective United States Ambassador to the emerging state of Ghana to be Negro or white? . . . Afro-Americans had always had, as their political "plum", the Liberian ambassadorship. . . . But the Ghanaians discretely let it be known that they would have none of this. Rumors flew about Accra that President Nkrumah himself would refuse to accept an American Negro as Ambassador. According to reports, he felt that since Negroes were regarded as second-class citizens in the United States, such an appointment would reflect an equivalent judgment of his country. Officially, Ghanaians issued heated denials of these rumors but they had served their function: to warn America that emerging Africa would demand full racial equality. (1965:384)

Ultimately Ghana's wish for a white ambassador from the United States was fulfilled, thanks in part to the cold war, according to Skinner. The real dilemma was how to reconcile the position of African Americans who wanted to improve relations between Ghana and the United States while securing greater rights for themselves with those of Africans who did not concur with racial stereotypes of African Americans but wanted their countries to be fully accepted as equals among nations. For white Americans, the only course open was to increase the number of African Americans in the foreign service in white countries as well as black. Both Africans and African Americans have been credited with making this suggestion.

As a political player Skinner became increasingly concerned with the dialectical tensions between Africans and African Americans, a relationship he has argued cannot be understood without "taking into account a significant third partner, the white American" (1965:381). At the time of his appointment, the civil rights movement gained momentum, coinciding with the overthrow of colonial rule in many African states. For African Americans the dilemma was not new, having already been articulated, as Skinner noted, by W. E. B. Du Bois: "The Negro is a sort of seventh son, born with a veil. . . . One ever feels his two-ness as American, a Negro; two souls, two thoughts, two unreconciled strivings; two warring ideals in one dark body, whose strength alone keeps it from being torn asunder. The history of the American Negro is the history of this strife—this longing to attain self-conscious manhood" (Du Bois 1903:5, qtd. in Skinner 1965:381). Du Bois was also a pioneering advocate of linking the plight of African Americans to the plight of Africans and people of color worldwide, a strategy that was at once beneficial to both parties and fraught with tensions. As Skinner notes, "Africans frequently stood up for the civil rights of Afro-Americans, but ironically enough, they often resented the fact that race and fate, if not love and duty compelled them to do so" (1965:381).

What exactly could lead to these dialectical tensions, on both sides, particularly for those African-American diplomats in the service of the government of the United States? As has often been noted, each interacting member of a triad will try to benefit from disagreements between the other two, but what has often been overlooked in this particular triad, according to Skinner, is "the manner in which white behavior affects relations between Africans and African-Americans" (1965:389).

For African Americans the issue goes further, to the heart of moral responsibility. An incident occurring at a conference on the immediate future of Africa illustrates this. Several former African-American ambassadors to Africa were asked to participate on a panel discussion, chaired by Skinner, concerning the relationship between African Americans and U.S. foreign policy in Africa. The initial speaker began by emphatically cheering the U.S. triumph in the cold war and went on to argue that "structural adjustment policies" were necessary and should be supported. Several African economists in the audience, who had already documented the reasons for their objections to such policies, immediately responded. They noted that as a representative of the U.S. government, was she not articulating that government's policy, a policy designed to further the interests of the United States, even at the expense of Africans? This clearly struck a moral chord, for the ensuing responses became somewhat defensive, as the former ambassadors tried to present their individual positions in a more positive light, one that acknowledged what Skinner has called the "bonds of love and duty, fate and kinship" between these groups. African Americans are not the only group to face such dilemmas. Clearly the American Jewish community has been divided over where to throw their support when conflicts arise between the policies of the United States and Israel. While private citizens in both groups have increasingly resorted to lobbying to promote their positions, there have been uneven results. Furthermore, the government official is overtly constrained, cross-cutting ties not withstanding, and must work often behind the scenes and informally to bring about favorable resolutions. Do such strategies really work? Are they in fact really undertaken at all? Is it not better, in terms of results, to be directly confrontational, rather than covert? We may never really be able to judge effectively, but African Americans have historically tried to influence U.S. policy in Africa in a variety of ways and continue to do so today through many organizations, such as TransAfrica and the Congressional Black Caucus. Skinner's *African-Americans and U.S. Policy toward Africa, 1850–1924* (1992) documents the early efforts in this area.

But what of Skinner's own role while serving as ambassador? To date he has not published his memoirs and his personal accounts are sealed. He has, however, published a number of articles pertaining to the dynamics of the relationship between African Americans and U.S. foreign policy in Africa. In testimony before the House Committee on Foreign Affairs, Skinner provided insight into his perspective:

> Mr. Diggs: Dr. Skinner, you have been one of the few black Americans who has served as a diplomat in any country—not only Africa, but in any of our diplomatic missions. There has been a long debate going on within the State Department and in other circles about the acceptance of black Americans in these roles.
>
> Statements, for example, that they attempted to corroborate with comments from African countries that if black Americans were second-class citizens in their own country, obviously they would be limited in what they would be able to do for a given country in a diplomatic post.
>
> Could you discuss that concept? I particularly would like to know what your experiences were as ambassador to Upper Volta, in terms of your own acceptance by that country, and any contiguous countries that you may have visited, and whether or not you see any changes within the State Department or within our Government with respect to that subject.
>
> Dr. Skinner: Well, I think that I am not a very good example, because I am unique as an American Ambassador. Very few American Ambassadors have first-class knowledge of the countries to which they are sent. I have known Upper Volta for a long time. I speak the language, somewhat,

so I am a very bad example, because I think that America can probably never get another Ambassador as well qualified to serve in Upper Volta.

With respect to the role of black ambassadors, I think that if there is one problem we don't have, it is the problem of conceiving the African as an "Untermensch." Most people—most Americans believe that they are not race-conscious—we are, very race-conscious. Most of our explanations are in racial terms.

We come out of a tradition where we emphasize blood, as the explanation for human behavior. Black Americans don't have that problem. To them Africans may be bright, stupid, but they are men and not Untermenschen.

Now Africans are very sensitive people, they are very aware politically, and some of them are concerned about the ability of American blacks who have not achieved complete equality in America to get for them the things that ambassadors should get for the country to which they are accredited. However, I think this is discounted by the recognition on the part of the Africans that in the black American they have not only a man who is interested in serving his country's interest, because after all that is the role of an ambassador, but a man who can interpret the problems of Africa, free from racism and the arrogance of whites.

In other words, the black man does not have certain hangups. The Africans are sensitive. But it seems to me that they are quite realistic, and I think in the light of what is happening, the fact that the Africans are decolonizing their own mentalities, and the black people in the United States are also decolonizing, or demystifying their own mentalities, should mean that there would be an even greater receptivity on the part of the Africans to black Americans.

I can understand the problem with the State Department. The State Department, after all, would like to place its own people. It is a club. They know each other. They will use every weapon, every tactic, to place their own people. We can't accept the fact that black Americans can't serve their country in Africa, or anywhere else.

At this point in time I think an Afro-American ambassador is superior to the best of the white ambassadors in Africa. It is just a question of historical time. Things will change, but I think as of this moment this is right. (House Committee 1970)

What is remarkable about this excerpt, in addition to its typical Skinnerian bluntness, is Skinner's skillful use of language that is at once inclusive and exclusive, underscoring the linguistic acrobatics that African Americans have learned to employ with respect to their identities. In speaking of his experiences as an ambassador and his preparation for that job through anthropology Skinner said:

> The experience of having to interpret the United States to the Voltaics, and the Voltaics to the United States convinced me that Franz Boas was correct in suggesting that anthropology was a discipline which addressed issues of more than academic importance. . . . I found it fairly easy to deal with the normal diplomatic traffic between ourselves and the Voltaics, provided of course, that I took into consideration the matter of scale. The United States as a major world power has complex global responsibilities and was involved in a Cold War which really had little meaning to the local people. On the other hand, many of their problems were so parochial, that they had little meaning to the State Department. . . . What was clear to me, but not appreciated either in Ouagadougou or in Washington DC, was that neither side understood the implications of the local and global factors involved. (House Committee 1970:7–9)

By all accounts, Skinner's tenure as ambassador was appreciated by the people of Upper Volta (Burkina Faso), whose president, Sangouli Lamizana, decorated him as the Commandeur del'Order National Voltaique (Commander of the Upper Volta National Order), the country's national decoration.

The Return to the Academy

When Skinner returned to Columbia at the end of the Johnson years, he was without doubt an established scholar whose credentials placed him in what he might refer to as "the big league." Columbia appointed him as the Franz Boas Professor of Anthropology in 1971. In 1974 Princeton University Press published *African Urban Life: The Transformation of Ouagadougou.* He was at that time the chair of the department of anthropology. The book was favorably received, having been reviewed positively by Lucy Mair in the *Times Literary Supplement* as well as in scholarly journals. Richard Basham and David De Groot, in reviewing anthropological approaches to the study of urban and complex societies for the *American Anthropologist*, opined: "The most basic problem for urban anthropologists has always been that of applying the two techniques central to the anthropological perspective—participant observation and holistic grasp of the culture at hand—to urban studies. Clearly the size and diversity of even the smallest city makes it impossible to study each of its inhabitants except in the most superficial manner and casts doubt upon the researcher's ability to extrapolate knowledge gained from intensive study of a few informants to the city's whole" (1977:427–28). They go on to argue, however, that Skinner's macro study of Ouagadougou was impressive: "Through long residence in the capital both as anthropologist and American ambassador, Skinner has been able to amass detailed ethnographic and historical information on seemingly every aspect of Ouagadougou life and each segment of the community. In approaching the city holistically he inevitably glosses over certain topics with which he undoubtedly is familiar and subsumes concern with theoretical explanation and problem orientation to description and inclusiveness. Surprisingly, however, he has produced a book which gives the reader both a holistic perspective and a sense of the quality of life in Ouagadougou. As such, *African Urban Life: The Transformation of Ouagadougou,* should serve both as an excellent reference book for other researchers in Ouagadougou and elsewhere in Africa and an interesting introduction to African urban life for the non-Africanist" (428–29). It is with this work that we begin to see Skinner's training as an ethnographer and his experience as ambassador come together in his writing, focusing attention on a dynamic area of increasing interest, and making it accessible to scholars, policymakers, and the lay public alike. That year the book won the annual Melville Herskovits Award for the best book published on Africa by an American scholar.

Social Change within the Academy

A considerable struggle in academe erupted over control of African studies. A new generation of Africanists, many of whom were African or African American, had emerged and were demanding not just a voice but a piece of the action. Nowhere was the call louder than in the African Studies Association (ASA) meeting of 1969. Until that time African studies, on both the departmental and the national level, had been firmly in the control of whites. The major departments at that time were at Northwestern, Boston University, UCLA, and the University of Wisconsin at Madison but, as Skinner recalls, "not a single one of them [was] controlled by blacks" (Skinner 1994c). Furthermore, these were monied, were staffed, had the legitimacy to really influence policy, and could affect positions of scholars coming up in and outside of the academy.

By 1969 matters had come to a head. Members of the black caucus had decided to interrupt the ASA meeting to demand representation on the board. According to Skinner, whose support they had enlisted, these black caucus members wanted half the seats on the board so that they could be involved with most of the commissions that were supported by the ASA. Skinner had, he suspects, "been brought along in terms of my age grade" and because he had served on the selection committee for the board. He was therefore a full-fledged member of the establishment. However, when he was asked for support, he felt he "could not turn them down." His decision was motivated by a number of factors. In part he understood yet resented that "to be a member of the academy, one had to go along with the canons of the academy, and these were developed by whites" (1994c). Skinner has often remarked that African Americans need to develop their own paradigms for discussion.

An even more compelling reason for his decision was the cover to the program: "a primeval scene with alligators and all that. And here we were talking about contemporary Africa [with] this woodcut, which went all the way back to the days of images of something like that. The thing that turned me off was the arrogance of the whites. They had contempt, absolute contempt, for the blacks" (1994c).

Eventually, African Americans and Africans were included in a meaningful way in the ASA. In 1985 the ASA awarded Elliot Skinner its Distinguished Africanist Award. By that time the number of African and Africana studies departments had increased dramatically and were staffed largely by blacks. Skinner, ever the pragmatist, cautioned that such departments run the risk of marginalization. When a younger generation of anthropology scholars formed a separate division within the American Anthropological Association and debated leaving it altogether, for similar concerns, Skinner was not initially forthcoming with support. This organization, the Association of Black Anthropologists (ABA), is now a well-established subdivision, but resentment on the part of some of its founders toward Skinner remains. Although Skinner was the first African American to run for president of the American Anthropological Association, he did not win the election.

The Continuing Dialogue

Skinner's return to academic life has not meant withdrawal from an active role in international affairs, particularly those concerning Africa. He is a member of the Council of Foreign Relations and has traveled widely in Africa giving lectures for the Foreign Service Institute of the U.S. Department of State. He was an outspoken critic of the Reagan policy of "constructive engagement" (n.d. "Reagan") pertaining to South Africa and a supporter of disinvestment (1984). He serves as a member of the TransAfrica Research Advisory Committee and also as the chair of its policy-making committee, which invites people to write papers on recommendations about foreign policy in Africa. He is also a member of the Association of Black Ambassadors. Though no longer interested in publishing articles for academic journals, he remains committed to the vital role anthropology can play in answering the larger questions concerning the rise of a "global civilization" and plans to continue writing.

Skinner feels that the future is largely in the hands of the new generation of academics and the demands they place upon themselves to maintain high standards and restructure the nature of the continuing dialogue.

References Cited

Basham, Richard, and David De Groot. 1977. "Current Approaches to the Anthropology of Urban and Complex Societies." *American Anthropologist* 79 (2): 414–32.

Hammond, Peter. 1965. Review of *The Mossi of the Upper Volta: The Political Development of a Sudanese People* by Elliot Skinner. *American Anthropologist* 67 (1): 133–34.

House Committee on Foreign Affairs. 1970. *Policy toward Africa in the Seventies.* Washington, D.C.: U.S. Government Printing Office.

Landgraf, John. 1996. Telephone interview with the author. Mar. 2.

Mair, Lucy. 1974. "Modernizing the Mossi." *Times Literary Supplement* (Nov. 15): 1279.

Skinner, Elliot P. 1960a. "Labour Migration and Its Relationship to Socio-Cultural Change in Mossi Society." *Africa* 30 (4): 375–401.

———. 1960b. "The Mossi Pogsioure." *Man* 5 (27–28): 20–22.

———. 1963. "Strangers in West African Societies." *Africa* 33 (4): 307–20.

———. 1964. *The Mossi of Upper Volta: The Political Development of a Sudanese People.* Stanford: Stanford University Press. Reprinted as *The Mossi of Burkina Faso: Chiefs, Politicians, and Soldiers.* Prospect Heights, Ill.: Waveland Press, 1989.

———. 1965. "African, Afro-American, White American: A Case of Pride and Prejudice." *Freedomways* 5 (3): 380–95.

———. 1974. *African Urban Life: The Transformation of Ouagadougou.* Princeton: Princeton University Press.

———. 1984. Letter to the editor. *Washington Post,* Feb. 10.

———. 1992. *African Americans and U.S. Policy toward Africa, 1850–1924: In Defense of Black Nationality.* Washington, D.C.: Howard University Press.

———. 1994a. Interview with the author. Columbia University, New York. Feb. 7.

———. 1994b. Interview with the author. Columbia University, New York. Feb. 14.

———. 1994c. Interview with the author. Columbia University, New York. Mar. 14.

———. 1996. Interview with the author. Columbia University, New York. Mar. 3.

———. n.d. "Anthropology, Area Studies Representatives, and Contemporary Education." Ms. Author's possession.

———. n.d. "The Reagan Doctrine and Southern Africa's Future." Ms. Author's possession.

Contributors

AMELIA MARIE ADAMS received a B.A. degree in anthropology from Smith College and an M.A. degree in anthropology from the University of Oklahoma. She is currently switching careers from anthropology to architecture.

JOYCE ASCHENBRENNER is a professor emeritus of anthropology at Southern Illinois University at Edwardsville, where she taught 1970–92. After conducting fieldwork in Pakistan, she received her Ph.D. from the University of Minnesota. She later did fieldwork in India, in southern Illinois, and in Chicago, under the auspices of the Urban Institute at the University of Chicago. She received an American Council of Learned Societies Award to research the anthropology of Katherine Dunham. Her publications include a monograph and a number of articles on Dunham as dancer, social activist, and anthropologist as well as a monograph and articles on African-American culture.

WILLIE L. BABER earned M.A. and Ph.D. degrees in anthropology at Stanford University, specializing in the Caribbean and economic anthropology. He held positions at Tuskegee Institute (1978–80) and Purdue University (1980–89) prior to his appointment at the University of North Carolina at Greensboro in 1989, where he chaired the African-American Studies Program from 1989 to 1991 and served as head of the department of anthropology from 1993 to 1997. He is currently a professor of anthropology and a Kellog Fellow. He is co-author (with Geneva Gay) of *Expressively Black: The Cultural Basis of Ethnic Identity.*

MICHAEL L. BLAKEY received his Ph.D. from the University of Massachusetts at Amherst in 1985. He is an associate professor of anthropology at Howard University and curator of the W. Montague Cobb Human Skeletal Collection and scientific director of the New York African Burial Ground Project at the Cobb Laboratory at Howard University. He was president of the Association of Black Anthroplogists from 1987 to 1989. He accomplished revision of the bylaws and reorganization of ABA officers during the first year of the American Anthropology Association reorganization; initiated *Transforming Anthropology* with editor Arthur Spears; and established ABA representation on the AAA board.

A. LYNN BOLLES is a professor of women's studies and anthropology at the University of Maryland at College Park. She received her Ph.D. in anthropology in 1981 from Rutgers University. Active in numerous professional organizations, she is currently president of the Caribbean Studies Association. Her publications include *Sister Jamaica: A Study of Women, Work, and Households* (1996) and *We Paid Our Dues: Women Trade Union Leaders in the Caribbean* (1996).

DALLAS L. BROWNE received his Ph.D. in anthropology from the University of Illinois at Urbana in 1983. He is an associate professor of anthropology at Southern Illinois University at Edwardsville, where he teaches courses in urban anthropology, political anthropology, African cultures, Latin American and Caribbean cultures, contemporary anthropological issues, and African-American culture. He is a member of the board of directors of the Katherine Dunham Museum Foundation and the Council on Foreign Relations. Currently, he is conducting research on African culture in Veracruz, Mexico.

CAROLE H. CARPENTER is a folklorist and professor in the Division of Humanities at York University, Toronto, where she teaches Canadian culture, folklore and culture, and the literature and culture of childhood. She has graduate degrees in folklore-folklife studies from the University of Pennsylvania. Widely published, she appears frequently on the radio and television and has written three major books on folklore in Canadian culture. Most recently she held the prestigious J. P. Robarts Chair in Canadian Studies (1994–95) and in 1996–97 was director of the Robarts Centre for Canadian Studies at York University.

FAYE V. HARRISON is a professor of anthropology and the graduate director of women's studies at the University of South Carolina at Columbia. She received her Ph.D. in anthropology from Stanford University in 1982. From 1989 to 1991 she was president of the Association of Black Anthropologists, the first to serve on the board of directors of the American Anthropological Association. *Transforming Anthropology* was first published under her presidency. She has also served as co-chair of the Commission on the Anthropology of Women, a unit of the International Union of Anthropological and Ethnological Sciences, since 1993. In addition to *Decolonizing Anthropology* (1991), her work has been published widely in books and journals, and she has also edited special issues of *Critique of Anthropology, Urban Anthropology,* and *American Anthropologist.* She is currently working on a book on black subaltern analysis in anthropology.

IRA E. HARRISON received a B.A. from Morehouse College (1955), an M.A. from Atlanta University (1959), a Ph.D. from Syracuse University (1967), and an M.P.H. from Johns Hopkins University (1971). He has been a member of the Caucus of Black Anthropologists; served as the firth southern regional representative and was a founding member of the Association of Black Anthropologists (ABA); accomplished the formal transition of the ABA into the American Anthropological Association in 1987; and was president of the ABA (1985–87). He has co-edited (with Z. A. Ademuwagun, John A. A. Ayoade, and Dennis M. Warren) *African Therapeutic Systems* (1979) and (with Sheila Cosminsky) the two-volume *Traditional Medicine* (1976–84). He has been researching and organizing symposiums on black anthropologists since 1978. He is currently on the editorial board of *Medical Anthropology Quarterly,* has written four books of poetry, and is an associate professor of anthropology at the University of Tennessee at Knoxville.

GWENDOLYN MIKELL is a professor of anthropology and foreign service and the director of the African Certificate Program at Georgetown University. She received her Ph.D. from Columbia University in 1975. She was the founding president of the Association for Africanist Anthropology within the American Anthropological Association, and she was president of the African Studies Association (1996–97). Her major publications include *Cocoa and Chaos in Ghana* (1989) and *African Feminism: The Politics of Survival in Sub-Saharan Africa* (1997). She has also published widely in journals and is completing a book on African women's peace activism.

YOLANDA MOSES has been president of the City College of New York and a professor of anthropology since 1993. She was previously vice president for academic affairs and a professor of anthropology at California State University at Dominguez Hills (1988–93) and dean of the College of the Arts and a professor of social science at California State Polytechnic University (1982–88). In 1995 Moses was elected the first African-American president of the American Anthropological Association. She is affiliated with numerous local, national, and international associations concerned with higher education, community and regional development, and service organizations. She is the author of numerous articles and monographs, including the groundbreaking *Black Women in Academe* (1989).

CHERYL MWARIA is an associate professor of anthropology and the director of African studies at Hofstra University. She received her Ph.D. in medical anthropology from Columbia University in 1985. She has conducted research in Africa, the United States, and Cuba, and has published on health-related issues in those areas. Currently she is completing a manuscript on African-American women with disabilities and serving as a board member of the American Ethnological Society.

LESLEY M. RANKIN-HILL is both a physical anthropologist and a medical anthropologist who earned an M.A. and a Ph.D. at the University of Massachusetts at Amherst. Her work with the First African Baptist Church Cemetery population, undertaken as a Smithsonian Institution Faculty Fellow, culminated in *The Biohistory of an Afro-American Cemetery Population* (1997). Currently she is the associate director of scientific research for the African Burial Ground Project at Howard University and an associate professor of anthropology at the University of Oklahoma. Her most recent research focuses on the adaptive strategies of Puerto Rican chronic arthritis patients.

HUBERT B. ROSS received his master's degree in sociology from Yale in 1942 and his Ph.D. in anthropology from Columbia in 1954. He was a fellow in the Johns Hopkins School for Advanced International Studies Summer Seminar on Africa in 1954. He began his teaching career at Lincoln University, where he was an instructor and an assistant professor until 1960, when he joined the faculty of Atlanta University. He eventually became a professor in the department of sociology and anthropology and remained active in teaching at this historically black university until his death in 1995. He was an African-American pioneer anthropologist.

PEGGY REEVES SANDAY received her B.S. degree in anthropology from Columbia University, where she studied under William S. Willis Jr., Margaret Mead, and Morton Fried. After receiving a Ph.D. from the University of Pittsburgh, where she studied under George Peter Murdock, she taught at Carnegie-Mellon University and then moved to the University of Pennsylvania, where she is now a professor of anthropology. She is the author or editor of six books and numerous articles, including *Female Power and Male Dominance* (1981), *Divine Hunger* (1986), and *Fraternity Gang Rape* (1990). At present she is completing a book based on her longtime fieldwork in West Sumatra.

LYNNE MALLORY WILLIAMS is currently teaching ninth-grade science and biology at Coronado High School for Colorado Springs School District Eleven. She is also a part-time biology instructor for Pikes Peak Community College. She has an M.A. in the history of science from the University of Oklahoma (1994) and an M.A. in instruction and curriculum with an emphasis in science education from the University of Colorado at Colorado Springs (1990). She has been teaching math and science to junior high school and middle school students for over fourteen years.